Dickens by Ch

CW00587831

A compilation by **Dr David Sutherland**
from the writings of Charles Dickens
for the 200th Anniversary of his birth
2012.

Cover: The young Charles Dickens at the height of his
fame. S Laurence.1837
Rear cover: Mr Pickwick meets Mrs Bardell in the Fleet by
Hablot Browne (Phiz).

*Please note that the main Dickens text based on his written and spoken words is depicted thus in a Times New Roman format; the compiler's linking text is in an Arial font as shown in this half of the sentence.

Printed by EPW Print & Design Ltd.: mark.epw@btconnect.com
ISBN 978-0-9563564-0-6
Designed & Published by:

davidsmuckle@aol.com
fax 01-642-706113

£8-99p. $13.00.   euro 10.00

Charles Dickens (**1812-1870**) was a complex, brilliant man whose genius defies explanation. Grandson of a butler and son of a minor naval clerk, he received only a meagre education. Yet, within a few years, he was world famous as an author, essayist, editor, lecturer, actor, and playwright. Through his books, he became an effective social reformer. Beneath the dazzling animation of cheerfulness, optimism, good humour and enthusiasm, there was a shadowy, tragic darkness that made him unflinchingly hard in his business deals and sometimes distant from his friends. He loved to travel in an era when long journeys were hazardous; and kept very fit through mammoth walks and rides. He was extremely popular and exceptionally kind to both his family and to his friends - many of whom were in the aristocracy. However, he never neglected the causes of the poor and oppressed. Beloved by his public - he was, in fact, the first western 'superstar'.

Thousands crowded him in the streets - for he was immediately recognisable wherever he went; a flotilla of boats greeted him in New York harbour; Queen Victoria delighted in his acting performances and invited him to Buckingham Palace; two Presidents of the United States gave him a personal interview; aristocracy supported his social projects; the learned read the magazines and the newspaper he edited; hundreds of thousands bought his books; and as many came to the Readings from his novels. Dickens seemed everywhere in the Victorian era – the merchandising of mugs, cards, tins, pictures etc. only added to his fame. Books were copied by third rate authors and plagiarised into third rate plays; the list is endless.

Yet despite his affability and good humour, he was a man who could be amazingly secretive, releasing only fragmentary insights through the characters and situations in his novels. Some facts he only revealed to a chosen few.

So this compilation was born. It keeps faithfully to his original writings; hence the title *Dickens by Charles Dickens.*

'There is nothing so infectious in the world, so irresistibly contagious, as laughter and good humour.'

Chapter One

"Whether I shall turn out to be the hero of my own life, or whether that station will be held by anybody else, these pages must show. To begin my life with the beginning of my life…" (David Copperfield)

Changes at Home. *David Copperfield*

Charles Dickens was born at Landport in Portsea on Friday the seventh of February, 1812; the son of John Dickens, a clerk in the Navy Pay Office stationed in the Portsmouth dockyard and Elizabeth Barrow, who was to have eight children. The eldest was Fanny (born in 1810) followed by Charles, and he was entered in the baptismal register as Charles John Huffham, although he only used this middle name on a few occasions, and when he did he spelled it Huffam.

For the record the others were: Alfred (died in childhood), Letitia (1816), Harriet (also died), Frederick (1820), Alfred (1822) and Augustus (1827)

Charles Dickens's birthplace in 1812: 387 Mile End Road, Landport. They lived there for five months. He had no sentimentality about the place. 'I can't say I usually care much about it,' he once remarked.

The origins of the family are largely unknown and Charles rarely spoke about his grandparents. On the maternal side they came from Bristol, with a family business making musical instruments and teaching music. His paternal grandparents were Butler and Housekeeper respectively to the rich Crewe family (who owned large houses in London and in the country). Charles's grandmother retained her position until she was seventy five. Many people recalled that she had the ability to extemporise stories for the delight of the Crewe children - a gift which was to skip a generation

Charles's grandfather, however, died before his son John (Dickens's father) was born, but Lord Crewe took a kindly interest in the children and, some sixteen years on, used his influence to obtain the position of naval clerk for John. This advancement in status suited John's aspirations, for he had already developed a taste for the 'good life', and the reckless spending that went with it. At the time he was described as having an 'idleness and general incapacity...with more than a shade of gentility...and a little pompous'; characteristics gained from his time mixing with the landed gentry. They were attributes that were both to help and hinder his progress through life.

John's work, although providing a £140 annual salary, never caught up with his spending power. However, it was through work that he met his future bride. One of his friends in the Navy Pay Office had a sister called Elizabeth. She was educated, vivacious, good humoured and a great mimic and quickly fell in love with the amiable John. So, in June 1809, Elizabeth Barrow married John Dickens; she was eighteen and he was twenty three.

Soon John was 'feeling the pinch' and could not afford the rent for the modest terrace house. At first they moved from Mile End to a cheaper, more cramped home in Hawk Street. However, finding the conditions not to their liking, they moved again to a larger dwelling in Southsea (Portsmouth). Elizabeth's sister came to the rescue by providing the additional money for the rent under the broad terms of living with them as a lodger. There was also a maid who helped with the general domestic duties and looked after Charles and Fanny. She was the first of many retainers who were to frequent the Dickens's household, whatever the financial circumstances, throughout his career.

Later in life Dickens was of the following firm opinion that 'the power of observation of young children to be quite wonderful for its closeness and accuracy, and the recollection of most of us can go farther back into such times than many of us can suppose.'

A friend was to recall being told how 'He remembered the small front garden to the house, from which he was taken away when he was two years old; and where, watched by a nurse through a low kitchen window almost level with the gravel walk, he trotted with something to eat, and his little sister with him.'

'I was carried from the garden one day to see the soldiers exercise and many years later, while writing *Nicholas Nickleby*, I recognized the exact shape of the military parade, as seen by me as an infant on the same spot, a quarter of a century before.'

In January 1815 John resumed his employment at Somerset House, the transfer taking the family from Portsmouth to Norfolk Street in London, close to the Middlesex Hospital. 'I recall leaving Portsea in the snow.' Otherwise his memories of that time are vague. The family stayed there for two years, but it was in a more oppressive world of noisy streets, smoke and incessant throngs of people. Charles missed the open fields, the fresh air and the sights and sounds of the country.

In 1816 the family increased in size with the birth of Letitia; and in 1817 they changed their abode, yet again - first to Sheerness and four months later to

8

Chatham (Kent). As John Dickens cheerfully resumed work in this naval port, his good humour was occasioned by a welcome increase in salary. He immediately looked for a house and chose Ordnance Terrace, a relatively new construction set on a hill. Here dwelled eight people - the parents, three children, two nurses and an Aunt in a six-room house.

Chatham merges into Rochester; curiously, the latter was to become a setting for both his first and last novel. Chatham, itself, was a bustling port, 'a mere dream of chalk, and drawbridges, and mastless ships in a muddy river.'

Charles lived there from the age of four until nine. He was never to lose his love of the sea; it was almost an addiction to live within sound and sight of the waves whenever he could, even on his journeys through France and Italy in later years.

In line with his salary, John Dickens's pretensions had risen. He engaged two servants; one was called Mary Weller. Mary, it is said (although not confirmed, for there were three other servants at different times) had a way of firing young Charles's imagination with ghoulish tales. In one, there was a sadistic sea Captain who baked his wives in pies and, in another, evil characters were tortured by rats. Charles, by his own admission, was left lying in bed in a state rigid with terror. However, by one of those curious twists of fate, the name of Weller was to be become one of the cornerstones to fame.

Next door was 'a peach faced creature in a blue sash' called Lucy who was of the same age and sat with him (and her brother) under the table eating all sorts of cakes at her birthday party. The three of them, and Fanny, loved to have magic-lantern shows, act simple plays and sing comic songs. However, and as usual, the Dickens family were overextending themselves financially; so the rent was proving to be too high. So John Dickens moved the family into a less salubrious area of Chatham, where Charles absorbed the sights and smells of the busy dockyard, images that stayed with him for life.

It was about this time he first saw Gad's Hill Place, on the highest ground on the main road between Rochester and Gravesend. On some occasion, his father looked at it with much admiration and said, "Charles, you might live in it, or in some such house, one day, if you work hard enough."

Gad's Hill Place, near Rochester

As a child he was subjected to 'violent spasms which often disabled me during periods of exertion; I was small and sickly. Thus I was never good at cricket or a first-hand at marbles or peg-top or prisoner's base. But I had pleasure in watching others at their games, reading while they played – one inestimable advantage for later life. I was in fact a very small and not-over-particularly-taken-care-of-boy. My mother taught me thoroughly well the rudiments of English and a little Latin. I faintly remember her teaching the alphabet; and when I looked upon the fat black letters in the primer, the puzzling novelty of their shapes, the easy good nature of O and S, always presents themselves before me.'

'A was an archer who shot at a frog. Of course he was. He was an apple pie also and there he is! He was a good many things in his time was A. And so were most of his friends, except X, who had so little versatility that I never knew him to get beyond Xerxes or Xantippe – like Y, who was always confined to a Yacht or Yew Tree; and Z condemned for ever to be a Zebra or a Zany.'

In 1818 he was sent to a preparatory day school with Fanny in Rome Lane, Chatham. It was over a dyer's shop; and as he went up steps to it, he frequently stumbled and grazed his knees.

'The mistress of the establishment holds no place in my memory; but rampant on one eternal door mat was a puffy pug-dog with a personal animosity towards us, who triumphs over time. The bark of that baleful Pug, a certain radiating way he had of snapping at our undefended legs, the ghastly grinning of his moist black muzzle and white teeth, and the insolence of his crisp tail curled like a pastoral crook, all live and flourish.

He belonged to some female, chiefly inhabiting a back parlour, whose life appears to us to have been consumed in sniffing, and in wearing a brown beaver bonnet.' (Reprinted Pieces)

'My father had left a small collection of books in a little room upstairs to which I had access and which nobody else in the house ever troubled. From

11

that blessed little room, *Roderick Random*, *Peregrine Pickle*, *Humphrey Clinker*, *Tom Jones*, the *Vicar of Wakefield*, *Don Quixote*, *Gil Blas* and *Robinson Crusoe* came out, a glorious host, to keep me company'. (David Copperfield)

'When I think of it, the picture always rises in my mind, of a summer evening, the boys at play in the churchyard, and I sitting on my bed, reading as if for my life.

So I took to writing a tragedy called *Misnar*, the Sultan of India, founded (and very literally founded, no doubt) on one of the *Tales of the Genii*. I sang small comic songs so especially well they used to elevate on chairs and tables, for more effective display of these talents; that on the later occasions of my own children's parties, my shrill, little voice of childhood did again tingle in my ears, and I blush to think what a horrible little nuisance I must have been to many unoffending grown-up people who were called upon to admire me'.

The chief ally and encourager in these displays was a youth of some ability and much older, named James Lamert. He was a stepson to Aunt Mary Barrow who was married for the second time to Doctor Lamert, an army surgeon. Her first husband, a commander in the Navy, had been drowned in Rio de Janeiro. It was James who first took Charles to the theatre at a young age. The venue was the Theatre Royal in Rochester where they sat in 'dear, narrow, uncomfortable, faded-cushioned, flea-haunted, single tear of boxes'

'It revealed to me many wondrous secrets of which not the least terrific were, that the witches in Macbeth bore an awful resemblance to the thanes and other proper inhabitants of Scotland; and that the good king Duncan couldn't rest in his grave, but was constantly coming out of it, and calling himself somebody else.'

During the last two years at Chatham, Charles and Fanny went to a school in Clover Lane, commencing in 1821. It was run by a twenty-three year old man called William Giles. He was the son of a Baptist minister but a Dissenter. Although he had taught grammar in an Oxford school, his beliefs kept him from gaining a university appointment. Charles was friendly with the family and, perhaps on account of this fact, the next move was to St Mary's Place where William's father was the Minister. 'The house was next to a Baptist Meeting House called Providence Chapel and I can vividly recall someone (who I wonder) humming an evening hymn to me, and I cried on the pillow – either with the remorseful consciousness of having kicked somebody else, or because somebody else had hurt my feelings in the course of the day.'

Charles was happy there and made many friends; they rowed on the Medway, skated when the ponds were frozen and he generally enjoyed himself in physical pursuits he had not engaged in before. But it was the advancement in his education that was pivotal for the ten-year-old. Giles's effect on his pupil's vocabulary and syntax is not to be underestimated and he pronounced Charles to be a 'boy of capacity'. When, several years later and half-way through the publication of *Pickwick Papers*, his old teacher sent Charles a silver snuff-box with the inscription 'the inimitable Boz', it was praise far more precious than obtained at any examination in the academy. It was an eponym Dickens loved and he used it universally throughout his life; it is still warmly used today. William's sister recalled Charles as 'a very handsome boy, with long curly hair of a light colour.' Mary Weller began to notice that Charles was becoming more serious. At Ordnance Terrace he would say, 'Now Mary, clear the kitchen, we are going to have a game.' She always recalled 'the sea songs, his especial favourites, sung in a clear treble voice'. But in St Mary's Place, Mary remembered that 'there was no such juvenile entertainment as I had seen at the Terrace.'

Meanwhile, events were once again overtaking the Dickens family as his father strolled his imprudent way through life. In 1819, just three week from the birth of another child, John borrowed the very large sum of two hundred pounds and was unable to keep up with the payments. His brother-in-law, Thomas Barrow (who had countersigned the debt) was forced to repay it. Understandably, there was a marked deterioration in the relationship between them. It was at this time that Charles first heard mention of 'the Deed,' representing a new crisis in family affairs. Later he was to find out that 'the Deed' was a composition of money owing to creditors.

In August 1820 came a son (Frederick) and more expenses which begat more debts. In May 1821 another brother-in-law (James Milbourne) generously paid off the Deed to the creditors. Then in March 1822 yet another son, Alfred, was born. There was a sudden grief in the family when Charles's baby sister died from smallpox shortly after Alfred's birth.

Mary Weller left to get married (many years later she turned up to hear Dickens perform at the height of his fame but she was too shy to approach him); and John was recalled to Somerset House, London. One result from the mounting debt soon showed itself as an enforced retrenchment in Bayham Street, Camden Town; then about the poorest part of the London suburbs. The Dickens family were suffering from their father's improvidence and had to sell most of the household goods to pay off the accumulating debts. Somehow, they managed to squeeze into a house of four rooms, a basement and a garret. Now, the ensemble consisted of the parents, six children (including the new baby Alfred), a maid and James Lamert.

Charles was not much over ten years old when the family were relocated from Chatham to London in 1822. He had to leave his 'good master'; and the 'old place' was endeared to him by recollections 'that clung all my life'. Chatham was the birth place of his happiness and his fancies, and what store it had set, he hardly knew, by its busy varieties of change and scene. The bright regiments always coming and going, the continual parading and firing, the successions of sham-sieges and sham-defences, the plays got up by his cousin in the hospital, the navy-pay yacht in which he sailed to Sheerness with his father, and the ships floating in the Medway with their far vision of the sea – he was to lose them all.

On the night before we left to London, my good master came flitting in among the packing-cases to give me Goldsmith's *Bee* as a keepsake; which I kept for his sake, and its own, a long time afterwards.

Curiously Charles stayed behind for a few weeks. No reason has ever been given but it was probably to complete his school term.

Through all the intervening years I have never forgotten the stage-coach journey, the smell of the damp straw in which I was packed and forwarded like

15

game, carriage-paid. There was no other inside passenger, and I consumed my sandwiches in solitude and dreariness, and it rained hard all the way, and I thought life sloppier than I expected to find it.

A side street off Gray's Inn Lane, London, a house To Let, still occupied despite its dilapidated condition. Charles spent much of his childhood in close proximity to London's poorer areas.

It was a mean small tenement, with a wretched little back garden abutting a squalid court. A washerwoman lived next door, and a Bow Street officer lived over the way.

He records in the essay *Our Next Door Neighbour* : 'the bill in the parlour window intimating that lodgings for a single gentleman were to be let within, had not been long in the window when a stout, good-humoured looking gentleman, of about five-and-thirty, appeared. In a day or two the single gentleman came in, and shortly afterwards his real character came out.

First of all, he displayed a most extraordinary partiality for sitting up till three or four o'clock in the morning, drinking whisky and water, and smoking cigars; then he invited friends home, who used to come at ten o'clock, and begin to get happy about the small hours, when they evinced their perfect contentment by singing songs with a half-a-dozen verses of two lines each; and a chorus of ten, which chorus used to be shouted forth, by the whole strength of the company, in the most enthusiastic and vociferous manner, to the annoyance of the neighbours, and the special discomfort of another single gentleman overhead.'

George Cruikshank

Our Next Door Neighbour

As I thought in the little back-garret in Bayham Street of all I had lost in losing Chatham, what would I have given, if I had had anything to give, to have been sent back to any other school, to have been taught something, anywhere!

I took in, from the very beginning in Camden Town, the struggling poverty which is nowhere more vividly shown than in the commoner streets of London.

'How much is conveyed by those two short words – "The Parish". And with how many tales of distress and misery, of broken fortune and ruined hopes, too often of unrelieved wretchedness and successful knavery, are they associated. A poor man, with small earnings and a large family, just manages to live on from hand to mouth, and to procure food from day to day; he has barely sufficient to satisfy the present cravings of nature and can take no heed for the future. His taxes are in arrears, quarter-day passes by, another quarter day arrives; he can procure no more quarter for himself, and is summoned by - the Parish. His goods are distrained, his children are crying with cold and hunger, and the very bed on which his sick wife is lying, is dragged from beneath her.' (Our Parish in Sketches by Boz)

How it came that I should be falling into misery and neglect about this time, I did not understand. I know my father to be as kind-hearted and generous a man as ever lived in the world. Everything that I can remember of his conduct to his wife, or children, or friends, in sickness or affliction, is beyond all praise. By me, as a sick child, he has watched night and day, unwearied and patiently. He never undertook any business, charge or trust that he did not zealously, conscientiously, punctually, honourably discharge. His industry has always been untiring. He was proud of me, in his way, and had a great admiration of the comic singing. But, in the ease of his temper, and the straitness of his means, he appeared to have utterly lost at this time the idea of educating me at all, and to have utterly put from him

19

the notion that I had any claim upon him, in that regard, whatever.

So I degenerated into cleaning his boots of a morning, and my own; and making myself useful in the work of the little house; and looking after my younger brothers and sisters (we were now six in all); and going on such poor errands as arose out of our poor way of living.

Chapter 2

His cousin, James Lamert, had finished his education at Sandhurst and was waiting, in hope, for a commission. He was spending some time living with the Dickens family in Bayham Street. Taking pity on the solitary child, James made a little theatre for him. But it could not supply what Charles missed most - the companionship of other children. Fanny, aged eleven, was showing great promise and was elected as a pupil to the Royal Academy of Music in April 1823.

But it was not without a stab to his heart, when he thought about his own disregarded condition. She left with the tearful good wishes of everyone in the house. Gradually all the dreaminess and romance Charles had invested in Chatham was transferred to London.

When I went out for the day it was to my mother's elder brother and to my Godfather who was called Mr Huffham and was a rigger, and mast, oar and block maker. He was an honest boat builder, a kind man and much taken by the comic songs, pronouncing me to his friends as a 'prodigy' My uncle, Thomas Barrow, worked with my father at

Somerset House as a fellow-clerk. However, he broke his leg in a fall and was laid up at his lodgings in Gerrard Street, Soho. In the upper part of the same house was a widow, the recently deceased being a partner in the celebrated book firm of Christie and Manson. Mrs Manson carried on the business and in her thoughtful and helpful way, having often seen me on the stairs, loaned me books for my amusement. One of them, George Coleman's *Broad Grins*, so impressed me with its description of Covent Garden that I stole down to the market to compare the description with the real thing. I recall the flavour of the cabbage leaves as if it were the very breath of comic fiction.

'Covent Garden Market, and the avenues leading to it, are thronged with carts of all sorts, sizes and descriptions, from the heavy lumbering wagons, with his four stout horses, to the jingling costermonger's cart, with its consumptive donkey. The pavement is already strewed with decayed cabbage-leaves, broken haybands, and all the indescribable litter of a vegetable market; men are shouting, carts backing, horses neighing, boys fighting, basket women talking, piemen expatiating on the excellence of their pastry, and donkeys braying.' (The Streets - Morning: in Sketches by Boz)

Although Charles mentions his uncle Thomas it appears that his broken leg was eventually amputated (without anaesthetic) and he was markedly incapacitated. Charles refers to himself as 'a little companion and nurse' in a letter to his uncle. Certainly Dickens had more than one reference to "wooden legs" in his writings. Despite the fact that his grandmother had retired from service and was domiciled in Oxford Street living with John Dickens's brother, Charles does not seem to have sought her out; there is mention of a silver watch (his grandfather's) which she gave him, and little else. She died in April 1824.

How did he spend his time? Chiefly by reading, doing errands and wandering around London, imbibing the sights and sounds. At first it was through the neighbourhood of ramshackle shops and derelict houses, rowdy taverns and factories where fumes poured out all day and workers poured out at night. Then he wandered farther afield into the more salubrious areas. He never forgot the city streets but there were the occasional problems (and dangers) for a lonely eleven year old boy wandering on his own through the crowded thoroughfares. On one occasion he got lost in the Strand. He had sixteen pence in his pocket given to him by his godfather. Feeling hungry and lonely he began to cry, but collecting himself he plucked up courage to enter a shop.

At last I saw a pile of cooked sausages in a window with the label, 'small Germans a Penny'. Emboldened by knowing what to ask for, I went in and said, 'if you please, will you sell me a small German? Which they did…thus I wandered about the city like a child in a dream, staring at the British merchants, and inspired by a mighty faith in the marvellous-ness of everything.

He slipped into a theatre where the 'conversation in the gallery was not improving' and when he came out in the dark and rain he was apprehensive. He had been frightened on one occasion; a threatening gang of boys had chased him. Fortunately, on leaving the theatre, he was accompanied home by a watchman 'with a dreadful cough'.

Sometimes Charles had a pang of conscience as he wandered around; especially when he thought about the worry he was causing his parents at such a late hour. 'They used to say I was an odd child, and I suppose I was.'

My uncle had a barber, very old and out of Dean Street, Soho, who never tired of reviewing the events of the last war and who, in a sagacious way, could detect Napoleon's mistakes and rearrange them on a plan of his own. His singular and eccentric speech was the basis of an essay I wrote, but sadly I never had the courage to show it to anyone. The canon's housekeeper in *Gil Blas* intrigued me and I, in my childish way, sketched a deaf old woman who waited on us in Bayham Street, and who had the propensity of making delicate hashes with walnut-ketchup. At the time I thought the piece immensely clever, but once again kept it to myself .

Another attack of fever laid him low and his spirits were not in the least revived by the resurgence of the mysterious 'deed'. The family fortunes were also low and affairs were going on badly. His mother, in her wisdom, decided on a plan to help the family. She enlisted the help of Charles's godfather down at Limehouse, who was reported to have an Indian connection. She had heard that people in the East Indies always sent their children home to be educated. Thus, she believed, it would be very rewarding to set up a school for such children.

We, it was reasoned, would all grow rich by it and perhaps even I might go to school myself.

A house was soon found for us at no 4 Gower Street North, we moved there and a large brass plate was affixed to the door announcing 'Mrs Dickens's Establishment'.

As a small actor in the comedy, I can report that I left at a great many other doors, a great many circulars calling attention to the merits of the establishment. Yet nobody ever came to school, nor do I recollect that anybody ever proposed to come, or that the least preparation was made to receive anybody. But I do know we got on very badly with the butcher and baker; that very often we had not too much for dinner.

Creditors continued to swarm around the Dickens's abode. 'They use to come at all hours, and some of them were quite ferocious. One dirty-faced man, I think he was a bootmaker, used to edge himself into the passage as early as seven o'clock in the morning, and call up the stairs, "Come! You ain't out yet, you know. Pay us, will you? Don't hide, you know; that's mean. I wouldn't be mean if I was you. Pay us will you! You just pay us, d'ye hear?" Receiving no answer to these taunts, he would mount in his wrath to the words, "swindlers" and "robbers"; and these being ineffectual too, would sometimes go to the extremity of crossing the street, and roaring up at the windows of the second floor.'(David Copperfield)

In 1824 John Dickens was arrested for debt (Charles had been working at the Blacking Factory for less than two weeks) and sent to the Marshalsea prison. It is believed that a baker who lived around the corner instigated the arrest for forty pounds or so, but other debts had accrued over many months. No help was forthcoming from relatives or friends. They had probably had enough. So on 20th of February, his father was incarcerated as an insolvent debtor; which could carry an indefinite period in jail. It was in the Marshalsea that Charles picked up his detailed knowledge into the lower grades of life. However, it was not an altogether wretched period.

The family lived more comfortably in prison than they had done for a long time out of it. We were still waited on by the maid-of-all-work, from Bayham Street, and the orphan girl from Chatham workhouse.

The criminal fraternity and prisons were to be an integral part of Dickens's novels and essays. His attitude towards them can vary from the jocular as in *Pickwick Papers*, to the measured central theme as in *Little Dorrit* (Amy Dorrit, the main character was born in the Marshalsea prison and married there) or to the horrific, as detailed in *Sketches by Boz – A Visit to Newgate,* when the condemned men and the final hours in the condemned cells are graphically written. Fagin, Pickwick, Jingle, Micawber are just a sample of the characters who end up in jail, one way or another. Although one can say that his childhood experiences were to psychologically traumatise him (as modern idiom would have it), Dickens's first foray into fictional incarceration is through Mr Pickwick and he treats it lightly, with the usual undercurrent of social deprivation and despair. In Little Dorrit he takes the opportunity to highlight the bureaucratic nonsense of the system.

'It was an oblong pile of barrack building, partitioned into squalid houses standing back to back, so that there were no back-rooms; environed by a narrow paved yard, hemmed in by high walls duly piked at top. Itself a close and confined prison for debtors, it contained within it a much closer and confined jail for smugglers. Offenders against the revenue laws, and defaulters to excise or customs, who had incurred fines which they were unable to pay, were supposed to be incarcerated behind an iron-plated door, closing up a second prison, consisting of a strong cell or two, and a blind alley some yard and a half wide, which formed the mysterious termination of the very limited skittle-ground in which the Marshalsea debtors bowled down their troubles.

Supposed to be incarcerated there, because time had rather outgrown the strong cells and the blind alley.

Hence the smugglers habitually consorted with the debtors (who received them with open arms), except at certain constitutional moments, when somebody came from some Office, to go through some form of overlooking something, which neither he nor anybody else knew anything about. On those truly British occasions, the smugglers, if any, made a feint of walking into the strong cells and the blind alley, while this somebody pretended to do his something; and made a reality of walking out again as soon as he hadn't done it – neatly epitomising the administration of most of the public affairs, in our right little, tight little island.' (Little Dorrit)

When Mr Pickwick was led into the Fleet Prison, the tone was one of detail and humour, designed to appeal to the expansive and enquiring mind of the main character. After a few days, however, the immortal Pickwick, so saddened by the squalor and ignorance he witnessed, locked himself away in a private room and did not venture out again.

The Marshalsea Prison

'Mr Tom Roker, the gentleman who had accompanied Mr Pickwick into the prison, turned sharp round to the right when he got to the bottom of the little flight of steps, and led the way through an iron gate which stood open, and up another short flight of steps, into a long narrow gallery, dirty and low, paved with stone, and very dimly lighted by a window at each remote end. "This," said the gentleman, thrusting his hands into his pockets and looking carelessly over his shoulder to Mr Pickwick, "This here is the hall flight."

"Oh!" replied Mr Pickwick, looking down a dark and filthy staircase, which appeared to lead to a range of damp and gloomy stone vaults beneath the ground, "and those, I suppose, are the little cellars where the prisoners keep their small quantities of coals. Ah! Unpleasant places to have to go down to; but very convenient, I dare say!"

"Yes! I shouldn't wonder if they was convenient," replied the gentleman, "seeing that a few people live there pretty snug. That's the fair that is!"

"My friend," said Mr Pickwick, "you don't really mean to say that human beings live down in those wretched dungeons?"

"Live down there. Yes, and die down there too, wery often," replied Mr Roker, "and what of that? Who's got to say anything agin it? Live down there! - Yes, and a wery good place it is to live in, ain't it?"

Mr Roker then proceeded to mount another staircase. "There," said Mr Roker, pausing for breath when they reached another gallery of the same dimensions as the one below, "this is the coffee-room flight: the one above's the third and the one above that's the top; and the room where you're agoing to sleep tonight is the warden's room and it's this way – come on."

"There," said Mr Roker, holding the door open, and looking triumphantly round at Mr Pickwick, "There's a room!"

Mr Sam Weller proceeded to inquire which was the individual bedstead that Mr Roker had so flatteringly described as an out-an-outer to sleep in.

"That's it," replied Mr Roker, pointing to a very rusty one in a corner, "It would make any one go to sleep, that bedstead would, whether they wanted to or not."

"I should think," said Sam, eyeing the piece of furniture in question with a look of excessive disgust, "I should think poppies was nothin' to it".

"Nothing at all," said Mr Roker.' (Pickwick Papers)

Chapter 3

My Father was waiting for me in the Lodge of the Marshalsea prison, and we went up to his room (on the top story but one) and cried very much. His last words before he was finally carried there, were to the effect that the sun was set upon him forever. I really believed at the time that they had broken my heart.

And he told me, I remember, to take warning by the Marshalsea, and to observe that if a man had twenty pounds a year, and spent nineteen pounds nineteen shillings and sixpence, he would be happy; but that a shilling spent the other way would make him wretched. I see the fire we sat before, now; with two bricks inside the rusted grate, one on each side, to prevent it burning too many coals.

Some other debtor shared the room with him, who came in by-and-by, and as the dinner was a joint-stock repast, I was sent up to Captain Porter in the room overhead, with Mr Dickens's compliments, and I was his son, and could he, "Captain Porter", lend me a knife and fork? Captain Porter lent the knife and fork, with his compliments in return. There was a very dirty lady in his little room; and two wan girls, his daughters, with shock heads of hair. I thought I should not have liked to borrow Captain Porter's comb. The Captain himself was in the last extremity of shabbiness; and if I could draw at all, I would draw an accurate portrait of the old, old, brown great-coat he wore with no other coat below it. His whiskers were large. I saw his bed rolled up in a corner; and what plates, and dishes and pots he had, on a shelf; and I knew (God knows how) that the two girls with the shock heads were Captain Porter's natural children and that the dirty lady was not married to Captain P. My timid, wondering station on his threshold, was not occupied more than a couple of minutes, I dare say, but I came down again to the room below with all this so surely in my knowledge, as the knife and fork were in my hand.

John Dickens – kind, gentile,
but recklessly improvident.

Mr Micawber - also kind, gentile
but recklessly improvident.

"I have no scruples," said Mr Micawber, "in
saying that I am a man who has, for some years,
contended against the pressure of pecuniary
difficulties. Sometimes I have risen superior to my
difficulties. Sometimes my difficulties have – in short,
have floored me."

"Copperfield, you are a true friend; but when
the worst comes to the worst, no man is without a
friend who is possessed of shaving materials." At this
dreadful hint Mrs Micawber threw her arms round Mr
Micawber's neck and entreated him to be calm. He
wept; but so far recovered, almost immediately, as to
ring the bell for the waiter, and bespeak a hot kidney
pudding and a plate of shrimps for breakfast in the
morning.'

'We had a beautiful little dinner and after dinner Mrs Micawber made us a bowl of hot punch with her own hands. Mr Micawber was uncommonly convivial. I never saw him such good company. He made his face shine with the punch, so that it looked as if it had been varnished all over.'

'As the punch disappeared, Mr Micawber became still more friendly and convivial. Mrs Micawber's spirits becoming elevated too, we sang "Au'd Lang Syne". When we came to "Here's a hand my trusty frere," we all joined hands round the table: and when we declared we would "take a right gude Willie Waught," and hadn't the least idea what it meant, we were really affected.

In a word, I never saw anyone so thoroughly jovial as Mr Micawber was, down to the very last moment of the evening, when I took a hearty farewell of himself and his amiable wife. Consequently, I was not prepared, at seven o'clock next morning, to receive the following communication: "My Dear Young Friend, The die is cast – all is over. Hiding the ravages of care with a sickly mask of mirth…I have discharged the pecuniary liability contracted at this establishment, by giving a note of hand, made payable fourteen days after date, at my residence, Pentonville, London. When it becomes due, it will not be taken up. The result is destruction. The bolt is impending, and the tree must fall.'

'My other piece of advice, Copperfield, annual income twenty pounds, annual expenditure nineteen nineteen six, result happiness. Annual income twenty pounds, annual expenditure twenty pounds ought and six, result misery. The blossom is blighted, the leaf withered, the god of day goes down upon the dreary scene and – and, in short, you are forever floored. As I am!" (David Copperfield)

The financial straits of the Dickens's household went from bad to worse; almost everything by degrees was sold or pawned - plate, jewellery, furniture and even Charles' precious books, his last refuge and comfort, were carried off from a little chiffonier, which his father called the library, to a bookseller in Hampstead Road.

'The keeper of this bookstall, who lived in a little house behind it, used to get tipsy every night, and to be violently scolded by his wife every morning. More than once, when I went there early, I had audience of him in a turned-up bedstead, with a cut in his forehead or a black eye, bearing witness to his excesses over night (I am afraid he was quarrelsome in his drink); and he, with a shaking hand, endeavouring to find the needful shillings in one or other of the pockets of his clothes, which lay upon the floor, while his wife, with a baby in her arms and her shoes down at heel, never left off rating him. Sometimes he had lost his money, and then he would ask me to call again; but his wife had always got some (had taken his, I dare say, while he was drunk), and secretly completed the bargain on the stairs, as we went down together.' (David Copperfield)

The pawnbroker became a familiar figure in his life, as well as the pawnbroker's clerk who officiated behind the counter, and liked, of all things, to hear Charles conjugate Latin verbs, and to add to this repertoire a declination or translation of nouns. Eventually, almost everything was sold and nothing was left in Gower Street, other than a few essential objects (a couple of chairs, a kitchen table and some beds) as circumstances would allow, in the two parlours of the empty house. 'My own little bed was so superciliously looked upon by a power unknown to me, hazily called 'The Trade', that a brass coal-scuttle, a toasting jack, and a bird cage were obliged to be put with it to make a Lot of it, and then it went for a song – so I heard mentioned, and I wondered what song – and thought what a dismal song it must be to sing.'

Elizabeth Dickens (nee Barrow) was accomplished but did little to encourage her eldest son.

Although there is some bitterness towards his father, diluted by that man's kindness, humour and good-nature; the feelings towards his mother, Elizabeth Barrow, are more enigmatic. She appears a more shadowy person in Charles' childhood; his bitterness towards her was only to surface later. He had, however, inherited her hazel coloured eyes, her love of dancing and mimicry, her delight in the ridiculous; and (according to many) came to resemble her as he grew older.

She was, through family ties and learning (as we have seen in the teaching of Latin and English), more sociably aware and, in some respects, more socially accomplished than her husband. It is generally agreed that she was a pretty, amusing and educated woman. In London her father had been the Chief Conductor of Moneys in Town, then a very senior post in the Navy Pay Office. However, the embezzlement of five thousand pounds, to support ten children, was only appeased (in his mind) by a confession and the subsequent flight abroad He was never to return to England.

Elizabeth was not prudent either. A few hours before Charles's birth, it is said although never proved, that she danced the night away at a ball; returning home in the small hours of the morning to give birth to her first son.

She appears in *Nicholas Nickleby* but there are glimpses elsewhere. Certainly Mrs Micawber's plea of, "I never will desert Mr Micawber!" has resonance in his mother's voice. What was Elizabeth's attitude to the grinding poverty and the uncertainty it engendered? With a growing family and frequent changes of abode, life must have been difficult, even depressingly hard, at times. There never appears in Charles's writings any sign of rancour between his parents. Indeed, it is hard to imagine a man like the affable John Dickens marrying a staid, humourless individual. Mrs Micawber's sublime optimism, like that of Mr Micawber, "that something is about to turn up," probably typifies the attitude of his parents to the challenging circumstance in which they regularly found themselves. Mrs Dickens had wealthy relatives who might just come to the rescue and they had to be ready 'in case of anything turning up'.

Perhaps, like Madame Mantalini, she was willing, on occasions, to overlook the frivolous attitude and impecunious state of her husband.

"I *am* miserable,' said Madame Mantalini, evidently pouting.

"Then you are an ungrateful, unworthy, demd unthankful little fairy", said Mr Mantalini.

"I am not," returned Madame, with a sob.

"Do not put itself out of humour," said Mr Mantalini breaking an egg. "It is a pretty, bewitching little demd countenance, and it should not be out of humour, for it spoils its loveliness, and makes it cross and gloomy like a frightful, naughty demd hobgoblin".

"I am not to be brought round in that way, always," rejoined Madame sulkily.

"It shall be brought round in that way it likes best, and not brought round at all if it likes that better," returned Mr Mantalini with his egg spoon in his mouth.

"It's very easy to talk," said Mrs Mantalini.

"Not so easy when one is eating a demnition egg." replied Mr Mantalini, "for the yolk runs down the waistcoat, and yolk of egg does not match any waistcoat but a yellow waistcoat, demmit." (Nicholas Nickleby)

Elizabeth Dickens in later life.

There is a similarity in the drawing by Hablot Browne (who worked in tandem with Dickens, as Phiz and Boz) between the two ladies, although bonnets were not exclusive to Mrs Dickens or to Mrs Nickleby, or for that matter either, in the Victorian era. However, Charles was always critical of the illustration for his books, examining every detail of every drawing. He had turned down Thackeray (of *Vanity Fair* fame) as an illustrator and, on occasions rejected a print after it had been published; the best example being the 'Fireside' print missing from the second issue of *Oliver Twist*. However, his depiction of Mrs Nickleby is universally assumed to represent his mother, as he later admitted.

Mrs Nickleby and Kate.

'This appeal set the widow upon thinking that perhaps she might have made a more successful venture with her one thousand pounds, and then she began to reflect what a comfortable sum it would have been just then; which dismal thoughts made her tears flow faster, and in the excess of these griefs she (being a well-meaning woman enough, but weak withal) fell first to deploring her hard fate, and then to remarking, with many sobs, that to be sure she had been a slave to her poor husband, and had often told him she might have married better (as indeed she had, very often),and that she never knew in his lifetime how the money went, but that if he had confided in her they might all have been better off that day; with other bitter recollections common to most married ladies, either during their coverture, or afterwards, or at both periods. Mrs Nickleby concluded by lamenting that the dear departed had never deigned to profit by her advice, save on one occasion; which was a strictly veracious statement, inasmuch as he had only acted upon it once, and had ruined himself in consequence.' (Nicholas Nickleby)

In March or April 1847, when Charles Dickens was thirty-five, he was asked by his trusted friend John Forster, if he remembered ever having seen in his boyhood their friend the elder Mr Dilke. He was John Dickens's acquaintance and contemporary, who had been a clerk in the same office in Somerset House. "Yes, he said, "he recalled seeing him at a house where his uncle Barrow lodged during an illness. Mr Dilke had visited him". Forster also asked if he could remember having had some juvenile employment in a warehouse near the Strand where his father and Mr Dilke had called to see him one day and given him a half-crown. Dickens was silent for several minutes and Forster felt that he had unintentionally touched a painful place in his memory.

Some weeks later Dickens made a further allusion to a time 'he never could lose the remembrance while he remembered anything, and the recollection of which, at intervals, haunted him and made him very miserable, even to this hour.'

Considering the dire straits that Dickens went through - the poverty, the imprisonment of the whole family, his seclusion; and the later incredible trappings of fame and fortune - it is curious that the events of the blacking warehouse should affect him so badly considering it was a relatively short period, of a few months, in his life. But there is no doubt that it left a painful and lasting impression.

To his sensitive young mind that period heralded the end of his world - the final rejection by his family, the final end to his visions of himself as an educated young man, established in a profession and wealthy.

Once again it was through the auspices of James Lamert, that the scene was set. He had left the Dickens house through want of space and got a job as chief manager in his cousin's firm. George Lamert was a man of some property, who had recently embarked in an odd sort of commercial speculation, and took James into his office and eventually obtained employment for the twelve year old Charles. He began on the 9th of February 1824.

This speculation was a rivalry of "Warren's Blacking, 30, Strand," - at that time very famous. One Jonathan Warren (famous one was Robert), living at 30 Hungerford Stairs or Market, Strand (for I forget which it was called then), claimed to have been the original inventor or proprietor of the blacking recipe, and to have been deposed and ill-used by his renowned relation. At last he put himself in the way of selling his recipe and his name and his 30 Hungerford Stairs, for an annuity; and he set forth by his agents that a little capital would make a great business of it. The man of some property was found in George Lamert. He bought this right and title, and went into the blacking business and the blacking premises.

In an evil hour for me, as I often bitterly thought. Its chief manager, James Lamert, the relative who had lived with us in Bayham Street, seeing how I was employed from day to day, and knowing what our domestic circumstances then were, proposed that I should go into the blacking warehouse, to be as useful as I could, at a salary, I think, of six shillings a week. I am not clear whether it was six or seven. I am inclined to believe, from my uncertainty on this head, that it was six at first, and seven afterwards.

At any rate the offer was accepted very willingly by my father and mother, and on a Monday morning I went down to the blacking warehouse to begin my business life.

It is wonderful to me how I could have been so easily cast away at such an age. It is wonderful to me, that, even after my descent into the poor little drudge I had been since we came to London, no one had compassion enough on me – a child of singular abilities, quick, eager, delicate and soon hurt, bodily and mentally – to suggest that something might have been spared, as certainly it might have been, to place me at any common school. Our friends, I take it, were tired out. No one made any sign. My father and mother were quite satisfied. They could hardly have been more so, if I had been twenty years of age, distinguished at a grammar school, and going to Cambridge.

The blacking warehouse was the last house on the left-hand side of the way, at old Hungerford Stairs. It was a crazy, tumble-down old house, abutting of course on the river, and literally overrun with rats. Its wainscotted rooms, and its rotten floors and staircase, and the old grey rats swarming down in the cellars, and the sound of their squeaking and scuffling coming up the stairs at all times, and the dirt and decay of the place, rise up visibly before me, as if I were there again.

Hungerford Stairs (left) was to haunt Dickens all his life.

The counting house was on the first floor, looking over the coal-barges and the river. There was a recess in it, in which I was to sit and work.

My work was to cover the pots of paste-blacking; first with a piece of oil-paper, and then with a piece of blue paper; to tie them round with a string; and then to clip the paper close and neat, all round, until it looked as smart as a pot of ointment from an apothecary's shop. When a certain number of grosses of pots had attained this pitch of perfection, I was to paste on each a printed label; and then go on again with more pots. Two or three other boys were kept at similar duty down stairs on similar wages. One of them came up, in a ragged apron and paper cap, on the first Monday morning, to show me the trick of using the string and tying the knot. His name was Bob Fagin;

and I took the liberty of using his name, long afterwards, in *Oliver Twist*.

Our relative had kindly arranged to teach me something in the dinner-hour from twelve to one, I think it was, every day. But an arrangement so incompatible with counting-house business soon died away, from no fault of his or mine; and for the same reason, my small work-table, and my grosses of pots, my papers, string, scissors, paste-pot and labels, by little and little, vanished out of the recess in the counting house, and kept company with the other small work-tables, grosses of pots, paper, string and scissors, and paste-pots, downstairs. It was not long before Bob Fagin and I, and another boy whose name was Paul Green, but who was currently believed to have been christened Poll (a belief which I transferred, long afterwards again, to Mr Sweedlepipe, in *Martin Chuzzlewit*), worked generally, side by side. Bob Fagin was an orphan, and lived with his brother-in-law, a waterman. Poll Green's father had the additional distinction of being a fireman, and was employed at Drury Lane Theatre; where another relation of Poll's, I think his little sister, did imps in the pantomimes.

No words can express the secret agony of my soul as I sunk into this companionship; compared these every day associates with those of my happier childhood; and felt my early hopes of growing up to be a learned and distinguished man crushed in my breast.

The deep remembrance of the sense I had of being utterly neglected and hopeless, of the shame I felt in my position; of the misery it was to my young heart to believe that, day by day, what I had learned, and thought, and delighted in, and raised my fancy and my emulation up by, was passing away from me, never to be brought back any more; cannot be written.

My whole nature was so penetrated with the grief and humiliation of such considerations, that even now, famous and caressed and happy, I often forget in my dreams that I have a dear wife and children; and wander desolately back to that time of my life.

My mother and my brothers and sisters (excepting Fanny in the Royal Academy of Music) were still encamped with a young servant-girl from Chatham-workhouse, in the two parlours in the emptied house in Gower Street North. It was a long way to go and return within the dinner-hour, and, usually, I either carried my dinner with me, or went and bought it at some neighbouring shop. In the latter case, it was commonly a saveloy and a penny loaf; sometimes, a fourpenny plate of beef from a cook's shop; sometimes, a plate of bread and cheese, and a glass of beer, from a miserable old public house over the way: the Swan, if I remember right, or the Swan and something else that I have forgotten. Once, I remember tucking my own bread (which I had brought from home in the morning) under my arm, wrapped up in a piece of paper like a book, and going into the best dining room in   Johnson's alamode beef-house in Clare Court, Drury Lane, and magnificently ordering a small plate of alamode beef to eat with it. What the waiter thought of such a strange little apparition, coming in all alone, I don't know; but I can see him now, staring at me as I ate my dinner, and bringing up the other waiter to look. I gave him a halfpenny, and I wish, now, that he hadn't taken it.

His father's creditors were not appeased and all hope of financial salvation went; so in the end, his mother and the whole encampment of Gower Street went to live in the Marshalsea.

The key of the house was sent back to the landlord, who was very glad to get it; and I was handed over as a lodger to a reduced old lady, long known to our family, in Little College Street, Camden Town, who took children in to board, and had once done so at Brighton; and, who, with a few alterations and embellishments, unconsciously began to sit for Mrs Pipchin in *Dombey* when she took me in.

She had a little brother and sister under her care then; somebody's natural children, who were very irregularly paid for; and a widow's little son. The two boys and I slept in the same room. My own exclusive breakfast, of a penny cottage loaf and a pennyworth of milk, I provided for myself. I kept another small loaf, and a quarter of a pound of cheese, on a particular shelf of a particular cupboard; to make my supper on when I came back at night. They made a hole in the six or seven shillings, I know well; and I was out at the blacking warehouse all day, and had to support myself upon that money all the week. I suppose my lodging was paid for, by my father. I certainly did not pay it myself; and I certainly had no other assistance whatever (the making of my clothes, I think, excepted), from Monday morning until Saturday night.

No advice, no counsel, no encouragement, no consolation, no support from anyone that I can call to mind, so help me God.

Sundays, Fanny and I passed in the prison. I was at the academy in Tenterden Street, Hanover

Square, at nine o'clock in the morning, to fetch her; and we walked back there together, at night.

I was so young and childish, and so little qualified – how could I be otherwise? – to undertake the whole charge of my own existence, that, in going to Hungerford Stairs of a morning, I could not resist the stale pastry put out at half-price on trays at the confectioners' doors in Tottenham Court Road; and I often spent in that, the money I should have kept for my dinner. Then I went without my dinner, or bought a roll, or a slice of pudding. There were two pudding shops between which I was divided, according to my finances. One was in a court close to St Martin's Church (at the back of the church) which is now removed altogether. The pudding at that shop was made with currents, and was rather a special pudding, but was rather dear; two penn'orth not being larger than a penn'orth of more ordinary pudding. A good shop for the latter was in the Strand, somewhere near where the Lowther Arcade is now. It was a stout, hale pudding, heavy and flabby; with great raisins in it, stuck in whole, at great distances apart. It came up hot, at about noon every day; and many and many a day did I dine off it.

We had half-an-hour, I think, for tea. When I had money enough, I used to go to a coffee-shop, and have half-a-pint of coffee, and a slice of bread and butter. When I had no money, I took a turn in Covent Garden market, and stared at the pineapples. The coffee shops to which I most resorted were, one in Maiden Lane; one in a court (non-existent now) close to Hungerford Market; and one in St Martin's Lane, of which I only recollect that it stood near the church, and that in the door there was an oval glass-plate with COFFEE ROOM painted on it, addressed towards the street. If I ever find myself in a very different kind of coffee room now, but where there is such an inscription on glass, and read it backwards on the wrong side MOOR-EEFFOC (as I often used to do then, in a dismal reverie), a shock goes through my blood.

I know I do not exaggerate, unconsciously and unintentionally, the scantiness of my resources and the difficulties of my life.

I know that if a shilling or so were given me by any one, I spent it in a dinner or a tea. I know that I worked from morning to night, with common men and boys, a shabby child. I know that I tried, but ineffectually, not to anticipate my money, and to make it last the week through; by putting it away in a drawer I had in the counting house, wrapped into six little parcels, each parcel containing the same amount, and labelled with a different day.

I know that I have lounged about the streets, insufficiently and unsatisfactorily fed. I know that, but for the mercy of God, I might easily have been, for any care that was taken of me, a little robber or a little vagabond.

But I held some station at the blacking warehouse too. Besides that my relative at the counting house did what a man so occupied, and dealing with a thing so anomalous, could, to treat me as one upon a different footing from the rest, I never said, to man or boy, how it was that I came to be there, or gave the least indication of being sorry that I was there. That I suffered in secret, and that I suffered exquisitely, no one ever knew but I.

The secret agony

How much I suffered, it is, as I have said already, utterly beyond my power to tell. No man's imagination can overstep the reality.

My rescue from this kind of existence I considered quite hopeless, and abandoned as such, altogether; though I am solemnly convinced that I never, for one hour, was reconciled to it, or was otherwise than miserably unhappy. I felt keenly, however, the being so cut off from my parents, my brothers, and sisters; and, when my day's work was done, going home to such a miserable blank; and *that*, I thought, might be corrected.

One Sunday night I remonstrated with my father on this head, so pathetically and with so many tears, that his kind nature gave way. He began to think it was not quite right. I do believe he had never thought so before, or thought about it. It was the first remonstrance I had ever made about my lot, and perhaps it opened up a little more than I intended.

A back attic was found for me at the house of an insolvent court agent, who lived in Lant Street in the borough, where Bob Sawyer lodged many years afterwards. A bed and bedding were sent over for me, and made up on the floor. The little window had a pleasant prospect of a timber yard; and when I took possession of my new abode, I thought it was paradise.

Meanwhile his father's small income was still on-going and the family lived in some comfort, although perhaps only relatively so, in the Marshalsea. To his delight and solace, Charles was able to breakfast with them in the prison, going there as early as the gates were opened. The maid from Bayham Street still lived with the Dickens' household, as before, and added to their comforts; as well as the little orphan girl rescued from the Chatham workhouse - 'sharp and quick of nature.' Her kindness and worldly ways became 'the Marchioness' in The Old Curiosity Shop. The warmth of his writing speaks of his eternal affection for her and the comfort she gave during these stressful times. Dickens never forgot an act of kindness.

"I begin to infer, from your manner and these appearances, Marchioness," said Mr Dick Swiveller after a pause, and smiling with trembling lip, "that I have been ill." "You just have!" replied the small servant, wiping her eyes. "Very ill, Marchioness, have I been?" "Dead, all but, I never thought you'd get better. Thank heaven you have!" The Marchioness, having arranged the bedclothes more comfortably, and felt that his hands and forehead were quite cool – a discovery that filled her with delight - cried a little more, and then applied herself to getting tea ready, and making some thin dry toast." (The Old Curiosity Shop).

The servant girl had lodgings in the neighbourhood so that she could report early for her duties, and when Charles met her on London Bridge, as he would sometimes do, he would astonish her with tales about the wharves and the tower, while they waited for the prison gates to open.

The 'Marchioness' – the maidservant to the Brass family (she has no given name in the book). (*The Old Curiosity Shop*)

Usually Charles had supper with his family, returning to his lodgings at nine. The landlord and his wife were very kind to the child; the landlord being fat, good-natured and lame; his old wife was quiet and caring, and they had an innocent grown up son, who was lame too.

One night Charles suffered from one of his attacks of abdominal spasm, and the caring trio sat by his bed all night. His affection showed when he made them the Garland family in *The Old Curiosity Shop* and highlighted their kindness and equanimity and common sense.

'Well, wasn't Mr Garland kind when he said, "Christopher, here's your money, and you have earned it well," and wasn't Mrs Garland kind when she said, "Barbara, here's yours, and I am much pleased with you"; and wasn't it beautiful to see how Mrs Garland poured out Barbara's mother a glass of wine; and didn't Barbara's mother speak up when she said, "Here's blessing you, m'am, as a good lady, and you, sir, as a good gentleman." (The Old Curiosity Shop)

Sometimes the painful spasms occurred at work, for no particular reason.

Bob Fagin was very good to me on the occasion of a bad attack of my old disorder. I suffered such excruciating pain that time, that they made me a temporary bed of straw in my old recess in the old counting house, and I rolled about on the floor, and Bob filled empty blacking bottles with hot water, and applied relays of them to my side, half the day. I got better and quite easy towards evening; but Bob (who was much bigger and older than I) did not like the idea of my going home alone, and took me under his protection.

I was too proud to let him know about the prison; and after making several efforts to get rid of him, to all of which Bob Fagin in his goodness was deaf, shook hands with him on the steps of a house near Southwark Bridge on the Surrey side, making believe that I lived there. As a finishing piece of reality in case of his looking back, I knocked at the door, I recollect, and asked, when the woman opened it, if that was Mr Robert Fagin's house.

(*The nature of the excruciating pain almost certainly had an organic basis. The fact that attacks occurred in happier, earlier days; and the fact that attacks occurred intermittently both in the lodgings and at work, supports this hypothesis. There is no mention of any abdominal symptoms such as vomiting, and there is no history of metabolic disease in his parents or their families, and none in his children either, although he did suffer from gout in later life – a not uncommon metabolic disease, especially with the meat-rich meals of the Victorian era. It is a disorder of nucleoproteins leading to uric acid crystals in the soft tissue and joints, and in the kidneys. The very nature of the sudden excruciating episodes would point to renal or ureteric colic. In middle age it is usually caused by renal stones which can be formed by gout crystals. Such stones cause blood to appear in the urine (there is no mention of this in his description, although modesty might have precluded in Victorian Britain). In children, however, there may be a congenital abnormality which can lead to an altered function of the ureter (the tube from the kidney to the bladder) which, in turn, causes violent ureteric spasms – always described as 'the most painful of all pains'. These spasms may cease as suddenly as they begin. Over the years the kidney tissue can be damaged and this renal damage plus atheroma plus gout, could be the multifactorial basis for the hypertension he suffered by his fifties.)

Chapter 4

While the Dickens family, lived not uncomfortably and in some style, at least in comparison to Captain Porter and associates, the creditors pressed on in their action, eager and determined to raise every penny they could. One incident involved the twelve year old Charles.

It was necessary, as a matter of form, that the clothes I wore should be seen by the official appraiser. I had a half-holiday to enable me to call upon him at his own time, at a house somewhere beyond the Obelisk. I recollect his coming out to look at me with his mouth full, and a strong smell of beer upon him and saying good-naturedly that "that would do," and "it was all right." Certainly the hardest creditor would not have been disposed to avail himself of my poor white hat, little jacket, or corduroy trousers. But I had a fat old silver watch in my pocket, which had been given me by my grandmother before the blacking days, and I had entertained my doubts as I went along whether that valuable possession might not bring me over the twenty pounds. So I was greatly relieved, and made him a bow of acknowledgement as I went out.

The reason for this curious happening resides in the fact that his father had applied for freedom under The Insolvent Debtors Act. This act required that all property be surrendered and that all goods with a combined value of over twenty pounds could be taken to pay off the debts; the family's possessions were also taken into account.

Charles missed his family and his old friends; at dinner time he would occasionally play on the coal barges with Bob Fagin and Poll Green. Generally, however, he would stroll alone, along the backstreets of London.

I was such a little fellow, with my poor white hat, little jacket, and corduroy trousers, that frequently, when I went into the bar of a strange public house for a glass of ale or porter to wash down the saveloy and the loaf I had eaten in the street, they didn't like to give it to me. I remember, one evening (I had been somewhere for my father, and was going back to the borough over Westminster Bridge), that I went into a public house in Parliament Street, which is still there though altered, at the corner of a short street leading into Cannon Row, and said to the landlord behind the bar, "What is your very best – *the very best* – ale, a glass."

For the occasion was a festive one, for some reason; I forget why. It may have been my birthday or somebody else's. "Two pence," say he. "Then," says I, "just draw me a glass of that, if you please, with a good head to it".

The landlord looked at me, in return, over the bar, from head to foot, with a strange smile on his face; and instead of drawing the beer, looked round the screen and said something to his wife, who came round from behind it, with her work in hand, and joined him in surveying me.

Here we stand, all three before me now, in my study in Devonshire Terrace. The landlord, in his shirt sleeves, leaning against the bar window frame; his wife, looking over the little half-door; and I, in some confusion, looking up at them from outside the partition. They asked me a good many questions, as to

'What is your very best ale?' (*David Copperfield*)

what my name was, how old I was, where I lived, how I was employed, &c. &c. to all of which, that I might commit nobody, I invented appropriate answers. They served me with the ale, though I suspect it was not the strongest on the premises; and the landlord's wife, opening the little half-door and bending down, gave me a kiss that was half-admiring and half-compassionate, but all womanly and good, I am sure.

At last, for John and Elizabeth Dickens, something turned up - in the shape of a legacy of

£450 in his mother's will. So, on the 28th of May John Dickens was released after only fourteen weeks in the Marshalsea. Just before the family was freed; there was re-enacted a curious little ceremony designed to get up a petition. It was for a bounty to be given to the prisoners so that they could drink his majesty's health on the King's forthcoming birthday. Charles's father and the erstwhile acquaintance Captain Porter were involved.

It is also the first time Dickens refers to his amazing powers of observation and his ability to record every mannerism and detail of those observed; in fact the prelude to his inimitable skill as an author.

When I went to the Marshalsea of a night, I was always delighted to hear from my mother what she knew about the histories of the different debtors in the prison; and when I heard of this approaching ceremony, I was so anxious to see them all come in, one after another (though I knew the greater part of them already, to speak to, and they me), that I got leave of absence on purpose, and established myself in a corner, near the partition.

The internal regulations of the place, for cleanliness and order, and for the government of a common room in the ale-house; where hot water and some means of cooking, and a good fire, were provided for all who paid a very small subscription; were excellently administered by a governing committee of debtors, of which my father was chairman for the time being. As many of the principal officers of this body as could be got into a small room without filling it up, supported him, in front of the petition; and my old friend Captain Porter (who had washed himself, to do honour to so solemn an occasion) stationed himself close to it, to read it to all who were unacquainted with its contents. The door was then thrown open, and they began to come in, in a long file; several waiting on the landing outside, while one entered, affixed his signature, and went out. To everybody in succession, Captain Porter said, "Would you like to hear it read?" If he weakly showed the least disposition to hear it, Captain Porter, in a loud sonorous voice, gave him every word of it. I remember a certain luscious roll he gave to such words as "Majesty – gracious Majesty – your gracious Majesty's unfortunate subjects – your Majesty's well-know munificence"; as if the words were something real in his mouth, and delicious to taste: my poor father meanwhile listening with a little of an author's vanity, and contemplating (not severely) the spikes on the opposite wall.

Whatever was comical in this scene and whatever was pathetic, I sincerely believe I perceived in my corner, whether I demonstrated or not, quite as well as I should perceive it now. I made out my own little characters and story for every man who put his name to the sheet of paper. I might be able to do that now, more truly; not more earnestly, or with a closer interest. Their different peculiarities of dress, of face, of gait, of manner, were written indelibly upon my memory. I would rather have seen it than the best play ever played; and I thought about it afterwards, over the pots of paste-blacking, often and often.

When I looked with my mind's eye, into the Fleet Prison during Mr Pickwick's incarceration, I wonder whether half-a-dozen men were wanting from the Marshalsea crowd that came filing in again, to the sound of Captain Porter's voice!

This scene is reproduced, almost verbatim, in *David Copperfield*: Captain Hopkins is the scrubbed and sonorous Master of Ceremonies, and the author contemplating his petition is Mr Micawber.

The family, after two quick moves, settled in SomersTown, only a few minutes walk from their old house in Bayham Street. His father, who had retired from his job on arrest to avoid potential dismissal, resumed his job in the Navy Pay Office. If his father's release was to be the immediate prelude to a new era in Charles's life, he was to be mistaken. The day's drudgery at Warren's warehouse continued, even after it moved to Chandos Street, Covent Garden.

The establishment was larger now, and we had one or two new boys. Bob Fagin and I had attained great dexterity in tying up the pots. I forget how many we could do, in five minutes.

Warren's blacking pots. The time spent in the blacking factory is unclear. 'I have no idea how long it lasted, whether for a year, or much more, or less.'

We worked, for the light's sake, near the second window as you come from Bedford Street; and

58

we were so brisk at it, that the people used to stop and look in. Sometimes there would be quite a little crowd there. I saw my father coming in at the door one day when we were very busy, and I wondered how he could bear it.'

I had the same wanderings about the streets as I used to have, and was just as solitary and self-dependent as before; but I had not the same difficulty in merely living. I never however heard a word of being taken away, or of being otherwise than quite provided for.

At last one day, my father, and the relative so often mentioned, quarrelled; quarrelled by letter, for I took the letter from my father to him which caused the explosion, but quarrelled very fiercely.

It was about me. It may have had some backward reference, in part, for anything I know, to my employment at the window. All I am certain of is, that, soon after I had given him the letter, my cousin (he was a sort of cousin by marriage) told me he was very much insulted about me; and that it was impossible to keep me, after that. I cried very much, partly because it was so sudden, and partly because in his anger he was violent about my father, though gentle to me. Thomas, the old soldier, comforted me, and said he was sure it was for the best. With a relief so strange that it was like oppression, I went home.

The young Charles was unsure about his future, what prospects lay ahead, whether an education was imminent; but there was a sting in the tail which he never forgot and never forgave.

My mother set herself to accommodate the quarrel, and did so the next day.

She brought home a request for me to return next morning, and a high character of me, which I am very sure I deserved. My father said, I should go back no more, and should go to school.

I do not write resentfully or angrily: for I know how all these things have worked together to make me what I am: but I never afterwards forgot, I never shall forget, I never can forget, that my mother was warm for my being sent back.

Mrs Dickens role as peacemaker did not result in Charles's reinstatement, due to his father's intervention. Perhaps seven shillings a week was sufficient inducement for her efforts, considering the dire financial straits they had recently endured or the fact may simply be that she did not recognise his potential. Many famous and successful men and women have acknowledged the influence and impetus their mother's teaching gave them when young; in Charles's case, it seems she hardly had any effect on his career. Indeed her name barely appears in his correspondence and he only refers to her on the rarest occasions. Perhaps, like Mrs Nickleby, she had an inconsequential and unworldly approach to life.

The period in the blacking factory seemed to have been a watershed in Dickens's youth. Spanning about 6 months he never forgot it. In the years ahead he never told his family. Yet it had one profound effect in later life, he was determined to succeed and have money. This meant that at times he could be hard and aggressive in his business dealings as numerous acrimonious forays, with those who published his works, were to testify. The young Charles - the suffering, innocent child - was to be reborn time and time again as Oliver Twist, David Copperfield, Paul Dombey, Jo, Nell Trent, Philip Pirrip and numerous others.

Until Old Hungerford Market was pulled down, until old Hungerford Stairs were destroyed, and the very nature of the ground changed, I never had the courage to go back to the place where my servitude began. I never saw it. I could not endure to go near it. For many years, when I came near to Robert Warren's in the Strand, I crossed over to the opposite side of the way, to avoid a certain smell of the cement they put upon the blacking-corks, which reminded me of what I was once. It was a very long time before I liked to go up Chandos Street. My old way home by the borough made me cry, after my eldest child could speak.

Chapter 5

There was a school in the Hampstead Road kept by Mr Jones, a Welshman, to which my father dispatched me to ask for a card of terms. The boys were at dinner, and Mr Jones was carving for them with a pair of holland sleeves on, when I acquitted myself of this commission. He came out and gave me what I wanted, and hoped I should become a pupil. I did.

At seven o'clock one morning, very soon afterwards, I went as day scholar to Mr Jones's establishment which was in Mornington Place... there was a board over the door graced with the words WELLINGTON HOUSE ACADEMY

'I should think there never can have been a man who enjoyed his profession more than Mr Creakle did. He had a delight in cutting at the boys, which was like the satisfaction of a craving appetite.' (David Copperfield)

Wellington House Academy, Hampstead Road. Dickens's school 1824-26

Although there was an inscription at the front of the house, "Mr Jones's Classical and Commercial Academy", it seems that Mr Jones's one qualification for office was his undoubted dexterity with the use of the cane, having been described by a fellow pupil later as "a most ignorant fellow, and a mere tyrant." Charles escaped, however, because he was a day-boy, who had the facility to carry home complaints, and, Mr Jones in his wisdom, decided that Charles should be treated with some leniency. Although in later writings about his education, Dickens was to record his grounding in Greek and Latin, and to be the recipient of certain prizes; these facts are not always corroborated by other pupils.

Indeed one wrote to Forster, "My recollections of Dickens whilst at school is that of a healthy looking boy, small but well-built, with a more than usual flow of spirits, inducing to harmless fun, seldom or ever I think to mischief, to which so many lads at that age are prone. I cannot recall anything that then indicated he would become a literary celebrity. But perhaps he was too young. He usually held his head more erect than lads ordinarily do and there was a general smartness about him."

Another school friend Doctor Danson wrote. "Dickens has given a very lively account of this place in his paper entitled '*Our School*' (*Household Words*, 1851) but it is very mythical in many respects, and more especially in the compliments he pays in it to himself. I do not remember that Dickens distinguished himself in any way, or carried off any prizes. My belief is that he did not learn Greek or Latin there, and you will remember that there is no illusion to the classics in any of his writings. He was a handsome, curly-headed lad, full of animation and animal spirits, and probably was connected with every mischievous prank in the school. Depend upon it he was quite a self-made man, and his wonderful knowledge and command of the English language must have been acquired by long and patient study after leaving his last school. At about that time Penny and Saturday Magazines were published weekly, and were greedily read by us. We kept bees, white mice, and other living things, clandestinely in our desks; and the mechanical arts were a good deal cultivated, in the shape of coach building, and making pumps and boats, the motive power of which was the white mice.

I think at the time Dickens took to writing small tales, and we had a sort of club for lending and circulating them. Dickens was also very strong in using a sort of lingo, which made us quite unintelligible to bystanders. We were very strong, too in theatricals."

They formed a small theatre groups, and in their enthusiasm got up 'very gorgeous scenery to illustrate the *Miller and his Men* and *Cherry* and *Fair Star*. Dickens was always the leader in these plays and at one representation, 'the fireworks in the last scene (to signify the destruction of the mill) were so very violent that the police interfered and knocked equally as violently at the doors.'

There was a Latin master at the school, a Mr Manville or Mandeville, who for many years was well-known at the Library of the British Museum (so there may be truth in Dickens's assertion of his learning these classical languages – he certainly refers to Classical mythology in his letters, especially when in Italy). It was the same master 'who plugged his ears with onions for his deafness. There was also a fat little dancing master who taught the hornpipes, a gruff serving man who nursed the boys in scarlet fever, and the principal himself who was always ruling ciphering books with a bloated mahogany ruler.'

So the picture emerges of Charles as a rather small boy, curly-headed, smart, hard-working and always cheerful. His teenage sense of humour could not be suppressed; he joined with his friends pretending, in a harmless way, to be beggars. They would enjoy the puzzled expressions of the passers-by and, when found out, laugh uproariously with them; or while sitting in the chapel, he would not attend in the slightest degree, but inciting those around him to laughter so "that they were lucky not to be thrown out."

Kit's writing lesson. (Martineau) (*The Old Curiosity Shop*)

Charles also recorded many years later in *The Uncommercial Traveller* a curiously comical account of one of the pupils least favoured, the school bully. Charles had received news that he was about to receive some treats from the West Indies including some guava jelly. 'It was now that Globson, bully no more, sought me out in the playground. He was a big fat boy, with a big fat head and a big fat fist, and…had raised such a bump on my forehead that I couldn't get my hat of state on, to go to Church. He said that after an interval of reflection (four months) he now felt this blow to have been an error of judgement, and that he wished to apologise for the same. Not only that, but holding down his big head…requested me, as an act of justice which would appease his awakened conscience, to raise a retributive bump upon it, in the presence of witnesses. This handsome proposal I modestly declined, and he embraced me, and we walked away conversing. We conversed respecting the West India Islands, and, in the pursuit of knowledge, he asked me with much interest whether in the course of my reading I had met with any reliable description of the mode of manufacturing guava jelly; or whether I had ever happened to taste that conserve, which he had been given to understand, was of rare excellence.'

A miniature of Charles Dickens, the first known portrait.

His time at the Wellington Academy was not particularly long, about two years; then, it is asserted, he attended another school near Brunswick Square, where his brothers were subsequently placed. However, many years later, when asked by a former pupil of Jones's school, if he had gone to any other school after he left the Academy, Dickens replied in the negative.

In 1827 there were two significant events.

John Dickens left the Navy Pay Office, it has been inferred that it was due to the period in the Marshalsea but there does not appear to be any firm evidence for this assumption. Once again he was hard-up and the family expense was stretched even tighter by the birth of another baby, Augustus. John had a small pension and an aptitude for languages. Thus he secured a new job as a parliamentary reporter for the *British Press*. But the rent was beyond them again and, as usual, they were short of money. With school fees also beyond them, Charles left school in May.

Thus at fifteen, Dickens's formal education ended; and it has been remarked that "he seemed to have acquired a very scant amount of classic lore while under the instructions of Mr Jones, and not too much lore of any kind."

When my father was asked, "Pray, Mr Dickens, where was your son educated?" He would reply, "Why, indeed sir- ha- ha! He may be said to have educated himself!"

Chapter 6

One May morning in 1827 Charles began a brief period working for a solicitor, Mr Molloy, in New Square, Lincoln's Inn Fields, London, followed shortly by a change of firms, moving to Gray's Inn where Ellis and Blackmore gave him regular employment in 1827.

"I was acquainted, "wrote Mr Blackmore, "with his parents, and then being in practice in Gray's Inn, they asked me if I could find employment for him. He was a bright, clever-looking youth, and I took him as a clerk. His modest salary at first was thirteen shillings and six pence a week, and afterwards fifteen shillings. Several incidents took place in the office of which he must have been a keen observer, as I recognised some of them in *Pickwick* and *Nickleby*. His taste for theatricals was much promoted by a fellow-clerk called Potter. They took every opportunity, then unknown to me, of going together to a minor theatre where, (I afterwards heard) they not infrequently engaged in parts."

'When the cloth was removed, Mr Thomas Potter ordered the waiter to bring in, two goes of his best Scotch whisky, with warm water and sugar…it was just half-past eight, so they thought they couldn't do better than go at half-price to the slips at the City Theatre, which they did accordingly. Mr Robert Smithers, who had become extremely poetical after the settlement of the bill, enlivened the walk by informing Mr Thomas Potter in confidence that he felt an inward presentiment of approaching dissolution, and subsequently embellished the theatre, by falling asleep, with his head and both arms gracefully drooping over the front of the boxes…such were the happy effects of the Scotch whisky...but Mr Thomas Potter conducted himself (*on stage) in a very different manner, and commenced going very fast indeed – rather too fast at last, for the patience of the audience to keep pace with him. On his first entry, he contented himself by earnestly calling upon the gentlemen in the gallery to "flare up", accompanying the demand with another request, expressive of his wish that they would instantaneously "form a union", both which requisitions were responded to, in the manner most in vogue on such occasions. "Give that dog a bone!" cried one gentleman in shirt sleeves, "Where have you been a having half a pint of intermediate beer?" cried a second… while numerous voices concurred in desiring Mr Thomas Potter to return to the arms of his maternal parent, or in common parlance to "go home to his mother!" All these taunts Mr Thomas Potter received with supreme contempt, cocking the low-crowned hat a little more to one side whenever any reference was made to his personal appearance, and, standing up with his arm a-kimbo, expressing defiance most melodramatically.'(Making a Night of It: Sketches by Boz)

So they went regularly to the theatre, entering after nine when the seats were cheaper. Both were dressed in the height of fashion, both had a penchant for chops and oysters, brandy and water, whisky and stout. Charles remained with the firm until November, picking up some legal knowledge and a profound observation of the men involved in its execution, both good and bad; from the kind and sympathetic solicitor, Mr Perker who represented Pickwick in the action by Bardell; to the gravity and greed of Tulkinghorn, the Dedlocks' family lawyer in *Bleak House*. Despite his best friend, Forster, being in the legal profession Dickens rarely hid his contempt for the excessive fees charged, the long delays occasioned; and the often unscrupulous and questionable practices where he found lawyers content to linger long over the minutiae and inconsequential details, to split hairs very slowly, and to grow rich on the distress of others – 'a very pleasant, profitable affair of private theatricals, presented to an uncommonly select audience.'

'This the Court of Chancery; which its decaying houses and its blighted lands in every shire, which has its worn out lunatic in every madhouse; and its dead in every churchyard; which has its ruined suitor, with his slip-shod heels and threadbare dress, borrowing and begging through the round of every man's acquaintance; which gives to *moneyed* might, the means abundantly of wearying out the right; which so exhaust finances, patience, courage, hope; so overthrows the brain and breaks the heart; that there is not an honourable man among its practitioners who would not give- who does not give- the warning, "Suffer any wrong that can be done to you, rather than come here." (Bleak House)

John Forster – a devout, life long friend and excellent biographer. Although slightly younger than Dickens he did not seem it. A mandarin presence, with an infectious laugh and north-country humour; his kindness in helping writers (critically and legally) was legendary.

I have that opinion of the law of England generally…that it puts all the honest men under the diabolical hoofs of all the scoundrels.

Mr Tulkinghorn's house was no 58 Lincoln's Inn Fields, actually occupied by John Forster. Dickens describes it, 'let off in sets of chambers now; and in those shrunken fragments of its greatness, lawyers lie like maggots in nuts.' His friend didn't seem to mind.

Without the necessary funds, Charles's chances of being articled were slim. His salary was even below that of the middle-aged copying clerk, always needy and uniformly shabby (so often depicted in his books). His own position was little better than a glorified office boy who had to copy wills and other legal documents as well as running errands to various lawyers and courts. During the copying he was to come across names like Bardell, Rudge, Corney and Newman Knott (easily corrupted to Knoggs for *Nicholas Nickleby*).

His perambulations and his errands only added to his vast knowledge of London – people, buildings and streets. His depth of facts appertaining to London has been described 'as wonderful, for describing every shop in any of the West End streets'. The work was mundane. He was bored. Thus with a complete change of direction, he decided to become a reporter like his father. Once again his father was feeling 'the pinch,' and the rent, as usual, was in arrears.

Outwardly Charles was fascinated by the theatre and having a good time with his friends in any bar, restaurant or eating house they could find. But he was beginning to develop a serious side and began learning shorthand, supplementing his education with many long hours in the British Museum. (The reader's ticket was obtained on his eighteenth birthday, the youngest permissible age, and he spent what he described as the most useful days of his life in the Reading Room.)

'The changes that were rung upon dots, which in such a position meant such a thing, and in such another position meant something else entirely different; the wonderful vagaries that were played by circles; the unaccountable consequences that resulted from marks like flies' legs; the tremendous effects a curve in a wrong place; not only troubled my waking hours, but reappeared before me in my sleep.'

When sufficiently confident in shorthand, which took eighteen months, he left Ellis and Blackmore in November 1828. He set up as a free-lance reporter in Doctors' Commons, near St Paul's. He shared a rented box with a family friend, and sat hour after hour taking down the court records of each case. He passed nearly two years there, assiduously writing and improving his skills.

He was nineteen years old when at last he entered the old Houses of Parliament's reporters' gallery with his father, who had been there for some time as a reporter for a morning newspaper. Charles's first parliamentary services were for a journal, the *True Sun*. Later he was engaged by the *Mirror of Parliament* (originated by an uncle on his mother's side); and at twenty three he began working for the *Morning Chronicle*.

'I have worn my knee by writing on them on the old back row of the old gallery of the old house of commons; and I have worn my feet by standing to write in a preposterous pen in the old house of lords, where we used to be huddled together like so many sheep. To the wholesome training of severe newspaper work, when I was very young man, I constantly refer my first success.

There never was anybody connected with newspapers, who, in the same space of time, had so much express and post-chaise experience as I. And what gentlemen they were to serve, in such things, at the old *Morning Chronicle*! Great or small it did not matter. I have had to charge for half-a-dozen breakdowns in half-a-dozen times as many miles. I have had to charge for the damage of a great-coat from the dripping of a blazing wax-candle, in writing through the smallest hours of the night in a swift flying carriage and pair. I have been upset in almost every description of vehicle known in this country.

I have been, in my time, belated on miry by-roads, towards the small hours, forty or fifty miles from London, in a wheel-less carriage, with exhausted horses and drunken post-boys, and have got back in time for publication. I have never forgotten the fascination of that old pursuit.'

Charles was becoming renowned for his speed, endeavour and accuracy of his reporting. Edward Stanley, the Chief Secretary, was anxious to publish his long speech on the Irish Question and noted that only part of it was accurately reported. He sent for the reporter who had taken down that section. When he saw Dickens he said, 'I had hoped to see the gentleman who had reported that part of my speech.' Once he had overcome his amazement at 'so young a man' he dictated the whole of his speech to Dickens who reported it accurately. Stanley wrote to Barrow complimenting him upon a reporter so able and so youthful.

But Charles was becoming bored and disillusioned. He was not impressed then (and never was) by politicians and parliament. 'Night after night I wrote predictions that never came to pass, professions that are never fulfilled, explanations that are only meant to mystify.'(David Copperfield)

Yet again, his mind took another somewhat slightly bizarre turn. He decided to become an actor. He had developed remarkable powers of mimicry and expression in his amateur performances. So he took lessons and at home practised gestures, voice, walking and movement. His icon and model was Charles Mathews – singer, comic, conjuror and impersonator – whom he had seen first in Chatham and recently in London. Such was Mathews' all-round ability that he took every part in short plays (an inspiration for Dickens's Readings on tour later). When he felt confident, he wrote to the Lyceum for an audition and an appointment was given. Fanny was to go with him. But, for posterity's sake, as it happened, fate played a hand in as much as he was 'laid up with a terrible bad cold' and had to postpone.

Charles was soon to embark of one act in his life that dominated his thoughts and drove him ambitiously forward – he fell in love.

Chapter 7

In 1855 Dickens wrote to Forster regarding the real-life Dora, whom David Copperfield had striven for, worked for, and idolised in an exaggerated way.

I fall into captivity (*David Copperfield*)

If you mean my own feeling, and will only think what the desperate intensity of my nature is…that it excluded every other idea from my mind for four years, at a time of life when four years are equal to four times four; and that I went at it with a determination to overcome all the difficulties, which fairly lifted me up in the newspaper life, and floated me away over a hundred men's heads; then you are right, because nothing can exaggerate that. I have positively stood amazed at myself ever since! And so I suffered, and so worked, and so beat and hammered away at the maddest romances that ever got into any boy's head.'

The Beadnell family lived in Lombard Street, London close to the bank where Mr Beadnell held an important, and in their eyes, a highly prestigious position. There were three sisters. One had dark ringlets, bright eyes and her laughter, which at times suddenly changes to a pouting expression, charmed him to distraction. Her name was Maria Beadnell and she was nineteen (a year older than Charles) when they met in the Spring of 1830. He made her acquaintance through his sister Fanny and the Beadnell's took little notice of the young man who looked much younger than his years. To them, as aspiring parents, he was of little interest.

Maria Beadnell. Dark hair and eyes, with a cold, captivating capriciousness. Small, she was often called "the pocket Venus."

Maria was flattered at first, but soon learned how to control his emotions and played on his love, both in a flirtatious and calculating way. They exchanged keepsakes and letters at regular intervals during their time together; the first surviving letter is from late1831 when he wants to present her with an Annual (hardly a romantic gift) with the reminder that '. Surely you will not refuse so trivial a present; a mere commonplace trifle; a common present even amongst the merest friends.' The use of the term "friends" seems to indicate that events had not really progressed even after a year or more. However, his ardour knew no bounds. Every hour he could, he spent with her (usually in the presence of her parents, as Victorian etiquette demanded), and wrote bad poems and entertained her in a lively manner. He, in a naïve and foolish expression of love, said he envied her dog, Daphne, which she clutched to her breast.

David Copperfield has a similar resentment of Dora Spenlow's attachment to her dog.

'Jip was there, and Jip would bark at me again. When I presented my bouquet, he gnashed his teeth with jealousy. Well he might. If he had the least idea how I adored his mistress, well he might!'(David Copperfield)

The more the hapless Charles tried, the more her attitude towards him became both ambiguous and perplexing. Her parents continued to treat him as just another young man, of relative unimportance, as shown by Mrs Beadnell's continuing habit of calling him "Mr Dickin". She may have been irritated by him or simply ignorant or perhaps belittling, it is hard to fathom out. Even when Charles did his best, such as escorting the family through the streets of London (they were going to be fitted for wedding clothes for sister Margaret's wedding) he was dismissed in an imperious tone, "And now, Mr Dickin, we'll wish *you* good morning!" No doubt the gallant heart did not notice, or if he did, it was not affected.

'I was resolute to declare my passion and know my fate. Happiness or misery was now out of the question…I passed three days in a luxury of wretchedness, torturing myself by putting every conceivable variety of discouraging construction on all that ever had taken place. How many times I went up and down the street, and round and round the square, before I could persuade myself to go up the steps and knock, is no matter now.'

Gradually Mr and Mrs Beadnell began to realise that Charles's attachment to their daughter was no passing fancy, no youthful crush. Fanny, who had distinguished herself with prizes at the Royal Academy of Music, was acceptable up to a point. But Charles's job was not very impressive, while his desire to become an actor was way beyond their comprehension. He also had a radical touch to his opinions which may have unsettled them. More important, in their eyes, his family had no social standing; and little by little, they began to unearth the Marshalsea episode. Still he was welcome (within reason) at their house and occasionally he was invited for dinner. Charles, however, found no fault with the family, who were tolerant of his mannerisms and humour. However, their forbearance must have been stretched to the limit, especially (on the occasion) when he gave a recitation after dinner of a long embarrassing poem, describing himself "as a cabbage without a heart". Her parents tried to isolate him, taking care not to let them spend any time together; Charles attempted to express his ardour in letters sent by a servant or more often through Henry Kolle who was engaged to Anne, Maria's sister.

So their answer to the conundrum was simply to send Maria, without warning, to Paris.

It seems to have worked. She came back more lukewarm than ever, but still predisposed to keep him wondering - mixing caprice and coldness with occasional endearment.

On his twenty-first birthday in Bentinck Street (yet another home for his family) Charles managed to way-lay her in a quiet corner and poured out his heart.

She heard him out 'with angelic gentleness' but, echoing her parents, called him 'a boy' and abruptly went home. That 'short and dreadful word' ended what had been 'a beautiful party'. He did what many young men would do under such disheartening circumstances – he got hopelessly drunk and awoke the following morning feeling even worse.

Still the star-struck Romeo, Charles persisted. His endearments, although somewhat histrionic and over stated by modern standards were by no means unusual. The twenty-six-year-old Napoleon was similarly afflicted in his hasty notes to Josephine.

Dickens, the thwarted lover, wrote repeatedly to Maria. In each letter, carefully composed, he added sonorous and emotional phrases, 'Whatever fancy, romance passion, aspiration and determination belong to me I never have separated and never shall separate from that hard-hearted little woman – you.' 'My feelings upon any subject …must be to you a matter of very little moment, still I have feelings…the miserable reckless wretch that I am.'

It was all to no avail. By May 1833 he was 'destitute of hope or comfort'.

He turned to her sister Anne for help; but no help was forthcoming. Her answer was curt, 'I really cannot understand Maria or venture to take responsibility of saying what her state of her affections is.'

Maria's friend Marianne Leigh compounded his wretchedness by revealing secrets he believed he had only shared with Maria. Marianne was candidly brutal, cruelly telling Charles what Maria really thought of him.

One month after the party, in a gesture that was meant to disarm her, he tied up all Maria's letters in a blue ribbon (the same colour of the blue gloves he had once matched for her) and sent them back, with all the keepsakes he had treasured.

'Our meetings of late have been little more than so many displays of heartless indifference on the one hand; while on the other they have never failed to prove a fertile source of wretchedness and misery…believe me that nothing will ever afford me more real delight than to hear that you, the object of my first and my last love, are happy.'

His final flourish, as he prepared the parcel, was 'I only wish that I could as easily forget that I ever received them.'

This dignified gambit failed, alas. She returned the letters with a note that contained a glimmer of encouragement; so that Charles's ardour, encouraged once more, prompted yet another note confirming that his love for her had not altered.

She returned this letter too.

In desperation he decided to play his trump card; that was to invite the Beadnell family to Bentinck Street and put on a dazzling display of amateur theatricals by the Dickens family and friends. She could not fail, or so he hoped, to be impressed by such versatility and accomplishment.

Sadly, she said nothing after the show and the crest-fallen Charles, feeling utterly crushed and miserable, took solace in talking to the scheming Marianne Leigh. This was a mistake! It gave Maria the chance to upbraid him, claiming that he had told her best friend intimate details of their romance and his feelings. Charles, mortified and driven by despair, went to see Maria and denied the charge; but he became infuriated when Fanny (his sister) supported the view that Charles had indeed confided to Marianne.

He then agonised over how Maria could have believed Marianne rather than himself. He claimed that there was a 'duplicity and disgusting falsehood...that had driven the two of them far apart.'

Charles would not give up. He was determined to get to the root of the matter. He asked if he could write to Marianne, and Maria replied that she had no objection providing she saw the letter first. She also added, sarcastically, 'that he could hardly dislike Marianne as much as he said he did - since he had, after all, often been noticed in deep conversation with her.'

'I have been so long used to inward wretchedness and real, real misery that it matters little, very little to me what others may think or of what becomes me. I have borne more from you than I do believe any living creature ever bore from a woman before,' he answered.

That evening Charles attended a bachelor dinner for Henry Kolle, who was marrying Anne Beadnell (Maria's sister) and, ironically, he was to be the best man. Getting drunk was now part of the scenario, and he accomplished the feat without any difficulty. In a final attempted reconciliation he declared, 'I have never loved and I can never love any but yourself.'

There was only a lukewarm reply and four years of adoration had finally come to an end. He once reflected that his love had 'excluded every other idea from my mind for four years'. But she did have one positive effect and the dye was cast. His tormented failure, this humiliating rejection, inspired him 'with a determination to overcome all the difficulties, which fairly lifted me up into the newspaper life.'

It also had another and negative effect. Many years afterwards, Dickens wrote that 'he had a habit of suppression which now belongs to me, which I know is no part of my original nature, but which makes me chary of showing my affections.'

The letters, which Charles had sent to her, were referred to in a fictional article, many years later. He wrote, perhaps regretful of the true facts and sensitive to the hurt they produced, 'I never had the remotest intention of sending any of those letters. But to write them, and after a few days tear them up, had been a sublime occupation.'

That should have been the end of the story of Maria and Charles, but it wasn't.

It was in 1855, while sitting quietly at home in front of some unopened correspondence, that he recognised the familiar handwriting of Maria Beadnell. He opened the letter, he told Maria, 'with the touch of my young friend David Copperfield when he was in love.'

Of course he was now world famous and she had written in the hope of renewing their friendship. Dickens replied with his usual unabashed ardour, recalling 'a Spring in which I was either much more wise or much more foolish than I am now.'

He was off to Paris. But when he returned she must come, with her husband Henry Winter, to dinner. After asking her what she would like as a present from

Paris, he promised to bring brooches for two of her daughters and, for her, a choker ornamented with stones, blue stones.

In Paris he mentioned her to Lady Olliffe, who asked him if it were true that he used to love Maria so very, very much?

'I told her there was no woman in the world, and there were very few men, who could ever imagine how much.'

He wondered if Maria, 'Had she seen little bits of herself in Dora' (*the wife of David Copperfield) and told her, 'People used to say to me how pretty all that was, and how elevated it was above the little foolish loves of very young men and women…I have never been so happy a man since, as I was when you made me wretchedly happy.'

Maria was thrilled and replied in confidence, "Though it is so late to read in the old hand what I had never read before, I have read it with great emotion…how it all happened as it did, we shall never know this side of Time; but if you had ever told me then, what you tell me now, I know myself well enough to be thoroughly assured that the simple truth and energy, which were in my love, would have overcome everything."

He responded, 'You ask me to treasure what you tell me, in my heart of hearts. Oh! see what I have cherished there, through all this time and all these changes!'

Maria now asked if she could meet him alone. Dickens replied that it was difficult in view of his fame, but if she could call at Tavistock House (his home) on a Sunday afternoon, asking first for Catherine, 'It is almost a positive certainty that there will be none here but I.'

So she arrived. Dickens had said in an earlier letter that he could not believe she was fat, old and toothless. He was wrong! She was all that she had said.

Maria (Mrs Winter) when Dickens renewed their acquaintance in 1855.

Flora (*Maria) in *Little Dorrit*

'Flora, always tall, had grown to be very broad too, and short of breath; but that was not much. Flora, whom he had left a lily, had become a peony; but that was not much. Flora, who had seemed enchanting in all she said and thought, *was* diffuse and silly. That was much. Flora, who had been spoiled and artless long ago, was determined to be spoiled and artless now. That was the fatal blow.'(Little Dorrit)

Maria had the hope (Dickens feared) that they would elope; and this terrified him. She kept up the correspondence, plying him with requests for another meeting. He only called on her once, going to her house with Kate. Daphne the dog was still in the hall, but stuffed for posterity.

She was to make one final attempt. Her husband's business failed and she wrote asking for money. The irony of once not being good-enough was not lost on Dickens, he declined the invitation to help – and that was the end of the matter.

Maria declared, twenty years later, that she had always been in love with him, but fame can certainly blur the past. It did in her case.

Chapter 8

'Mr Augustus Minns was a bachelor, of about forty as he said – of about eight-and-forty as his friends said. He was always exceedingly clean, precise, and tidy; perhaps somewhat priggish and the most retiring man in the world.'

With these words Charles Dickens's amazing literary career began as a short story, '*Mr Minns and his Cousin*' (originally called '*A Dinner at Poplar Walk*').

Today it is seldom referred to, other than in the historical sense, and even less seldom read. It is a simple parable of greedy expectation.Not surprisingly, Mr Minns is a clerk in Somerset House (like Dickens's father), and is driven to despair by the constant pressure of his cousin, Octavius Budden, to dine with them and their friend. The dinner does not go well; Mr Minns is irritated by the precocious seven-year-old son and the incessant fawning of the cousin and his wife. The final ignominy, however, is a soaking because Mr Minns had mislaid his umbrella and, while searching for it, misses the last coach. These events rendered him 'cold, wet, cross and miserable' when he finally reaches home at three o'clock in the morning; with a resolve 'to make his will the next day, so that none of them would appear therein'. This story was the first of a number of essays which would eventually be compiled into 'Sketches by Boz'.

'The whole of these sketches were written and published, one by one, when I was a very young man. They were collected and republished while I was still a very young man; and sent into the world with all their imperfections (a good many) on their heads.'

The era of Defoe, Smollett, Fielding and Jane Austen had passed; the new era of the Bronte sisters, Collins, and Gaskell had yet to come. There was a hiatus in English Literature around the 1820s and 30s; a gap that was to be filled by Charles Dickens.

His stories are replete with ghosts (Jacob Marley in A Christmas Carol), goblins (in another Christmas story The Chimes), and coincidences (none greater than Oliver Twist turning out to be the long lost nephew of the girl whose pictures he gazes on while ill, in the home of the kindly old man who rescues him; who also happens to be his departed father's friend). However, there was one coincidence which was to please him for the rest of his life. It was to make him feel that he was on a predetermined course to fame.

Posting with 'fear and trembling', his first sketch into the
editor's box

Late one November evening in 1833, the
twenty-one year-old approached 'a dark letter-box in
a dark office up a dark court in Fleet Street' and into it
posted 'with fear and trembling' a long envelope.

A few weeks later Dickens went into a book
shop at 186 Strand on his way to the House of
Commons. He paid a precious half-crown for the
December issue of the *Old Monthly Magazine*.
Nervous with anticipation, with shaking hands, he

opened up the copy and for the first time saw his work, unsigned, in print.

'On which occasion I walked down to Westminster Hall, and turned into it for half an hour, because my eyes were so dimmed with joy and pride, that they could not bear the street, and were not fit to be seen there.'

The bookseller was William Hall and within two years, by a strange coincidence, he was to have the most remarkable effect on Dickens's life.

The *Monthly Magazine* belonged to Captain Holland, recently returned from South America. He was pleased to accept articles from numerous authors, but payment was poor or non-existent. For Dickens, however, help was on hand. He was engaged by the liberal paper, the *Morning Chronicle*, at five guineas a week which was a handsome salary in those days. He enjoyed working for a paper which shared his strong liberal views. On the parliamentary staff was Thomas Beard who became his life long friend. They remained close and shared advice over the years (Dickens regularly turned to him). Yet Thomas always remained in the shadows; by nature a shy, retiring man.

At twenty-three Dickens was no ordinary reporter - fast, accurate and ingenious, he was determined to succeed and leave the memories of the blacking factory buried forever. When the House was in sitting he reported it regularly; but as a special correspondent he travelled the country to innumerable provincial places. He records a trip to Edinburgh, for example, to cover a ceremony in which Earl Grey was to be given the freedom of that beautiful city. The banquet turned out to be a farce as guests, who could not contain their greed until the great man arrived, tucked into the food shouting "Shame!" with their mouths full to others equally laying into the fare, and as Charles observed, it was 'one of the few instances on record of a dinner having been virtually concluded before it began.'

The start of his cynicism regarding politicians and Courts of Law had taken root and was to flourish in later works. The pomposity and silliness, the grotesqueness and the dishonesty were there to be ridiculed and parried. He took it all in; he was not the star reporter for nothing.

The era of Maria Beadnell was passing and with renewed vigour he poured his frustrations into a series of sketches for the *Monthly Magazine*, which was delighted to accept them; so was the *Morning Chronicle*. He even visited the theatre one evening and was amazed to hear one of his essays rehashed into a dramatic scenario. The most famous writer at that time, Harrison Ainsworth, sought out Dickens to introduce him to his own publisher John Macrone. Ainsworth, who became a close friend, was very much like Dickens in his writing skills, humour and mercurial personality; allied to his extraordinary conviviality was his generosity in providing expansive dinners.

But 'the damnable shadow' in his life', his father's improvidence, reappeared once again. Mr Dickens was arrested by a score of tradesmen to whom he owed money in what he loosely described as 'a domestic tragedy.' Stung by this further humiliation Charles decided to stem the tide. He paid off as many as he could, arranged securities for the rest and persuaded his family to decant into cheaper lodgings. However, he had had enough. He fled the scene in December 1834, moving out of the family abode and into rented rooms in Furnival's Inn, Holborn. His brother Fredrick joined him. Macrone went to visit them and found the rooms "uncarpeted and bleak-looking, with a deal table, two or three chairs and a few books." Dickens was barely making ends meet.

It is interesting, although not totally unusual in authors then, that Charles decided to disguise his name by writing under the pseudonym of Boz. It was the nickname of his brother Augustus, who in honour of the *Vicar of Wakefield* the family had dubbed Moses. It was facetiously pronounced as Boses and, in time, finally shortened to Boz.

'Boz was a very familiar household word to me, long before I was an author, and so came to adopt it.'

Dickens, however, was the one who had vouched for his father's debts. Thus there was the threat of jail if he was unable to meet these financial obligations. He may have thought that anonymity would be the wisest course, in view of his family's past.

A sister paper the *Evening Chronicle* was launched on January 31st 1835. Dickens began writing for it too, producing "*Sketches of London*" – the number one being 'Hackney-coach Stands'. But he only agreed to contribute after demanding a pay rise from five to seven guineas per week. In addition, he informed the *Old Monthly Magazine* that he could not continue to write for nothing. James Grant, the proprietor, could not afford even the modest sum of half-a-guinea per page. "Only imagine," wrote Mr Grant several years later, "Mr Dickens offering to furnish me with a continuation, for any length of time I might have named, of his *Sketches by Boz*, for eight guineas a sheet, whereas in little more than six months from that date, he could have got a hundred guineas per sheet of sixteen pages from any leading periodical of the day.'

After twenty sketches for the *Evening Chronicle*, he wrote twelve more for *Bell's Life in London*; this diversity in commission explains the difference in scene and mood in his sketches, some with a strong social theme, others almost purely descriptive of street life in the capital.

Public Dinners (Sketches by Boz) Dickens appeared in four of the illustrations; here seen left, before the column, Cruikshank is on the right, black whiskers and white waistcoat, both acting as ushers.

In 1836 he also wrote two articles in a humorous vein for *The Library of Fiction*, published by Chapman and Hall.

He was beginning to mix in artistic society; often being a guest at Ainsworth's famous literary parties, where he met the young Daniel Maclise and the illustrator George Cruikshank, as well as the politicians Bulwer-Lytton and Disraeli. John Macrone, a young and energetic publisher, suggested that Dickens's 'capital sketches' should be compiled into a book, with illustrations by Cruikshank, known in the book world as an eminent artist.

George Cruikshank. Already famous, he was asked to illustrate *Sketches by Boz* to give some prestige to the venture; his powerful opinions and assertiveness led to the inevitable clashes with Dickens over the years.

Of much more significance, was his friendship with the editor of the *Evening Chronicle*, George Hogarth. He was a Scotsman who had been a friend of Walter Scott. Hogarth recognised and fostered the latent talent, with many invitations to his home in Chelsea where Charles would meet and court the eldest daughter, the nineteen-year-old Catherine.

Catherine (Kate). Pretty, with sleepy, deep blue eyes; her good humour, cheerfulness and amiable nature were very attractive. She was deeply in love with the mercurial Charles and remained devoted to him all her life.

John Macrone was excited at the prospect of reprinting the short pieces and in 1835 offered one hundred pounds for the copyright. Dickens eagerly took the money. It would offer some financial stability. But it was a deal made out of necessity and innocence and was to ferment acrimony within a few years.

The decision as to what should constitute the title gave a future indication of Dickens's self-assertiveness when it came to his writing. At that time the author generally followed the illustrator who created the theme. One of the titles accepted by Macrone was 'Sketches by Boz and Cuts by Cruikshank' – the more famous name coming second. Dickens not only baulked at this overlong title but immediately began badgering the artist for the illustrations and also a change of title. An 'unpleasant turn' of events was Cruikshank's blunt comment.

The first two volumes of *Sketches by Boz* appeared on his birthday in 1836. He received one hundred and fifty pounds from Macrone. It was a boost towards his hope of marriage and settling down. For in 1835 he had fallen in love with Catherine Hogarth.

Catherine was a pretty, plump girl, with none of the artifice of Maria. But she often lacked confidence in herself which made her uneasy with events and occasionally mistrustful. In addition she suffered from periodic bouts of depression and at such times her petulance hurt Charles; no doubt they made him hark back to Maria and her moods.

Upset, he would write:

'My dear Catherine, It is with great pain that I sit down before I go to bed tonight, to say one word which can bear the appearance of unkindness or reproach; but I owe a duty to myself as well as to you, and as I am wild enough to think that an engagement of even three weeks might pass without any such display as you have favoured me with thrice already, I am the more strongly induced to discharge it.

The sudden and uncalled for coldness with which you treated me before I left last night surprised and deeply hurt me – surprised because I could not have believed that such a sullen and inflexible obstinacy could exist in the breast of any girl in whose heart love had found a place; and hurt me because I feel for you far more than I have ever, and feel a slight from you more than I can tell.'

Catherine, in fairness, both then and in the future, was always contrite when reproached and begged for his pardon and his love. The peace-loving and easy-going companion that Dickens cherished was quickly reborn.

And he would acknowledge her love: 'If you would only determine to show the same affection and kindness to me, when you are displeased and feel disposed to be ill-tempered, I declare unaffectedly I should have no one solitary fault to find with you. You asking me to "love you once more" is quite unnecessary – I have *never* ceased to love you for one moment since I knew you; nor *shall I*!'

Catherine would respond to Charles's gentle firmness, respecting it throughout her life and do her best to control the sulking episodes which accompanied her depression. She enjoyed his humorous letters, some beginning 'dearest mouse', 'darling tatie' or simply - 'my dearest love.'

He liked to entertain the Hogarth family, and they too responded to his good nature and pranks. On one occasion as Dickens recalled years later, 'a young man dressed as a sailor jumped in at the window, danced a hornpipe, whistling the tune, jumped out again, and a few minutes later Charles Dickens walked gravely in at the door, as if nothing had happened, shook hands all round, and then, at the sight of the puzzled faces, burst into laughter.'

Charles – a new found determination and
confidence were noted by his friends, although
they were never shaded with conceit.

Some days Catherine would bring her sister,
the fourteen-year-old Mary, and call at his rooms for
breakfast. Mary doted on Charles from the very
beginning. He took them to the theatre, which was
having a great influence on him at the time, writing a
libretto and adapting a one-act play from his sketches.
It was a happy group when joined by the other
Hogarths, including the youngest girl, Georgina aged

seven. As events turned out, all three sisters were to play a prominent role in his life

But Dickens was finding the work schedule exhausting and his kidney spasm returned. The concerned Catherine reprimanded him, saying that his devotion to work, especially until one or two in the morning, was making her "coss".

In turn, he felt hurt, complaining that, 'I am doing my best with the stake I have to play for – you and a home for both of us.'

'If the representation I have so often made to you, about my working as a duty, and not as a pleasure, be not sufficient to keep you in the good humour, which you, of all people in the world should preserve – why then my dear, you must be out of temper, and there is no help for it.'

The *Monthly Magazine* (the prefix '*Old*' being dropped) asked for more articles. But Dickens replied that with other writing commitments he would have very little spare time.

Because there had been a sudden and unexpected turn of events. He had been visited by a representative of a new publishing venture, a Mr William Hall. Dickens was amazed and overjoyed when he recognised the bookseller from whom he had bought the first copy of his first sketch. Hall, puzzled at first by the warmth of his reception, explained that, with a friend Mr Chapman, he wanted to discuss the publication of a series of comic sporting stories. They were to accompany illustrations by a popular artist at that time, Robert Seymour. The publication was to be twenty instalments in monthly parts.

'The idea propounded to me was that the monthly something should be a vehicle for certain plates to be executed by Mr Seymour; and there was a notion, either on the part of the admirable humorous artist, or of my visitor, that a "Nimrod Club", the members of which were to go out shooting, fishing and so forth, and getting themselves into difficulties through their want of dexterity, would be the best means of introducing these. I objected, on consideration, that although born and partly bred in the country I was no great sportsman, except in regard to all kinds of locomotion; that the idea was not novel, and had already been much used; that it would be infinitely better for the plates to arise naturally out of the text: and that I would like to take my own way, with a free range of English scenes and people, and was afraid I should ultimately do so in any case, whatever course I might prescribe to myself at starting. My views being deferred to, I thought of Mr Pickwick.' (*he recalled a coach proprietor from Bath called Moses Pickwick).

'My dearest Kate, They have made me an offer of fourteen pounds a month…the work will be no joke, but the emolument is too tempting to resist.'

Dickens was bursting with enthusiasm and within a week of Hall's visit he wrote, 'Pickwick is begun in all his might and glory.' It would add £14 a month to his income but require almost twelve thousand words per month, for twenty instalments. However, Dickens was undaunted. Now they could get married.

The Times of the 26th of March gave notice that on the 31st there would be published the first shilling number of the "*Posthumous Papers of the Pickwick Club*", edited by Boz.

A few days later, the same paper announced that Mr Charles Dickens had married Catherine, the eldest daughter of Mr George Hogarth, on the 2nd of April.

They were married at St Luke's Church, Chelsea, and the rector was Rev Charles Kingsley (incidentally the father of Charles who wrote *Westward Ho!*). The best man was Thomas Beard. Charles gave Kate a sandalwood work box inlaid with ivory. The breakfast was the quietest possible. The Hogarth family, the Dickens family and Thomas Beard comprised the whole assembly. A few pleasant things were said by both parties, their health was drunk and all seemed imbued with happiness, not the least Charles and his beautiful young wife.

Their honeymoon was in the village of Chalk, near Rochester in Kent,

Thus "*Sketches*" had been published on his twenty-fourth birthday, and here was "*Pickwick*", his first novel, coinciding with his wedding. Dickens must have felt he had reached a pinnacle of happiness. Two factors were to temporarily mar the road to the summit.

Four hundred copies of Pickwick were printed and the public was disappointed, sales were modest in the extreme. The book was not a series of popular sketches nor was it a defined story. Indeed, it has been called a novel without a plot. Even the author's friends spoke slightingly about the production which they called "a low cheap form of publication."

Pickwick Papers concerns the perambulations of four members of the Pickwick Club from London into the country; the four being the benevolent Mr Pickwick, the portly and amorous Tupman, the poetical Snodgrass and the nervous sportsman Winkle.

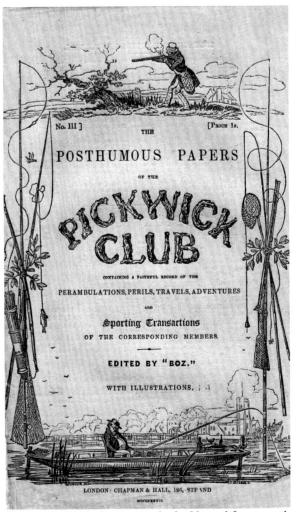

Original jacket by Seymour who had hoped for a sporting theme.

They are befriended by hospitable Mr Wardle, father of amongst others – Emily and the fat boy Joe – and are invited to Dingley Dell. They are also taken-in by the lying and smooth talking Jingle who elopes with Wardle's sister, but the plot is foiled. Sam Weller becomes Mr Pickwick's faithful and jovial servant. Mrs Bardell, with whom Mr Pickwick lodges, inadvertently mistakes her lodger's intentions; leading to a breach of promise-of-marriage trial. Mr Pickwick is imprisoned for refusing to pay the damages and only relents when Sam refuses to leave him and is determined to be jailed also; and he is aghast when he meets Mrs Bardell in The Fleet. She has also been imprisoned for failing to pay the artful solicitors' costs. He is released on settling her debts. The story ends happily with the marriage of Sam to a pretty housekeeper, called Mary (thus immortalising the girl who looked after him in his childhood), Mr Snodgrass (to Emily) and Mr Winkle to Arabella Allen.

After the first monthly part, numbers two to five sold fifty copies each. Chapman and Hall seriously began to debate whether they should cease publication.

The cover was to mirror Seymour's idea of a sporting club, but Dickens had decided otherwise. He began with the main characters. The first sketch of Mr Pickwick was a long thin man but Dickens would have none of it. Chapman suggested his friend at Richmond, "a fat, old beau who would wear, in spite of the ladies' protest, drab tights and black gaiters". The publisher's friend was (amazingly) John Forster and he became the immortal Pickwick. Mr Winkle, the sportsman, appeared on the cover at Seymour's bidding, blasting away at what appears to be a sparrow. Dickens was quickly to discard Winkle's sportsmanship and he was relegated to a more minor role; Dickens was not going to play second fiddle to anybody.

The first chapter is both tedious and over-facetious. Samuel Pickwick emerges with an array of superfluous honours and the badge of absurdity; a self-contained man and self-satisfied by his own literary and scientific prowess; certainly as the author of a paper on the "Speculations on the Source of the Hampstead Ponds, with some Observations on the Theory of Tittlebats", his academic standing verges on the ridiculous rather than funny. Chapter III becomes a short story, *The Stroller's Tale* and in Chapter IV another – *The Convict's Return* (perhaps both written in desperation to recapture the *Boz* spirit). Dickens must have seen the prospects of fame and fortune diminishing monthly.

The tenuous sporting theme emerges only briefly in the book. The terrified Winkle's attempts to shoot rooks which 'produced a scream as of an individual – not of a rook – in corporeal anguish. Mr Tupman had saved the lives of innumerable unoffending birds by receiving a portion of the charge in his left arm.'

While cricket is fleetingly referred to in the Dingley Dell match with All-Muggleton; Dickens, never a sportsman as such (although extremely fit through ten to fifteen mile marathon walks and three hour rides) was now on his own course, for Seymour was no longer around.

Dickens only met him once, two days before at Furnival's Inn and, on that occasion, the author had asked for a correction to a plate for the second issue. The original intention had been to have twenty four pages per issue and four illustrations. Seymour had completed three for the second issue when he shot himself.

Chapman and Hall were mortified and in despair. Dickens was being handsomely paid, sales were plummeting and their famous illustrator was dead. They turned to R W Buss, a painter who had exhibited at the Royal Academy, but who did not know how to etch. Putting aside all other work on the understanding that he was commissioned for *Pickwick*, he assiduously began learning the technique. Dickens looked at the first two illustrations, inconsequential and poorly executed, and was appalled. As quickly as he arrived, Buss left; and few know of his brief moment of fame in *Pickwick Papers*.

R.W. Buss; his two illustrations were suppressed by Dickens, as quickly as possible.

In his place came 'Phiz' (Hablot Browne) who had worked on a pamphlet by Dickens called *Sunday Under Three Heads* which was a rapid riposte to a bill in Parliament that would have prohibited all public recreation on Sunday. The enraged young author felt that 'if they legislate in ignorance, they are criminal and dishonest; if they do so with their eyes open, they commit a wilful injustice; in either case, they bring religion into contempt.'

George Cruikshank and Hablot Browne were to do the majority of illustrations for the succeeding novels.

Although still popular and an integral part of Dickens's works, their styles are one of caricature and exaggeration; sometimes the draftsmanship sits uneasily with the author's forced humour.

So Chapter X was reached in the fourth number and success eluded him.

Dickens, having introduced a whole plethora of characters and scenes without any lasting effect, realised that since the majority of the sales were in London, and no humour goes down better in the capital than cockney wit, introduces Sam Weller in this chapter.

"Sam!" said a smart chambermaid.

"Hallo," replied the man with the white hat.

"Number twenty-two wants his boots."

"Ask number twenty-two wether he'll have 'em now, or wait till he gets 'em" was the reply... look at these here boots – eleven pair o' boots; and one shoe as b'longs to number six, with the wooden leg."

From the introduction of Mr Pickwick's faithful servant sales began to increase and then soar.

Sam has been described as 'one of those people that take their place among the supreme successes of fiction.'

Mr Pickwick meets Sam Weller – a pivotal moment that was to launch Dickens's career.

The repartee is never better than when Sam and his father are engaged. The old coachman's second marriage is marred by the frequent visits of the hypocritical and drunken vicar (Reverend Stiggins) to his public house, the Marquis of Granby. 'Take example by your father, my boy, and be very careful o' widders all your life, especially if they've kept a public house.'

One interesting character, Joe, anticipates the description of a medical condition due to a tumour

106

within the brain (later described by Frohlich and the syndrome is still named after him) which produces gluttony, obesity and a capacity to fall asleep in a second.

'Everyone was excited, except the fat boy, and he slept as soundly as if the roaring of cannon were his ordinary lullaby. The fat boy, who had been effectually roused by the compression of a portion of his leg between the finger and thumb of Mr Winkle, rolled off the box once again, and proceeded to unpack the hamper, with more expedition than could have been expected from his previous inactivity.'(Pickwick Papers).

Dickens was busy on other fronts. His love of the stage surfaced with the *Strange Gentleman*, acted in September 1836 at St James's theatre, and the comic operetta, *Village Coquettes* in December. Fanny had made many friends in the theatre and introduced her brother, who was eager to show his prowess as a thespian. He was described as 'a very young gentleman with long brown hair falling in silky masses over his temples, dressed up to the height of existing fashion, his eyes full of power and strong will, and with a touching expression of sweetness and kindliness on his lips.'

In one performance, Dickens responded to the cries of Boz by actually taking a bow. Most critics felt that the operetta had small merit and that those who produced it were cashing in on his fame. One paper sarcastically wrote that "some critics in the gallery were said to have expected Sam Weller."

One of the reviewers had become the literary editor of the Examiner. He gave a bad review but in such a humorous way that Dickens was not particularly offended. The writer was John Foster, a lawyer who had graduated from University College,

London. By coincidence it was John Forster who had been suggested by Chapman (his friend) as the loose model for Mr Pickwick. They had much in common. Forster was at times loud and brash, (Dickens once remarked that, 'his whisper seems to go in at your ear and comes out at the sole of your boot'). He was the son of a Newcastle-upon-Tyne butcher and a herdsman's daughter, and had begun training at the Inner Temple but found law boring compared to journalism. In addition he and Dickens shared the same high spirits and boisterous manner. They both liked to perform impromptu dances and impersonations at parties, loved the theatre, delighted in eating and drinking (sometimes to excess). He kept Dickens amused, either directly or as the brunt of his humour, to a degree that often had the author creased double with laughter. Finally, like Charles, John Forster had a radical but caring nature. His kindness and generosity were obvious to everyone and he quickly became a close friend after their first meeting at *Village Croquettes*. It was a friendship that was to last a lifetime.

Chapter 9

With the death of Seymour the number of pages increased to thirty two each month with only two illustrations. Dickens, as ever the opportunist as far as money was concerned, asked for a raise and got it. He was to earn a considerable sum from this book.

On the sixth of January 1837 (the first day of Epiphany) a son was born in Furnival's Inn. He was named after himself.

'I shall never be so happy again in these chambers – never if I roll in wealth and fame.'

Kate took some time to recover, complicated by an episode of depression and to her dismay she could not breast feed, having to rely on a wet-nurse instead. She was not alone in her ill-health, for Dickens was suffering from daily headaches due to overwork. Their remedy was to go to the Medway at Chalk taking the baby and Mary, and to rent the same cottage in which they had spent their honeymoon. Despite the pressure of writing, Charles was very solicitous to Kate, constantly looking after her comforts and wishes and cheering her up in his inimitable way.

They stayed for two months. He wrote as quickly as he could, trying to keep up with the busy schedule; but there was the added monotony of proof-reading which often meant (in his case) page upon page of alteration and addition. Not content with this workload, Dickens kept rushing up to London to supervise the rehearsals of the bawdy play "*Is She His Wife?*" at his usual venue, St James's theatre. The subject matter was curious for his ensemble, the theme being bigamy and seduction. Its success, however, showed that the theme did not affect the audiences' Victorian sensibilities.

Plans were made to move to a more fashionable and substantial address in Doughty Street, London. It was a private road with a gate at each end, agreeably locked at night to deter the undesirables.

In March 1837 he agreed to the rent of £80 per year and moved in, a fortnight later. It was a twelve room house occupying four floors and required a cook, a housemaid a nurse and eventually a man-servant. The rooms, lit by lamps, had mirrors to add to the brightness; the carpets and walls were also striking in colour, some pink with floral carpets. The furniture was of the highest quality of its time.

Doughty Street housed many literary figures including Sidney Smith and Edmund Yates, who wrote, " It was a broad airy, wholesome street, none of your common thoroughfares to be rattled through by vulgar cabs and earth-shattering Pickford vans; but a self-included property, with a gate at each end, and a lodge with a porter in a gold-laced hat and the Doughty arms on the buttons of his mulberry-coloured coat, to prevent any one, except with a mission to one of the houses, from intruding on the exclusive territory."

Dickens wrote to Forster, 'I have delayed writing you a reply to your note meaning to call on you. I have been so much engaged in the "pleasant" occupation of moving that I have not had time; and I am obliged at last to write and say I have been long engaged to the Pickwick publishers to a dinner in honour of that hero which comes off tomorrow. I am consequently unable to accept your kind invite, which I frankly own I should have liked much better.'

When he was fed up, Dickens broke the monotony of writing with long walks and even longer rides. This was when he would write to Forster:

'What a brilliant morning for a country walk!' 'I start precisely – precisely mind- at half-past one. Come, come, come, and walk in the green lanes. You will work the better for it!'

Or 'You don't feel disposed, do you, to muffle yourself up, and start off with me for a good brisk walk over Hampstead Heath? I know a good 'ouse there where we can have a red-hot chop for dinner, and a glass of good wine.'

As for riding, 'I think Richmond and Twickenham, thro' the park, out at Knightsbridge, and over Barnes common – would make a beautiful ride, I shouldn't object to an early chop at some village inn' or ' a hard trot for three hours.'

There was always the call for punctuality. 'I start precisely – precisely mind - at half past one' Dickens hated unpunctuality, almost amounting to a phobia. He would hurry others to be present some ten to fifteen minutes before departure and could not tolerate being kept waiting. Missives to Forster, like the one above, always stressed being punctual. (He also disliked untidiness, his room epitomised both neatness and order - chair, writing table, quills etc were arranged in the same way throughout each book.) Punctuality, however, was a problem before 1840 because time varied from place to place (e.g. Bristol time was eight minutes after London). Railway Time was to standardise the clock throughout Britain, probably to his relief.

Mary (drawn by Phiz)

Life had progressed very agreeably at Furnival's Inn just before the move to Doughty Street. Mary Hogarth lived with Charles and Kate. She was a sweet, happy seventeen-year-old; and both were devoted to her. They would enjoy each other's company either at the theatre or around the fireside after his busy days' work. As the twelfth issue of *Pickwick* approached, Dickens was to be so affected by a catastrophe that he could not work for two months.

On 7th of May, 1837, Charles, Kate and Mary went to see the Dickens farce *Is She his Wife* at the St James's Theatre. They came home in high spirits. 'Mary went upstairs to bed at about one o'clock in perfect health and her usual delightful spirits.'

No sooner had she closed the bedroom door than there was a choking cry. He rushed up and found her gasping for breath. A doctor was sent for but he could do nothing.

'She sank under the attack and died - died in such a calm and gentle sleep, that although I held her in my arms for some time before, when she was certainly living (for she swallowed a little brandy from my hand) I continued to support her lifeless form, long after her soul had fled to Heaven. The very last words she whispered were of me. They think her heart was diseased.'

Charles took the ring from her lifeless hand and wore it as his own, until he died. He saved a lock of hair and placed her clothes neatly for posterity. Mrs Hogarth fainted on hearing the news and was in shock for a week, resting in bed. Kate tried to console her mother, while hiding her own grief. Soon afterwards she had a miscarriage.

Dickens misery was inconsolable.

'She had been the grace and life of our home. We might have known that we were too happy together to be long without a change... I have lost the dearest friend I ever had, the dear girl whom I loved, after my wife, more deeply and more fervently than anyone on earth.

I wish you could know how I weary now for the three rooms in Furnival's Inn, and how I miss that pleasant smile and those sweet words which, bestowed upon our evening's work, in our merry banterings round the fire, were more precious to me than the applause of a whole world could be.'

Some years later he wrote to Mrs Hogarth.

'After she died I dreamed of her every night for many months, sometimes as a spirit, sometimes as a living creature, never with bitterness of my real sorrow, but always with a kind of quiet happiness, which became so pleasant to me that I never lay down at night without a hope of the vision coming back in one shape or another.'

He wrote her epitaph for the gravestone in the cemetery in Kensal Green; "Young, beautiful, and good, God numbered her among His angels at the early age of seventeen."

The writing of *Pickwick* was delayed for two months, and also the early work on *Oliver Twist*. As to why the writing had ceased, there were a whole series of circulating rumours, "that the work was so varied, so extensive, and yet true in his observations, that it could not be the production of any single individual; that it was the joint production of an association, the different members of which transmitted their various ideas and observations; that one of their number, whose province it was to reduce them to a connected form, was, and had been for many years, a prisoner in the King's Bench." Another rumour surmised "that the author was a youth of eighteen who had been bred to the Bar, and whose health had so seriously suffered through his literary exertions that there was not the slightest chance of his ever publishing another number of *Pickwick*." To quash these rumours Dickens decided to issue an Address in the fifteenth number, explaining the actual reasons for the delay.

Kate, with her vulnerable emotions, must have suffered as much (if not more) than anyone in the family; but she faced her mother's grief and Charles's collapse as best she could, despite the miscarriage.

As he began to recover, Charles's writing showed a fresher and more vigorous style. The Trial of Bardell v Pickwick was published and became the high point of the book. In this section the landlady, Mrs Bardell, mistakenly thinks Mr Pickwick, is about to propose and promptly faints into his arms. When he does not propose, an action for breach of promise is taken out. For the first time in his novels Dickens has his sights on the judiciary and is scathing in his attack on the Judge and the lawyers involved; an attack made more effective by the absurd proceedings, which effectively belittles the legal system.

Mr Perker (Mr Pickwick's solicitor) wonders what the jury have had for breakfast, 'a good, contented, well—breakfasted juryman is a capital thing to get hold of. Discontented or hungry jurymen, my dear sir, always find for the plaintiff.'

'Mr Justice Stareleigh was a most particularly short man, and so fat that he seemed all face and waistcoat. He rolled in, upon two little turned legs, and having bobbed gravely to the bar, who bobbed gravely to him, put his little legs under the table, and his little three-cornered hat upon it; and when Mr Justice Stareleigh had done this, all you could see of him was two queer little eyes, one broad pink face, and somewhere about half of a big and very comical-looking wig.

The Judge had no sooner taken his seat, than the officer on the floor of the court called out "Silence!" in a commanding tone upon which another officer in the gallery cried "Silence!" in an angry manner, whereupon three or four more ushers shouted "Silence!" in a voice of indignant remonstrance.

"For the defendant Serjeant Snubbin and Mr Monkey", said the Judge writing down the names.

"Beg your Lordship's pardon, Phunky."

"Oh! Very good," said the judge, "I never had the pleasure of hearing the gentleman's name before." Here Mr Phunky bowed and smiled, and the judge bowed and smiled too, and then Mr Phunky blushed into the very whites of his eyes.

"Go on," said the judge.

The ushers again called silence, and Mr Skimpin proceeded to "open the case"; and the case appeared to have very little inside it when he opened it, for he kept such particulars as he knew, completely to himself, and sat down, after a lapse of three minutes, leaving the jury in precisely the same advanced stage of wisdom as they were in before.

Serjeant Buzfuz, then rose with all the majesty and dignity which the grave nature of the proceedings demanded. Drawing forth two scraps of paper, he proceeded. "Dear Mrs B., I shall not be at home till tomorrow. Slow coach. Don't trouble yourself about the warming pan!" And what does this allusion to the slow coach mean? For aught I know it may be a reference to Pickwick himself, who has most unquestionably been a criminally slow coach during the whole of this transaction, but whose speed will now be very unexpectedly accelerated, and whose wheels, gentlemen, as he will find to his cost, will very soon be greased by you!"

Mr Serjeant Buzfuz paused to see whether the jury smiled at his joke, but nobody took it but the greengrocer, whose sensitiveness on the subject was very probably occasioned by his having subjected a chaise-cart to the process in question on that identical morning, so the learned Serjeant considered it advisable to undergo a slight relapse into the dismals before he concluded "But enough of this gentlemen, it is difficult to smile with an aching heart." He had proceeded with such volubility, that his face was perfectly crimson, here paused for breath.

The silence woke Mr Justice Stareleigh, who immediately wrote down something with a pen without any ink in it, and looked unusually profound, to impress the jury with the belief that he always thought most deeply with his eyes shut.'

The trial proceeds in grave and inconsequential pomposity, finally:

'Mr Justice Stareleigh summed up, in the old established and most approved form. He read as much of his notes to the jury as he could decipher on so short a notice, and made running comments on the evidence as he went along. The jury then retired to their private room to talk the matter over, and the judge retired to *his* private room, to refresh himself with mutton chop and a glass of sherry.' (Pickwick Papers)

Mr Pickwick is found "Guilty" and in lieu of the 'breach of promise' ordered to pay seven hundred and fifty pounds; which, of course, he refuses to pay and is eventually sent to the Fleet Prison.

The trial of Bardell v Pickwick

Sales had reached the astonishing figure of over fifty thousand a month and Dickens was in the full vigour of success. So in August 22, 1836, he entered into an agreement with Richard Bentley (a short, energetic, florid faced man) to edit a new

117

monthly magazine, *Bentley's Miscellany*, for £40 a month; and to contribute a serial story. The fact that he just finished the tenth instalment of *Pickwick* in January 1937, when he began Oliver Twist is quite amazing. In addition he was also writing an operetta called *The Village Coquettes*, as well as planning a new novel for Macrone provisionally called *Gabriel Vardon*. Kate and Charles both agreed that it was time he lessened his workload, and confident of future success, Dickens was overjoyed to resign from his tedious parliamentary duties at the *Morning Chronicle*. Thus ended five years of assiduous penmanship.

Dickens was now the literary superstar and Pickwick mania was at is height. The book was plagiarised by a whole series of imitators – Pickwick Abroad, A tour in France, Posthumous Papers of the Cadgers' Club, Posthumous Notes of the Pickwickian Club, The Penny Pickwick, Pickwick in America, Pickwick in India and so on and so forth. Dickens was disgusted at such unabashed plagiarism but nobody annoyed him more than his first publisher, and friend, Macrone.

He had given Dickens £400 for his writings, and it had netted some £4,000 for the publisher; but Macrone was not content. He was anxious that Dickens should begin the story *Gabriel Vardon* and, on finding out about the other commitments, accused Dickens of breaking his contract. The contract, Macrone said, would only be relinquished in return for his retention of the copyright of *Sketches by Boz* for £100.

'I heard half-an-hour ago, on authority which leaves me in no doubt (from the binder of Pickwick in fact), that Macrone intends publishing a new issue of my *Sketches* in monthly parts of nearly the same size and in just the same form as *Pickwick Papers*. I need not tell you that this is calculated to injure me most seriously, or that I have a very natural and most decided objection to him being supposed to presume upon the success of the *Pickwick* and thus foist this old work upon the public in its new dress for the mere purposes of putting money in my own pocket. Neither need I say that the fact of my name being before the town, attached to three publications at the same, must prove seriously prejudicial to my reputation.

I wish him to be reminded that no intention of publishing them in this form was in the remotest manner hinted to me, by him or on his behalf, when he obtained possession of the copyright.'

Forster, in his legal capacity, went to Macrone, who proved obdurate. That he had bought the book for a small sum when Dickens needed the money before his marriage and had made a considerable profit, did not alter the publisher's resolve. Thus it was decided that Chapman and Hall, Forster and Dickens should buy back the copyright for £2,000. The *Sketches* were reissued in 1837; but Dickens was bitter about the whole episode.

In later years, Dickens's wide circle of friends often remarked on his humour, vivaciousness and brilliance of writing, but everyone agreed that his compassion and kindness stood above all else.

When Macrone died a short while afterwards, Dickens produced a book, compiled by him and others, solely to help the publisher's family.

He called it 'The *Pic-nic Papers*.'

THE

PIC-NIC PAPERS.

BY

CHARLES DICKENS,

W. H. MAXWELL, THOMAS MOORE, MISS STRICKLAND,
HORACE SMITH, LEITCH RITCHIE,

AND OTHER CELEBRATED WRITERS.

EDITED BY CHARLES DICKENS, ESQ.,

AUTHOR OF "THE PICKWICK PAPERS," "NICHOLAS NICKLEBY," ETC.

With Illustrations on Steel
BY GEORGE CRUIKSHANK AND PHIZ.

LONDON :
WARD AND LOCK, 158, FLEET STREET

A curiosity piece by Dickens to help the
Macrone family.

When the last instalment was published, Mr
Pickwick was the genial and good-natured father-
figure the public loved; Dickens had received £2,500
as well as the monthly payments and a share in the
copyright; Chapman and Hall made a clear profit of
£14,000 (from a work they nearly abandoned as
hopeless); Thackeray had stated ' that a man who, a
hundred years hence, should sit down to write a
history of our time, would do wrong to put the great

contemporary history of Pickwick aside as a frivolous work'; and Dickens had the final word:

'If I were to live a hundred years and write three works in each, I should never be so proud of any of them as I am of Pickwick, feeling as I do, that it has made its own way, and hoping, as I must own I do hope, that long after my hand is withered as the pen it held, Pickwick will be found on many a dusty shelf with many a better work.'

He was right and, in many people's eyes, there are few better.

Chapter 10

"Please, sir, I want some more."

People with only the vaguest notion and slightest interest in Dickens can still place these words in the mouth of the starving Oliver Twist (perhaps Scrooge's "Humbug" ranks a close second in the public's memory.)

The novel began in the second issue of *Bentley's Miscellany* in February 1837 with Cruikshank as illustrator.

It was to be the first novel in the English language with a child as the central character.

When Mr Bumble (the sanctimonious and dishonest beadle) mentions a 'blackin' bottle' he recreates a small, but never-to-be forgotten episode in Dickens's life (Weller senior had mentioned "Warren's blackin' in the previous novel). Once again he saw himself as the champion of the poor and oppressed.

Charles's private life was hectic, with endless dinners and suppers in literary societies, clubs and at 48 Doughty Street.

Preliminary drawing by Cruikshank for *Oliver Twist* 'Mr Bumble degraded in the eyes of the paupers.'

However, even in the midst of friends, he would have to concentrate his thoughts on the impending book; sometimes retiring to his room, as his brother-in-law Henry Burnett recalled, 'the mind and muscles working in company, as new thoughts were being dropped upon the paper – and to note the working brow, the set of the mouth, with the tongue tightly pressed against the closed lips, as was his habit.'

He worked feverishly on his third book, *Oliver Twist* and the final episodes of *Pickwick*. Charles and Kate enjoyed several holidays including, in July 1837, their first trip abroad; going to the French and Belgian coast and taking Phiz with them. But as in most holidays, they rarely had time alone, besieged by friends and acquaintances. Dickens craved company.

He wrote from Calais in July 1837: 'We have arranged for a post-coach to take us to Ghent, Brussels, Antwerp, and a hundred other places, that I cannot recollect now and couldn't spell if I did. We went this afternoon in a barouche to some gardens where the people dance, and where they were footing it most heartily – especially the women who in their short petticoats and light caps looked uncommonly agreeable.

A gentleman in a blue surtout and silken berlins accompanied us from the hotel, and acted as curator. He even waltzed with a very smart lady (just to show us, condescendingly, how it ought to be done) and waltzed elegantly too. We rang for slippers after we came back, and it turned out that this gentleman was the Boots.'

On Bentley offering Dickens £40 per month, he gave up his job in the *Morning Chronicle*. However, the author and the paper parted less than amicably and, on departing, he sent the *Morning Chronicle* an acid note.

Later, when the paper gave a favourable review of the *Miscellany*, Dickens was not mollified one bit and stuck by a letter he had sent, telling the editor, 'I cannot retract one syllable'

In September they had another seaside holiday in Broadstairs. Charles had been ill and wrote,

'I am much better...I have been compelled for four-and-twenty mortal hours to abstain from porter or other malt liquor!!

Extraordinary Gazette.

SPEECH OF HIS MIGHTINESS

ON OPENING THE SECOND NUMBER

OF

BENTLEY'S MISCELLANY,

EDITED BY "BOZ."

On Wednesday, the first of February, "the House"
(of Bentley) met for the despatch of business, in pur-
suance of the Proclamation inserted by authority in
all the Morning, Evening, and Weekly Papers, ap-
pointing that day for the publication of the Second
Number of the Miscellany, edited by "Boz."

Bentley's Miscellany including *Oliver Twist*. Dickens is
triumphantly leading the stout porter who is lumbering
along under a pile of the magazines.

I have done it though – really...I have
discovered that the landlord of the Albion has
delicious hollands and that a cobbler who lives
opposite to my bed-room window is a Roman Catholic
and gives an hour and a half to his devotions every

124

morning behind his counter. I have walked upon the sands at low-water from this place to Ramsgate, and sat upon the same at high, till I have been flayed with the cold. I have seen ladies and gentlemen walking upon the earth in slippers of buff, and pickling themselves in the sea in complete suits of the same. I have seen stout gentlemen looking at nothing through powerful telescopes for hours, and, when at last they saw a cloud of smoke, fancying a steamer behind it, and going home comfortable and happy. I have found out that our next neighbour has a wife and something else under the same roof with the rest of his furniture – the wife deaf and blind, and the something else given to drinking.'

Oliver Twist: Oliver Twist is a child who is given his name by the workhouse, where he is born, run by the cruel tyrant Mr Bumble, the parish beadle. He runs away to London and is ensnared by the old Jew Fagin and his gang of thieves, including Bill Sikes, Nancy and 'the Artful Dodger'. Although rescued by Mr Brownlow, he is kidnapped by the gang. He accompanies Bill Sikes on a robbery and is shot, and is nursed back to health by Mrs Maylie and Rose. In the background is the sinister figure of Monks, who is aware of Oliver's parentage. Nancy contacts Rose about Monks, but Fagin believes her to be a traitor and she is brutally murdered by Sikes. Rose turns out to be Oliver's aunt and Monks is Oliver's half-brother, a man who has stolen the whole of his deceased father's fortune. Monks emigrates and dies in prison, Mr Bumble ends up destitute in the workhouse over which he formerly ruled and Oliver is adopted by the kindly Mr Brownlow (who turns out to be an old friend of his father).

Oliver Twist has two of Dickens's most famous villains – Fagin and Bill Sikes, and his most famous victim, Nancy – Sikes's girl and a lady of the impoverished streets of London. She was an untypical Dickens's woman, away from the virginal recreations that at times marred his work who, by their innocence, recreated Mary in one guise or another.

The public were unprepared for a Dickens book with a plot, but rapidly took to it. Although the plot is almost too theatrical and improbable at times, it remains today a perennial favourite, served up in many ways including plays, films and a popular musical.

Oliver is the typical 'lost child' – sweet and uncontaminated by the iniquity that surrounds him; showing (as Dickens felt about his time alone in London) that purity and a good disposition are sufficient to stave off and resist all evil influences. The scenes in the workhouse, at Fagin's den of thieves, the murder of Nancy and the horror-haunted Sikes - are amongst his best.

But many minor characters prevail including Mr Bumble, the Artful Dodger and the dog.

Pickwick ended in November 1837 and Kate and Charles visited Brighton.

'It is a beautiful day and we have been taking advantage of it, but the wind until today has been so high and the weather so stormy that Kate has been scarcely able to peep out of doors. On Wednesday it blew a perfect hurricane, breaking windows, knocking down shutters, carrying people off their legs, blowing the fires out, and causing universal consternation. The air was for some hours darkened with a shower of black hats (second-hand) which are supposed to have been blown off the heads of unwary passengers in remote parts of town, and have been industriously picked up by the fishermen. Charles Kean was advertised for *Othello* "for the benefit of Mrs Sefton, having most kindly postponed for this one day his departure for London" I have not heard whether he got to the theatre, but I am sure nobody else did.'

'I am glad you like *Oliver* this month. I hope to do great things with Nancy. If I can work out the idea I have formed of her, and of the female who is to contrast with her. I have had great difficulty in keeping my hands off Fagin and the rest of them in the evenings; but I came down here for a rest. I have resisted the temptation, and steadily applied myself to the labour of being idle.'

Although Oliver was an orphan born in the workhouse, the book is not just about the harsh New Poor Law which caused much suffering; but about the thousands of deprived and abandoned children, especially in the big cities such as London. It also deals with topics not found in English novels at the time, such as child abduction, prostitution and brutal murder (hardly topics for a musical, although it was to be adapted as one in time).

Dickens had wandered the streets as a child and knew the problems that lurked there - the starving and neglected child; the child working in dank unhygienic conditions for long hours and often wracked with pain and illness; the child as a vagabond and thief; and the prostitution that brought a precarious and squalid income often ending with disease and a violent death. Many knew this but chose to ignore it. However, Dickens, in the words of the old adage "that the pen is mightier than the sword" became the social reformer who, in this respect, transcends Shakespeare, Scott, Austen and the

Brontes. Through him the public's awareness changed at a stroke; and he was to perform this feat time and time again. That is, without doubt, one of his greatest legacies.

Remembering the kindness bestowed upon him by Bob Fagin (especially during one episode of illness in the blacking warehouse) it is curious that Dickens chose the name 'Fagin' for his most villainous and repulsive character, the corrupter of children.

Oliver is introduced to the respectable old gentleman

"We are very glad to see you, Oliver, very,' said the Jew. 'Dodger, take off the sausages, and draw a tub near the fire for Oliver. Ah, you're a-staring at the pocket-handkerchiefs! Eh, my dear! There are a good many of 'em, ain't there? We've just looked 'em out, ready for the wash; that's all, Oliver; that's all Ha! Ha! Ha!"

The other is the vicious burglar, Bill Sikes.

'He had a brown hat on his head and a dirty belcher handkerchief round his neck, with long frayed ends of which he smeared the beer from his face as he spoke. He disclosed, when he had done so, a broad heavy countenance with a beard of three days' growth, and two scowling eyes; one of which displayed various partly-coloured symptoms of having been recently damaged by a blow'

Nancy's death was one of the most dramatic scenes in the story.

"Then spare my life for the love of Heaven, as I spared yours," rejoined the girl, clinging to him "Bill, dear Bill, you cannot have the heart to kill me…Bill, Bill, for dear God's sake, for your own, for mine, stop before you spill my blood! I have been true to you, upon my guilty soul I have." The housebreaker freed one arm, and grasped his pistol. The certainty of immediate detection if he fired flashed across his mind even in the midst of his fury; and he beat it twice with all the force he could summon, upon the upturned face that almost touched his own.'

There is a small gem – the white dog called Bull's Eye, "whose very feet were bloody" **and whose ghostly presence is to follow, haunt and betray Sikes.**

'If any description of him were out, it would not be forgotten that the dog was missing, and had probably gone with him. This might lead to his apprehension as he passed along the streets. He resolved to drown him, and walked on looking about for a pond; picking up a heavy stone and tying it to his handkerchief as he went. The animal looked up into his master's face while these preparations were making; whether his instinct apprehended something of their purpose. Or the robber's sidelong look at him was sterner than ordinary, he skulked a little farther in the rear than usual, and cowered as he came more slowly along. When his master halted at the brink of a pool, and looked round to call him, he stopped outright. "Do you hear me call? Come here!"

The animal came up from the very force of habit; but as Sikes stooped to attach the handkerchief to his throat, he uttered a low growl and started back. "Come back!" said the robber. The dog wagged his tail, but moved not. Sikes made a running noose and called him again. The dog advanced, retreated, paused an instant, turned, and scoured away at his hardest speed. The man whistled again and again, and sat down and waited in the expectation that he would return. But no dog appeared, and at length he resumed his journey.'(Oliver Twist)

Towards the end of *Pickwick Papers,* Chapman and Hall announced a new venture. Thus Dickens was left with the daunting task of thinking about three major novels at once. He was also aware that his imprudent father was not adverse to pointing out to the publishers the value of his son, when in the usual financial straits, and asking for a loan.

There was the customary "falling out" with the publisher, even more serious than the one with Macrone. Dickens disliked Bentley's meddling with the *Miscellany*; he could not endure being told what to do. He threatened to resign, also claiming that the serial

Oliver Twist should be counted as one of the two novels contracted.

Bentley disagreed. Dickens's initial contract included his next two novels; they would belong to Bentley for £500 each. As Macready, his friend remarked, "Dickens makes a contract which he considers advantageous at the time, but subsequently finding his talents more lucrative than he had supposed, he refuses to fulfil the contract."

And so it proved! The increasingly famous author insisted that *Oliver Twist* should be considered as one of the two and the payment should rise to £700. Bentley refused claiming that he was already being well-paid as editor and that the novel, *Oliver Twist*, represented Dickens's contribution. Bitterness rose on both sides as further demand and counter-demands were made.

Dickens downed tools and refused to write another word.

'It is no fiction to say that at present I *cannot* write this tale. The immense profits which *Oliver* has realised to its publisher, and is still realising; the paltry, wretched, miserable sum it brought me…the consciousness that I have still the slavery and drudgery of another work on the same journeyman terms; the consciousness that my books are enriching everybody connected with them but myself, and that I with such a popularity as I have acquired, am struggling in old toils, and wasting my energies in the very height and freshness of my fame, and best part of my life, to fill the pockets of others, while for those who are nearest and dearest to me I can realise little more than a genteel subsistence: all this puts me out of heart and spirits.'

Bentley went to see him but Dickens was cold and irritable, threatening not to write the book at all. So the publisher gave in, agreeing to make *Oliver* one of the two novels for which the advance had been paid. Because Bentley knew that going to court would be futile and there was no point in having a hostile editor in his employ. He conceded to the payments of £1,300 in total.

Still Dickens was not satisfied. He wanted a clear demarcation between his editorial duties on the *Miscellany* and Bentley's. Forster represented Dickens and matters were not helped by Bentley's dislike of someone he described as "an ill-mannered man". After lengthy negotiations Bentley backed down. Both men were furious and when the publisher started making niggling deductions from Dickens's fees, if his work was slightly trimmed to make room for other articles by other writers, things became even more acrimonious.

As the months went on and his fame grew, Dickens's iron will became increasingly apparent. He expected to be right at all times and to be recognised as such. When crossed, he was mercurial in his anger and easily roused; yet equally quick to forgive. Above everything he disliked being "used". Yet he rarely lost a friend. Not because he was famous, many were equally famous. Even after major quarrels there was usually a rapid rapprochement and a renewed friendship. There is no doubt that the saving grace was his humour, his "inimitable funny way". Everyone around him enjoyed his spontaneous wit, and when he roared with laughter, he often reduced himself (and those around him) to a state verging on collapse. High spirits, theatrical comedy and excellent mimicry ensured a happy circle.

Dickens's busy schedule did not let up in 1838. Bentley pressed him to do the new novel to be called *Gabriel Vardon* (eventually *Barnaby Rudge*), hopefully to be completed by November. Dickens, who initially agreed, now felt a sense of "something hanging over him like a hideous nightmare." He had promised the impossible, even with his frenetic writing skills. For the editing of the *Miscellany*, in addition to supplying monthly parts, were proving too taxing.

'I no sooner get myself up, high and dry, to attack Oliver manfully, than up come the waves of each month's work, and drive me back again into a sea of manuscripts.'

In February 1838 he wrote to Bentley: 'I have been thinking a great deal about *Barnaby Rudge*. I see it will be wholly impossible for me to produce it by the time I had hoped, with justice to myself or profit to you.'

After some wrangling by Dickens, part of it being related to monies to be paid, (and negotiated once again by Forster), it was agreed by all that *Barnaby* should begin when *Oliver* ceased. At times work was slow.

'I have been sitting patiently at home waiting for Oliver Twist who has not yet arrived.'

In March 1838 his first daughter was born and they were delighted, calling her Mary (although affectionately called Mamie). From July to September he wrote rapidly, completing eight chapters, and having a change of scene by spending some time on the Isle of Wight. On his return he largely shunned his friends – being out of town, as he said. When they did entertain, long hours of work were needed after dinner; something he referred to in later life with abhorrence.

Of the closing sequences in *Oliver Twist*, he took great care. A nice touch is that he involved his wife with his writing, asking her opinion on each scene and (most especially) the final one involving Nancy

'I showed what I have done to Kate last night who was in an unspeakable "state", from which and my own impression I augur well.'

So the story unfolded, to great public acclaim. In September 1838 he wrote to Forster, for once eschewing an invitation to go riding, 'My missis is going out to dinner, and I ought to go, but I have a bad cold. So do come, and sit here, or work or do something, while I write the last chapter of Oliver, which will be 'arter a lamb chop, and a bit o' so'mat else.'

After lunch, they sat down and discussed the fate of Charley Bates and the Artful Dodger (two young thieves used by Fagin). Dickens sat for a while, then, with a sudden burst of writing, composed the final Chapter. Forster never forgot seeing Dickens write the last full stop and throwing down his pen with a flourish.

Bentley brought out the book in three volumes. It was the first to bear the name of Charles Dickens, to expose him for public acclaim.

But a quarrel had been brewing between them for some time, partly due to Bentley's lack of graciousness and diplomacy; and partly due to Dickens continually stretching his contractual rights. So another novel came to its triumphant close with Dickens out of sorts with the publisher. So far he had quarrelled with both Macrone and Bentley and come out on top.

Cruickshank's fireside print only made
the first edition of *Oliver Twist* before
Dickens deleted it.

It had been an exhausting period, for in
addition he had edited the '*Memoirs of Joseph
Grimaldi*' for Bentley, the original manuscript having
been prepared by a Mr Wilks from the celebrated
clown's notes. Of passing interest is the fact that
Dickens had an indifferent opinion of the mass of
Wilks' notes (which he bluntly described as "twaddle")
and the modifications and additions were dictated to
his father, probably one of the few times they worked
together in this way.

With the last chapter of *Oliver Twist*, Dickens
resigned from *Bentley's Miscellany*. Bentley was livid

that Dickens had worked on yet another small comic book for Chapman and Hall. However, he hid his wrath and asked the author to continue as editor in name only, for £40 a month; but Dickens refused and insisted that his friend Ainsworth be appointed as editor. His valedictory editorial summed up his feelings, 'that the magazine had always been literally "Bentley's" *Miscellany* and never mine.'

Dickens agreed to pay Bentley £2000 for the copyright of *Oliver* and was released from his contract to write *Barnaby Rudge*. Chapman and Hall advanced £3000 for the future work.

'Chapman and Hall just sent me three "extra-super" bound copies of Pickwick,' he wrote to Forster, 'The first I forward to you, the second I have presented to our good friend Ainsworth, and the third Kate has retained for herself.'

Oliver Twist was his second run-away success. Now Dickens wanted to concentrate on a new project, *Nicholas Nickleby*.

Chapter 11

"Ah!" said that gentleman, smacking his lips "here's richness!" as he tasted the watered-down twopenn'orth of milk.

The irascible headmaster of Dotheboys Hall, Wackford Squeers, never said a truer word. For *Nicholas Nickleby* was to be the third major success in as many years, rich in characterisation and dramatisation. Dickens had been 'out of town' when *Pickwick* was published and determined to be so when *Nicholas Nickleby* came out in April 1838.

He wrote to Forster, "Meet me at the Shakespeare on Saturday night at eight; order your horse for midnight, and ride back with me."

"The smallest hours were sounding from St Paul's into the night before we started, and the night was none too pleasant", wrote Forster.

Dickens was elated on two fronts. A daughter had been born in early March and Kate was well-enough in April to celebrate their second wedding anniversary and, coincidently, John Forster's twenty-sixth birthday, on the same day. Dickens kept this celebration up, 'except when they were living out of England, for twenty successive years, it was a part of his love of regularity and order, as well as his kindness of nature, to place such friendly meetings as these under rules of habit and continuance,' Forster noted.

In addition sales of *Nicholas Nickleby* reached fifty thousand on the day of publication.

Nicholas Nickleby: The nineteen year old Nicholas, his mother and his sister Kate are left penniless, and they appeal to Ralph Nickleby, the deceased's brother. Nicholas is sent to a Yorkshire school where the children are starved and maltreated by the headmaster Wackford Squeers. One of the pupils, Smike, a simple minded boy of about Nicholas's age has been abandoned and is regularly beaten by Squeers. The infuriated Nicholas thrashes the headmaster and runs away with Smike. They become actors with the provincial company of Vincent and Mrs Crummles. Kate is apprenticed to Mrs Mantalini, a dressmaker, whose husband wastes her money while casting a professional eye over the young ladies in her business. Ralph colludes with Sir Mulberry Hawk to get money out of the weak Lord Verisopht. Nicholas falls in love with Madeline Bray, saves her from a wretched marriage to the 'ancient' usurer, Gride. After being befriended by the munificent Cheeryble brothers, Nicholas marries Madeline and Kate marries Frank Cheeryble, the nephew.

The internal economy of Dotheboys Hall

Charles Dickens knew of the plight of the poorer, inner-city child, free to roam the slums (where sewage flooded the streets, and buildings rotted) – many such children were abandoned, starving and neglected. There was another form of cruelty in which children were equally abandoned and starving - but were not free. In fact they suffered a form of tortured imprisonment.

He had heard of the Yorkshire Schools where boarding was cheap and confidential. To be fair, some schools attempted to educate and improve their pupils, and conditions were tolerable; while in others they were simply juvenile prisons of "slave" labour.

These children of the disreputable establishments were abandoned. They were often the unwanted step-children whose presence could complicate wills and annuities, to their step-fathers' disadvantage. Better by far to remove them two hundred and fifty miles from London and leave them, in effect, to perish.

Such an establishment was Dotheboys Hall, at Bowes near Barnard Castle. Today the building still stands (in County Durham not Yorkshire) - remote, solitary and windswept, especially when the Pennine breeze is at its height.

'I cannot recall to mind how I came to hear about Yorkshire schools when I was a not very robust child, sitting in bye-places near Rochester Castle; but I know that my first impressions of them were picked up at that time.'

Dickens, like his fictitious hero Nicholas, decided to travel there. He was in a hurry to find out. This haste to find details is shown by the fact that he decided to set off in severe wintry conditions, in a journey that took four days. So on a bleak January morning in 1838, he began, with Phiz (Hablot Browne) as his travelling companion. Knowing that his fame might have preceded him and he could be recognised, and his presence in the schools resented, he consulted Mr Smithson (a solicitor friend who had Yorkshire connections). They concocted a story in the letters of introduction about placing a little boy in a school, the child having been left with a widowed mother. Thus travelling *in cognito* they were entertained by a mistress of one of the schools, 'a very queer old body' who carried a letter from the father of one boy 'containing a severe lecture (enforced and aided by many texts from the Scriptures) on his refusing to eat boiled meat. She was very communicative, drank a great deal of brandy and water, and towards evening became insensible.' There was also a 'most delicious lady's maid who begged them to watch out for the coach that would be sent to meet her…the coach did not come and a very dirty girl did.'

In an era of horse-drawn vehicles, four days from home and without the use of telephones or modern electronic communication, meant that the North of England was as conveniently remote as one could get from London. On arrival they met the solicitor who had been sent the letter of introduction, but received a curiously lukewarm response. It is almost certain that the locals were suspicious of a man who was generally instantly recognisable despite the feigned identity. Many probably knew of the harsh realities of the schools and wanted to spare their own.

But there is no doubting that life was harsh in the Yorkshire Schools; as an account by a pupil later told of 'eighteen boys, two were totally blind. In November he was quite blind…and sent to a private room where there were nine other boys blind.' Malnutrition, beatings and disease were certainly the order of the day.

Thus in a gloomy mood and on a bitterly cold day, with deep snow scattered around a churchyard in Bowes, he came across the gravestone of a nineteen year-old boy from Wiltshire, who had died at the Shaw Academy in 1822. 'I think his ghost put Smike into my head upon the spot.'

The opening issue of *Nicholas Nickleby* was in April 1838. Charles and Kate wanted to get away from the City and took a house in Petersham, remaining there until late August; although he visited London frequently. At Petersham the grounds were large and Dickens enjoyed racing, high jumping, bowling and quoits; pursuits in which he, with his usually fervour, excelled.

He loved 'living in these remote and distant parts, with the charm of mountains formed by Richmond Hill presenting an almost insurmountable barrier.'

Nicholas Nickleby ranks as one of his most popular works. But at times he struggled to complete the full quota (unlike Pickwick when he often ran over).

'I could not write a line 'til three o'clock and have five slips to finish and don't know what to put in them.'

'I am writing incessantly until it was time to dress; and have not yet got the subject of my last chapter, which *must* be finished tonight.'

It was November 1838 and already the constant plagiarism had begun before the book was finished. This time Dickens seemed to take it in good fun. A theatrical adapter named Stirling 'had seized upon it without leave while only a third was written; hacked, cut and garbled its dialogue, invented a plot and ending of his own, and produced it at the Adelphi. The acting was not of the finest. Of Ralph Nickleby there was indeed nothing visible save a wig, a spencer and a pair of boots,' commented Forster ruefully. Dickens was magnanimous, all things considered, praising "the skilful management and dressing of the boys, the capital manner and speech of Fanny Squeers" and sundry other matters.

But work was pressing: 'I must be alone in my glory today and see what I can do. I perpetrated a great amount of work yesterday, and have every day indeed since Monday, but I must buckle-to again and endeavour to get the steam up. If this were to go on long, I should "bust" the boiler.'

There are many reasons for the run-away success of *Nicholas Nickleby* at that time (and its popularity since). Ralph Nickleby (the uncle and the other main character - old, hard and inflexible) is the perfect foil for the dashing Nicholas. Mrs Nickleby is garrulous, and Mrs Mantalini is dominated by her spend-thrift husband. Smike, the downtrodden youth, ill-treated at Dotheboys Hall and befriended by Nicholas, struck a cord in the Victorian era that does not vibrate so violently today. Kate Nickleby is as sweet as any Dickens's heroine, and Sir Mulberry Hawk is 'a dastardly' figure in his wooing of her and his use of the aristocratic fop, Lord Verisoft, for money.

However, there is a "child" who stands out in comic relief, away from the melodramatic sadness of Smike. That "child" is the 'infant phenomenon'. Her father, the kindly and exaggerating Vincent Crummles, runs a theatrical company, joined by the journeying Nicholas and his companion, the runaway Smike. They watch a rehearsal.

'As Mrs Vincent Crummles recrossed back to the table, there bounded on to the stage from some mysterious inlet, a little girl in a dirty white frock with tucks up to the knees, short trousers, sandaled shoes, white spencer, pink gauze bonnet, green veil and curl-papers; who turned a pirouette, cut twice in the air, turned another pirouette, then, looking off at the opposite wing, shrieked, bounded forward to within six inches of the footlights, and fell into a beautiful attitude of terror, as a shabby gentleman in an old pair of buff slippers came in at one powerful slide, and chattering his teeth, fiercely brandished a walking stick. "They are going through the Indian Savage and the Maiden," said Mrs Crummles. "This sir," said Mr Vincent Crummles bringing the maiden forward, "This is the infant phenomenon – Miss Ninetta Crummles. She is ten years of age, sir".

"Not more!"

"Not a day!"

"Dear me!" said Nicholas, "it's extraordinary." It was; for the infant phenomenon, though of short statue, had a comparatively aged countenance, and had moreover, been precisely the same age – not perhaps to the full extent of the memory of the oldest inhabitant, but certainly for five good years.' (Nicholas Nickleby)

Another masterstroke is the Squeers' family - Mr and Mrs, Fanny and the son.

Mrs Squeers who: 'came in, still habited in the primitive night-jacket which had displayed the symmetry of her figure on the previous night, and further ornamented with a beaver bonnet of some antiquity, which she wore, with much ease and lightness, on the top of the nightcap. "If the young man comes to be a teacher here, let him understand, at once, that we don't want any foolery about the boys. They have the brimstone and treacle, partly because if they hadn't something or other in the way of medicine they'd be always ailing and giving a world of trouble, and partly because it spoils their appetites and comes cheaper than breakfast and dinner.'

Mrs Squeers calls Nicholas "Knuckleboy"; shades of Mrs Beadnell and her mispronunciation of Charles as "Mr Dickin".

The jewels in the crown are the headmaster, Mr Wackford Squeers and his daughter, Fanny. His vicious ignorance and lack of concern for the pupils is heightened by the humour, as is her ignorance and conceit.

It is of note that many of the infectious diseases which spread rapidly in overcrowded, malnourished children – measles, diphtheria, scarlet fever – induced blindness (usually partial but sometimes complete). Congenital venereal disease regularly produced cataracts and conjunctival scarring. Serious suppurative infections always caused the loss of the eye which became a ball of pus. Thus Dickens felt it fitting that Squeers should have a more-than distinctive face.

'Mr Squeers's appearance was not prepossessing. He had but one eye, and the popular prejudice runs in favour of two. The eye he had was unquestionably useful, but decidedly not ornamental.'

Nicholas and the Headmaster arrive at Dotheboys Hall, late at night, to be greeted by Mrs Squeers.

'How is my Squeery?" "Quite well, my love," replied Squeers. "How's the cows?"

"All right, everyone of 'em," answered the lady.

"And the pigs?"

"As well as they were when you went away."

"Come that's a blessing," said Squeers, pulling off his great coat. "The boys are all as they were, I suppose?"

"That young Pitcher's had a fever."

"No!" exclaimed Squeers, "Damn that boy, he's always at something of that sort."

"Never was such a boy, I do believe," said Mrs Squeers, "whatever he has is always catching too. I say it's obstinacy, and nothing shall ever convince me that it isn't. I'd beat it out of him; and I told you that, six months ago."

Miss Fanny Squeers is in her three-and-twentieth year and quickly falls for Nicholas. However, at their first afternoon together, her best friend riles her to jealousy (shades of Maria and Marianne) as Nicholas partners the friend, Miss 'Tilda Price, at cards, and her boyfriend John Browdie partners Fanny Squeers..

The deal fell to Nicholas and the hand prospered. "We intend to win everything," said he.

"'Tilda *has* won something she didn't expect, I think, haven't you dear?" said Miss Squeers maliciously.

"Only a dozen and eight, love," replied Miss Price, affecting to take the question in a literal sense.

"How dull you are to-night!" sneered Miss Squeers.

"No, indeed," replied Miss Price, "I am in excellent spirits. I was thinking *you* seemed out of sorts."

"Me!" cried Miss Squeers, biting her lips, and trembling with very jealousy; "oh no!"

"That's well," remarked Miss Price. "Your hair's coming out of curl, dear."

"Never mind me," tittered Miss Squeers, "you had better attend to your partner".

"I've never had such luck, really," exclaimed coquettish Miss Price, after another hand or two. "It's all along of you, Mr Nickleby, I think. I should like to have you for a partner always"

"We have all the talking to ourselves, it seems," said Nicholas, looking good-humouredly round the table as he took up the cards for a fresh deal

"You do it so well," tittered Miss Squeers, "that it would be a pity to interrupt, wouldn't it, Mr Browdie? He! he! he!"

"Why, and here's Fanny in tears now!" exclaimed Miss Price, as if in fresh amazement. "What can be the matter?"

"Oh! You don't know miss, of course you don't know. Pray don't trouble yourself to inquire," said Miss Squeers, producing that change of countenance which children call making a face."

"You needn't take the trouble to make yourself plainer than you are, ma'am, however," rejoined Miss Price," because that's quite unnecessary."

"'Tilda," exclaimed Miss Squeers with dignity, "I hate you."(Nicholas Nickleby)

The identity of Dotheboys Hall and its illustrious headmaster were disguised in the original preface to *Nicholas Nickleby*.

Dickens wrote 'of his great amusement and satisfaction, during the progress of this work, to learn, from country friends and from a variety of ludicrous statements concerning himself in provincial papers, that more than one Yorkshire schoolmaster lays claim to being the original Mr Squeers...that Mr Squeers is the representative of a class and not of an individual…where imposture, ignorance, and brutal cupidity are the stock-in-trade of a small body of men, and one is described by these characteristics, all his fellows will recognise something belonging to themselves, and each will have a misgiving that the portrait is his own.'

Nicholas astonishes Mr Squeers and family.

Dickens recorded in his note book, under the date February 2,1838, 'Shaw, the schoolmaster we saw today, is the man in whose school several boys went blind some time since from gross neglect. The case was tried, and the verdict went against him. It must have been between 1823 and 1826. Look this up in the newspapers.'

There is no doubt that William Shaw was Squeers, and his advertisement is found in contemporaneous issues of the *Times*.

"Education – by Mr Shaw, at Bowes Academy, Greta Bridge, Yorkshire. YOUTH are carefully INSTRUCTED in English, Latin, and Greek languages, Writing, Common and Decimal Arithmetic, Book-keeping, Mensuration, Surveying, Geometry, Geography, and Navigation, with the most useful branches of the Mathematics, and provided with Board, Clothes, and every necessary, at 20 guineas per annum each. No extra charges. No vacations. Further particulars, may be known on application to Mr J Metcalfe, agent, 38 Great Marylebone Street. Mr Shaw attends at the George and Blue Boar, Holborn, from 12 to 2 daily."

"Boys, I've been to London, and have returned to my family and you, as strong and as well as ever."

According to half-yearly custom, the boys gave three feeble cheers at this refreshing intelligence.

"This the first class in English spelling and philosophy, Nickleby,' said Squeers, beckoning Nicholas to stand beside him. "We'll get up a Latin one, and hand that over to you. Now, then, where's the first boy?"

"Please, sir, he's cleaning the back parlour window," said the temporary head of the philosophical class.

"So he is, to be sure," rejoined Squeers. "We go upon the practical mode of teaching, Nickleby; the regular education system. "C-l-e-a-n, clean, verb active, to make bright, to scour. W-i-n, win, d-e-r, der, winder, a casement. When the boy knows this out of book, he goes and does it. Where's the second boy?"

"Please, sir, he's weeding the garden," replied a small voice.

"To be sure," said Squeers, by no means disconcerted. "So he is. B-o-t, bot, t-i-n, tin, bottin, n-e-y, bottinney, noun substantive, a knowledge of plants. When he learns that bottinney means a knowledge of plants, he goes and know's 'em. Third boy, what's a horse?"

"A beast, sir," replied the boy.

"A horse is a quadruped, and quadruped's Latin for beast, as everybody that's gone through grammar knows, or else where's the use of having grammars at all?"

"Where indeed!" said Nicholas abstractedly.

"As you're perfect in that," resumed Squeers, turning to the boy, "go and look after *my* horse, and rub him down well, or I'll rub you down." (Nicholas Nickleby)

William Shaw lies buried in Bowes churchyard, close to a grave believed to be the original 'Smike'. He always denied being 'Squeers'. There is no doubt that rather than exaggerating the situation in Yorkshire Schools, Dickens may have underplayed it to a degree, after all his visit was brief, being only a few days. Shaw was prosecuted in 1832 and seemed to have escaped serious punishment. The indictment included five boys sleeping in a bed, a supper of warm milk water and bread, and on Sundays they had a pot of skimmings for tea, in which there were vermin. In his and other schools, blindness, disease and violence were common; filth and suffering everywhere. Shaw's advertisement appeared for the last time in 1840 and by 1848 only one such school remained. Dickens had produced the effect he desired.

He celebrated his birthday in 1839 with an impromptu dinner which Leigh Hunt (the essayist), Ainsworth and Forster were guests. 'Twenty seven years old. Who'd have thought it? I *never* did! But I grow sentimental.'

In March he travelled down to Devon to find a new house for his parents, evidently wanting to locate them some distance away and take their improvidence with them. The final straw, of many, was his father's habit of cutting out his son's signature from correspondence, and selling them for a few shillings. Dickens found it intolerable that his father was trading off his reputation; so Dickens rented a cottage called Mile End Cottage at Alphington, one mile outside of Exeter. In his usual haste he had been walking and searching and saw a "jewel of a place with an excellent parlour, a capital closet and a beautiful little drawing room." The house belonged to a Devonshire widow.

'She is a fat, infirm, splendidly-fresh-faced country dame, rising sixty and recovering from an attack "on the nerves". The good lady's brother and his wife live in the next nearest cottage, and the brother transacts the good lady's business, the nerves not admitting of her transacting it herself, although they leave her in her debilitated state something sharper than the finest lancet.'

He furnished the house, and secreted them off to Devon with no choice in the matter, giving them an allowance of seven pounds and ten shillings a quarter. Perhaps it was on condition that they kept away from London, certainly it has been said that, in future, they were subdued in his presence.

His circle of friends grew and they visited Charles and Kate often. They included his doctor and the lawyer Smithson who had arranged connections in Yorkshire.

But the most frequent visitors were the actors, artists and writers.

In addition to Forster and Browne there were, amongst others, Maclise, the artist (who was became one of the closest of friends), while Tom Beard remained from earlier days, Macready (the famous actor to whom *Nicholas Nickleby* was dedicated), the artist George Cattermole (Dickens spoke at his wedding and they became collaborators); the barrister Talfourd, Jerrold, Sir Emerson Tennent, Samuel Rogers, Sydney Smith (the witty Canon of St Paul's); the then famous writers Ainsworth and Thackeray, plus Dickens's relatives. The artists Sir Edwin Landseer RA (of "Monarch of the Glen" fame), Sir David Wilkie RA and Clarkson Stansfield RA were soon to join the circle.

Not all his close friends were male. He often came up from Petersham to dine with Miss Angela Burdett-Coutts (later Baroness), a rich, young heiress from the Coutts banking family.

Her calmness and philanthropic nature impressed Dickens, while her impressions of him were of 'restless, vivacity, impetuosity, generous impulses, earnestness and frank sincerity.'

In addition there was Lady Holland, the leading socialite of her day. She inquired of Sir Edward Bulwer-Lytton (first Baron Lytton, prolific writer and later MP) as to what manner of person Dickens was, to be assured that 'he was presentable'.

She invited Dickens to Holland House. Dickens was overawed by the sumptuous surroundings and the liveried footmen.

Women also suffered in the industrial system of the day.
Baroness Burdett-Coutts and Dickens were always
supportive of projects to help women; seen here dragging
with a harness a load of coal in the mine, while another carries
a heavy basket.

After all, it seemed to him only a short while
since the 'blacking warehouse and Marshalsea days'.
The twenty-seven year old behaved modestly and

quietly amongst the honoured guests and was classed as 'very unobtrusive and altogether pre-possessing.'

Baroness Angela Burdett-Coutts, a close friend whom Dickens admired.

Dickens always dressed in the height of fashion, with his brown hair immaculately groomed. It is said that he kept a comb 'at the ready' at all times' and refreshed his locks regularly. He loved bright colours (for example a crimson waistcoat embellished with a gold watch and chain was one of his favourites) and he was often referred to as 'colourful' or 'dandified'. But he could not compete with another person of exceptional outfits. This was Count d'Orsay, who frequented Holland House. Curiously his wife's stepmother (the witty and attractive Countess of Blessington, the host of a glittering saloon at Gore House) regularly accompanied the Count. So Dickens was encouraged to more exquisite outfits by the outlandish d'Orsay.

Whatever feelings Dickens had about this elite society and the snobbish world they lived in, he kept it to himself. He was self-assured and confident. He was not daunted when he was invited to breakfast with Samuel Rogers (the highly successful banker and poet, admired by Byron) and his friends. Rogers gave his celebrated breakfasts for over forty years. They were of average fare, being a man of economy. However, a prerequisite was that guests had to be modest, witty and wise, for as his friend Sydney Smith pointed out, 'no one is conceited before one o'clock.' Thus in one place or another, Dickens also met Captain Marryat (the author), Wellington, Disraeli, Lord Durham and Prince Louis Napoleon.

He was popular wherever he went, they admired him; and it must be recalled that he was still under thirty and generations removed from some of them. He was elected a member of the prestigious Athenaeum at the same time as another famous Charles…Darwin, who was to revolutionise scientific thought for all time.

Kate and the family prospered. Dickens's parents were at first sullen about their move, but gradually came to accept the change and even enjoy their new neighbours and the countryside. He records an anecdote about his mother who clearly did not detect the resemblance of herself to Mrs Nickleby.

Dickens wrote to Lane in1844, 'Mrs Nickleby herself sitting bodily before me in a solid chair, once asked me whether I really believed there ever was such a woman.'

His sister Fanny inspired the creation of Kate Nickleby, and her husband Henry Burnett was Nicholas. He states that Phiz took him as the model and on entering a room at the Opera House he heard a shout, "Welcome, Nicholas Nickleby".

The Grant brothers, Daniel and William, whom he met at Manchester, became the amiable and humane twins, the Cheeryble brothers.

When one died in 1855 Dickens, wrote from Niagara Falls to an American friend: 'William, one of the noblest hearts who sat for the Cheeryble brothers is dead. If I had been in England I would certainly have gone into mourning for the loss of such a glorious life. His brother is not expected to survive him. I am told that it appears from a memorandum found among the papers of the deceased that in a lifetime he gave away in charity £600,000, or three million dollars!'

By September 1839 he was in Broadstairs where they had taken a house 'two doors from the Albion Hotel where we had a merry night two years ago.'

Dickens loved houses with a view of the sea and to walk along the shore, and note the sea in all its moods.

It has been blowing great guns for the last three days, and last night there was such a sea! I staggered down to the pier, and, creeping under the lee of a large boat which was high and dry, watched it breaking for nearly an hour. Of course I came back wet through.

On the 9th of September: 'I am hard at it, but these windings-up wind slowly, and I shall think I have done great things if I have entirely finished by the 20th.' But by the 18th, 'I have had pretty stiff work, as you suppose, and have taken great pains. The discovery is made, Ralph is dead, the loves have come all right, Tim Linkinwater has proposed, and I have now only to break up Dotheboys and the book together.

The story was finished at Broadstairs on the 20th as scheduled in his punctual way. 'Finished *Nickleby* this day at two o'clock, and went to Ramsgate with Fred (his brother) and Kate.'

Broadstairs, Dickens favourite holiday place

The final issue appeared in October 1839, the same month his third child, Kate (Katey) Macready, was born.

A dinner to mark the end of the book was arranged by Chapman and Hall.

'I have fixed the Nickleby dinner for Saturday the 5th of October. Place, the Albion in Aldersgate Street, Time, six for half-past exactly.'

The publishers presented him with a portrait by Maclise and his friends gathered in high spirits to complement the book, which had outstripped all his others.

Dickens was paid £150 per issue for the twenty instalments plus a bonus reaping £4,500 in all. It was time to buy a more imposing property and they settled on No 1, Devonshire Terrace, Regent's Park.

Writing to Macready in November 1839, he said, 'You must come and see my new house when we have it to rights...a house of great promise (and great premium), undeniable situation, and excessive splendour.'

Charles Dickens had reached an unsurpassed pinnacle in authorship, loved by all classes. His star was on the ascendancy, it was time for a change of direction, to try something new and, for him, original.

Chapter 12

While staying at the King's Head, Barnard Castle, County Durham, Dickens wandered into the shop of William Humphreys, who as a celebrated horologist had build a grandfather clock which was placed inside the door and attracted the author's notice.

As he looked around at the grandfather clock he had an idea for the next stage of his literary career.

He reassured everyone that the time was right to stop monthly instalments of his books, and issue a weekly magazine, in a manner similar to Addisons' *Spectator* (then extremely popular).

By issuing a cheap weekly publication priced three pence (monthly at one shilling, or if enlarged three pence beyond that) he could accept contributions from others and thus relieve his work load. He also felt that publishing at such short intervals, that the 'wretched imitators' and 'plagiarists' would be circumvented. He had described them in various magazines and reviews before the publication of *Nicholas Nickleby* as 'dishonest dullards, resident in cellars and bye-streets, who impose upon the unwary and credulous, cheap and wretched imitations.'

The contract with the publisher's was exceptional in the extreme, namely £8,000 per year in all if the magazine sold fifty thousand copies weekly, as expected. As a bonus they also handed over £1,500 for *Nicholas Nickleby*.

The plan was to start 'with some pleasant fiction to introduce a little club or knot of characters, and to carry their personal histories and proceedings through the work; to introduce fresh characters constantly; to re-introduce Mr Pickwick and Sam Weller, the latter who might furnish an occasional communication with great effect; to write amusing essays on the various foibles of the day as they arise.'

Dickens, after some procrastination settled on the title, *'Master Humphrey's Clock'* 'From week to week Master Humphrey will set his clock'.

The idea was that in the clock's case, manuscripts would be stored, while various characters would surround the old clockmaker. It was launched in April 1840 and nearly seventy thousand copies sold, on the basis of Mr Pickwick's and the Weller's (father and son) return. Dickens, as usual, left town and went with friends to Birmingham, spending so much money on eating and drinking, that they had to pawn their watches to fund the journey home.

The public were not fooled. What they expected was a novel, not essays, short stories or sketches. However, the sales soon plummeted. Master Humphrey, sitting by his clock, had no intention of telling a yarn; and, sadly, the flat repartee of Mr Pickwick and Sam and Tony Weller did not improve matters. It has been said that despite having no cuckoo in it, thankfully, Master Humphrey was soon ejected from the nest. He disappeared pretty quickly, although he did make a fleeting return to the first chapter of volume 2. The only way to save the flagging circulation was to produce a consecutive tale.

'The first chapter of this tale appeared in the fourth number of *Master Humphrey's Clock* when I had already been made uneasy by the desultory character of that work, and when, I believe, my readers had thoroughly participated in that feeling.'

On the 4th of March 1840 he wrote to Forster, seeking advice.

'If you can manage to give me a call in the course of the day or evening, I wish you would. I am laboriously turning over in my mind how I can best effect the improvement we spoke of last night, which I will certainly make by hook or by crook, and which I would like you to see *before* it goes finally to the printers. I think of lengthening *Humphrey*, finishing the description of the society, and closing with the little-child story, which is *sure* to be effective.'

He perseverated about the title, having a number including "*The Old Curiosity Dealer and the Child*" (which, as it turned out, would have been more to the point than "*The Old Curiosity Shop*" – because there is hardly anything in the book about old curiosities, or the shop).

However, his work was interrupted for a few days, because he was called for Jury service at an inquest on the body of a baby, alleged to have been murdered by its mother. Dickens was saddened by the facts of the case but had pity for the girl and, though his exertions, convinced the fellow jurymen to charge her with only the concealment of the birth. The coroner accepted their verdict.

'The poor desolate creature dropped upon her knees before us with protestations that we were right (protestations among the most affecting that I have ever heard in my life), and was carried away insensible. I caused some extra care to be taken of her in prison, and counsel to be retained for her defence when she was tried at the Old Bailey; and her sentence was lenient, and her history and conduct proved that it was right.'

Early in 1840, Kate and Dickens went with Maclise and Forster to spend three days with Walter Savage Landor at Bath. It was there that he thought of the central character being a young girl called Little Nell – the first child heroine in literature.

'I feel the story extremely myself, which I take to be a good sign; and am already warmly interested in it. I shall run it on now for four whole numbers together, to give it a fair chance.'

* *The Old Curiosity Shop*: Nell lives in a gloomy atmosphere of the curiosity shop kept by her grandfather. She is devoted to him. He borrows money to help Fred (Nell's brother) from a loathsome and grotesque dwarf, Daniel Quilp. But the old man gambles the money and they have to flee to escape the enraged Quilp. Nell guides her grandfather, old and infirm, around the countryside, suffering great hardship. They find a cottage by a country church, but Nell succumbs, followed shortly after by her grandfather.

A rest by the way. Looking back at St Paul's they felt they were clear of London. (*The Old Curiosity Shop*)

The book was a huge success and Little Nell became a universal favourite on both sides of the Atlantic. People wept over her death. The apocryphal tale of a crowd on New York pier shouting to a ship coming in from England, 'Is Little Nell dead?' Thousands of letters poured in pleading for a happy outcome. His friend, Lord Jeffrey stated that he sobbed in his library over that episode, 'I am a great goose to have given way so,' he lamented. Edgar Allan Poe, Landor, Carlyle and Macready were said to be similarly affected; although Thomas Carlyle who was considered at the time to be England's greatest author, often referred to the younger Dickens as 'little fellow' and could not hide his overall contempt of fiction writing. The even older Walter Savage Landor was also beginning to be disenchanted with Dickens and was to become more critical over the years. However, at the time Dickens had never been so idolised by his public.

Today, the pathos of Little Nell makes uncomfortable reading; mawkish and strained, with the author striving throughout for a high pitch of pathos, pomp and rhetoric, suitable for a state funeral.

'And now the bell- the bell she had so often heard, by night and day, and listened to with solemn pleasure almost as a living voice – rang its remorseless toll, for her, so young, so beautiful, so good. Decrepit age, and vigorous life, and blooming youth, and helpless infancy, poured forth – on crutches, in the pride of strength and health, in the full blush of promise, in the mere dawn of life- to gather round her tomb.' (The Old Curiosity Shop)

To help his work he went to their favourite haunt, Broadstairs, both in June and September. 'It is now four o'clock and I have been at work since half-past eight. I have really dried myself up into a condition which would almost justify me in pitching off the cliff, head first – but I must get richer before I indulge in a crowning luxury.'

Forster, as always consulted, suggested Nell's demise and Dickens agonised over the writing. The enshrined memory of Mary came back to haunt him.

'It casts the most horrible shadow upon me, and it is as much as I can do to keep moving at all.

It is such a very painful thing to me, that I really cannot express my sorrow. Old wounds bleed afresh when I only think of the way of doing it: what the actual doing it will be, God knows. I can't preach to myself the schoolmaster's consolation, though I try. Dear Mary died yesterday, when I think of this sad story.'

It is said that the pubic mourned her death in a way never experienced before for a fictitious character; Lord Jeffrey (as mentioned) sobbed terribly after reading it, O'Connell the great Irish agitator was so overcome with its pathos, that he wept, saying "He should not have killed her. She was too good!" Writing to George Cattermole respecting the design for the death-chamber, Dickens said, "I am breaking my heart over this story, and cannot bear to finish it."

He reluctantly wound up the story on the morning of January 17th 1841. 'It makes me very melancholy to think that all these people are lost to me for ever, and I feel as if I never could become attached to any new set of characters.

The Old Curiosity Shop is a book without a hero, unless Richard Swiveller can be considered one. The villainous dwarf, Quilp, is well etched; so is the crooked attorney Sampson Brass and his grim sister, Sally; the kindly Marchioness and the benevolent Mrs Jarley, who runs a waxwork show, are enjoyable characters; while the golden-hearted Kit loves Nell, she is a worthy person in the true Dickens mould.

Quilp's character deserves special mention. Dickens was a champion of woman's welfare, of which Baroness Burdett-Coutts was a leading light. It is often remarked that Betsey Trotwood (David Copperfield's aunt) is the first feminist in literature; Quilp is the first wife-beater, or spousal abuser, in modern terminology. Over a century was to pass until this crime became etched in the public's awareness, yet Dickens's skill made the wicked Quilp more heinous, and the crime more obvious, by the dull slant of humour in the dwarf's dealings with Mrs Quilp.

"You'd better walk in then," said the dwarf. "go on, Sir, go on. Now Mrs Quilp – after you ma'am". Mrs Quilp hesitated, but Mr Quilp insisted. And it was not a contest of politeness, or by any means a matter of form, for she knew very well that her husband wished her to enter the house in this order, that he might have a favourable opportunity of inflicting a few pinches on her arms, which were seldom free from impressions of his fingers in black and blue colours. Mr Swiveller, who was not in on the secret, was a little surprised to hear a suppressed scream, and, looking round, to see Mrs Quilp following him with a sudden jerk.'

On a one occasion, while dining at Dickens's house, Forster had begun an argument which became increasing heated and dogmatic ('an endless stream of talk which he thinks argument' – Macready noted). Dickens, as usual, could not contain his own opinions and an increasing exasperation. He pointed out that they were in his house and would Forster kindly leave. His friend stood up immediately – only to be stayed by Macready, who pointed out the value of their friendship. Dickens apologised (in a fashion); although he could not desist from saying that if Forster was to begin provoking him again he could get out. Forster was furious at this further slight, but controlling his anger – he sat without speaking for the rest of the evening. Fortunately for posterity, their friendship continued undiminished.

Macrone and then Bentley had advertised, without any end result, a new novel entitled *Gabriel Varden*. It was originally designed to follow *Oliver Twist* in *Bentley's Miscellany*, now it followed *The Old*

164

Curiosity Shop, Master Humphrey popped up to introduce the story...*Barnaby Rudge*.

Dickens had the advantage of having been formulating the plot for some time. The book is named after a mentally-impaired youth who gets involved in the Gordon riots of 1780 when anti-popery feeling led to an assault by a mob on Newgate Jail to free the misguided Gordon.

'It is necessary to say that those shameful tumults, while they reflect indelible disgrace upon the time in which they occurred, and all who had part in them, teach a good lesson. That what we falsely call a religious cry is easily raised by men who have no religion, and who in their daily practice set at naught the commonest principles of right and wrong; that it is begotten of intolerance and persecution; that it is senseless, besotted, inveterate, and unmerciful; all history teaches us.'

The unemployed rioters by Hablot Browne (Barnaby Rudge)

Barnaby Rudge: The plot concerns the love of Edward, Lord Chester's son, and Emma (the niece of Geoffrey Haredale, who is a Roman Catholic). Sir John Chester is opposed to Roman Catholicism and foments a riot, which burns down Haredale's house. However, Haredale and Emma are saved by Edward, who marries Emma. Barnaby, although simple minded, finds contentment in his own world and, although encouraged to riot, is saved from the death penalty.

Dickens was now living in luxury, dining and entertaining lavishly, and dressing in the opulent height of fashion; while many of his friends had an even more luxurious life style. But his deep feelings for the oppressed and unemployed are mirrored in the riots of *Barnaby Rudge*. By going back sixty years, he was able to sidestep recent issues. He could vent his feelings obliquely and not through any obvious support of the many riots which were currently breaking out in various English towns. His conscience could not fully condemn the unemployed who did not, and would not, wait patiently for the slow machinations of the government to help them. Gabriel Varden, the upright locksmith, vanquishes his starring role as the book unfolds and largely disappears into the pages. However, his coquettish daughter, Dolly, became an endearing favourite with the readers.

Two minor characters are well-written. Many secret societies - some for the employees, others for the employers - were being formed in the late eighteenth century and at least one, The Freemasons, was to become a major force. The rituals of such secretive meetings are sarcastically enshrined in the following section.

The leader of a group, which is to become violently involved in the riots, is the anarchic and diminutive Simon Tappertit, Varden's apprentice; and the secret group are the 'Prentice Knights. Their meetings offer humour mingled with a taste of the bitter, almost psychopathic, rebelliousness, that was later to flourish in many of the uprisings of the twentieth century.

"Lead on," said Mr Tappertit, with a gloomy majesty, "and make remarks when I require you. Forward!" This latter word of command was perhaps somewhat theatrical and unnecessary, inasmuch the descent was by a very narrow, steep, and slippery flight of steps, and any rashness or departure from the beaten track must have ended in a yawning water-butt. But Mr Tappertit being, like some other great commanders, favourable to strong effects, and personal display, cried "Forward!" again, in the hoarsest voice he could assume, and led the way, with folded arms and knitted brows, to the cellar down below, where there was a small copper fixed in one corner, a chair or two, a form and a table, a glimmering fire, and a truckle-bed covered with a ragged patchwork rug.

"Welcome noble captain!" cried a lanky figure, rising as from a nap.

The captain nodded. Then throwing off his outer coat, he stood composed in all his dignity, and eyed his follower over. "What news tonight?" he asked when he had looked into his very soul.

"Nothing particular," replied the other stretching himself – and he was so long already that it was quite alarming to see him do it – "how come you to be so late?"

"No matter…the comrade – is he here?"

There soon appeared at the same door, two other 'pretices, having between them a third, whose eyes were bandaged, and who was attired in a bag-wig, and a broad-skirted coat, trimmed with tarnished lace; and who was girded with a sword, in compliance with the laws of the Institution regulating the introduction of candidates, which required them to assume this courtly dress, and kept it constantly in lavender, for their convenience. One of the conductors of this novice held a rusty blunderbuss pointed towards his ear, and another a very ancient sabre, with which he carved imaginary offenders as he came along in a sanguinary and anatomical manner.

The long comrade read aloud as follows "Mark Gilbert, age, nineteen. Bound to Thomas Curzon, hosier Golden Fleece, Aldgate. Loves Curzon's daughter. Cannot say that Curzon's daughter loves him. Should think it probable. Curzon pulled his ears last Tuesday week"

"Write Curzon down, denounced" said the captain, "Put a black cross against the name of Curzon. 'Prentice, do you love your constitution?" To which the novice (being to that end instructed by his attendant sponsors) replied "I do!" "The Church, the State, and everything established – but the masters?" quoth the captain. Again the novice said, "I do!"
(Barnaby Rudge)

Simon is not above loving his employer's daughter, Dolly, but relies upon the waspish servant Miss Miggs (who adores him) to let him into the shop (where he resides) when a secret meeting ends in the early hours of the morning.

"Come down, and undo the shop window, that I may get in that way."

"I dursn't do it Simmun," cried Miggs.

"But Miggs," cried Mr Tappertit, getting under the lamp, that she might see his eyes. "My darling Miggs -"

Miggs screamed slightly. "I know if I come down, you'll go and –"

"And what, my precious?" said Mr Tappertit.

"And try," said Miggs hysterically, "to kiss me or some such dreadfulness; I know you will!"

"I swear I won't," said Mr Tappertit, with remarkable earnestness. "Upon my soul I won't!" (Barnaby Rudge).

Miss Miggs, the Varden's disloyal servant, has her own views on men.

As a general principle and abstract proposition, Miggs held the male sex to be utterly contemptible and unworthy of notice; to be fickle, false, base, sottish, inclined to perjury, and wholly undeserving. When particularly exasperated against them (which, scandal said, was when Sim Tappertit slighted her most) she was accustomed to wish with great emphasis that the whole of the race of women could but die off, in order that the men might be brought to know the real value of the blessings by which they set so little store.(Barnaby Rudge)

Dickens was to witness a hanging and the spectacle of the jovial, drunken, cheering crowds disgusted him (Thomas Hardy also saw one, reproduced in *Tess of the D'Urbervilles*, which appalled him too).

Thus Dickens introduced sinister Dennis the hangman, one of the riot leaders, who eventually

meets his own fate, cringing and pleading, as he is led to the gallows.

'A   squat, thickset personage, with a low, retreating forehead, a coarse shock head of hair, and eyes so small and near together, that his broken nose alone seemed to prevent their meeting and fusing into one of unusual size. In his grimy hands he held a knotted stick, the knob of which was carved into a rough likeness of his own vile face.'

"These smalls", said Dennis rubbing his legs, "these very smalls – they belonged to a friend of mine that's left off such encumbrances forever: this coat too –I've often walked behind this coat, in the streets, and wondered whether it would ever come to me: this pair of shoes have danced a hornpipe for another man, afore my eyes, full half-a dozen times at least: and as to my hat," he said taking it off, and twirling it round upon his fist –"Lord! I've seen this hat go up Holborn on the box of a hackney coach –ah, many and many a day!"

"You don't mean to say their old wearers are *all* dead, I hope?" said Mr Tappertit, falling a little distance from him as he spoke. "Every one of 'em," replied Dennis.'(Barnaby Rudge)

'It may be further remarked,' Dickens stated, 'that Mr Dennis's allusions to the flourishing condition of his trade in those days have their foundation in Truth. Even the case of Mary Jones dwelt upon with so much pleasure by the same character, is no effort of invention. Under the Shop-lifting Act, one Mary Jones was executed, whose case I shall just mention; it was at the time when press-warrants were issued on the alarm about the Falkland Islands. The woman's husband was pressed, their goods seized for some debts of his, and she, with two small children, turned into the streets a-begging. It is a circumstance not to be forgotten that she was very young (under nineteen), and most remarkably handsome. She went to a linen-draper's shop, took some coarse linen off the counter, and slipped it under her cloak; the shopman saw her, and she laid it down; for this she was hanged. Her defence was 'that she had lived in credit and wanted for nothing till a press-gang came and stole her husband from her; but, since then, she had no bed to lie on; nothing to give her children to eat; and they were almost naked; and perhaps she might have done something wrong, for she hardly knew what she did.' The parish officers testified the truth of this story; but it seems that there had been a good deal of shop-lifting about Ludgate; an example was thought necessary; and this woman was hanged for the comfort and satisfaction of the shopkeepers of Ludgate Street. When brought to receive sentence, she behaved in such a frantic manner as proved her mind to be in a distracted and desponding state; and the child was suckling at her breast when she set out for Tyburn.'

One of the 'principal characters' is Grip, Barnaby's companion, and a singular raven. At various times, Dickens had two ravens as pets. When Victoria was due to marry Albert, Dickens feigned anguish and despair, expostulating his 'love' for Victoria. His eccentricity drove his family and friends to distraction for several days. They coined the phrase, "Raven mad".

Dickens's love of this species and the importance of the two pet birds in his life, are seen when he devotes over half of the preface of *Barnaby*

Rudge to a history of his ravens. Obviously, it was a bird that appealed to his sense of whimsy.

'The raven in this story is a compound of two great originals, of whom, I have been at different times, the proud possessor. The first was in the bloom of his youth when he was discovered in modest retirement in London by a friend of mine, and given to me. He slept in a stable – generally on horseback – and so terrified a Newfoundland dog by his preternatural sagacity that he has been known to walk off unmolested with the dog's dinner, from before his face.'

On March 12th 1841 he sent a letter to Maclise under an enormous black seal, to be forwarded to Forster:

'You will be greatly shocked and grieved to hear that the Raven is no more. He expired to-day at a few minutes after twelve o'clock at noon. He had been ailing for a few days, but we anticipated no serious result conjecturing that a portion of white paint he swallowed last summer might be lingering about his vitals without having any serious effect upon his constitution. Yesterday afternoon he was taken so much worse that I sent an express for the medical gentleman, who promptly attended, and administered a powerful dose of castor oil. Under the influence of this medicine, he recovered so far as to be able at eight o'clock pm to bite Topping (* the coachman). His night was peaceful. This morning at daybreak he appeared better.

Towards eleven o'clock he was so much worse that it was found necessary to muffle the stable-knocker. On the clock striking twelve he appeared slightly agitated, but he recovered, walked twice or thrice along the coach-house, stopped to bark,

172

staggered, exclaimed "*Halloa old girl*! (his favourite expression), and died.

Kate is as well as can be expected but terribly low as you may suppose. The children seem rather glad of it. He bit their ankles. But that was play.'

Maclise 'commiserates' with Dickens on the pet raven's death

Despite the brilliant descriptive writing (riots have never been more vividly portrayed) the sales of *Barnaby Rudge* fell to thirty thousand, having been over three times that figure for *The Old Curiosity*

Shop. With its emphasis on social unrest, religious intolerance and hanging, it is a much more profound and socially conscious work than the *Shop*.

Their fourth child had been born in February 1841. 'I mean to call the boy Edgar, a good honest Saxon name.' Eventually they decided on Walter Landor, after his friend.

And they both decided that it was time for a holiday.

Chapter 13

A holiday in Ireland had been the initial thought, but a celebratory dinner in Edinburgh had been planned, and Charles and Kate decided on a grand tour of Scotland, with an emphasis on the remote Highlands.

It seemed no time since the young Dickens had attended the dinner for Earl Grey (seven years before) as a junior reporter. Now, in the land of Burns and Scott, a rousing and overwhelming welcome awaited. When they arrived in June 1841 enthusiastic crowds besieged them everywhere,.

Dickens was apprehensive about the dinner and the celebrity status and all the trappings that went with it, as one would expect a twenty-nine year-old to be. He wrote to Forster:

'I have been this morning to Parliament House and am now introduced (I hope) to everyone in Edinburgh. The hotel is perfectly besieged, and I have been forced to take refuge in a sequestrated apartment at the end of a long passage, wherein I write this letter. They talk of three hundred at the dinner. We are very well off in point of rooms, having a handsome sitting room, another next to it for *Clock* purposes, a spacious bedroom, and a large dressing room adjoining. The castle is in front of the windows and the view noble.

We are engaged everyday of our stay already; but the people I have seen are so very hearty and warm in their manner that much of the horrors of lionization gives way before it. I am glad to find that they propose giving to me for a toast on Friday, the Memory of Wilkie (*recently deceased). I should have liked it better than anything, if I could have made my choice. Communicate all the particulars to "Mac". I would to God you were both here. Do dine together at Gray's Inn on Friday and think of me. All sorts of regard from Kate. She has gone with Miss Allan to see the house she was born in.'

Dickens felt a sense of relief when the dinner passed off successfully and wrote to Forster, who was also keeping in touch with the young family:

'The great event is over; and being gone, I am a man again. It was the most brilliant affair you can conceive; the completest success possible from first to last. The room was crammed, and more than seventy applicants for tickets were refused yesterday.

There were nearly two hundred ladies present. The place is so contrived that the cross table is raised enormously: much above the heads of the people sitting below: and the effect of first coming in (on me, I mean) was rather tremendous. I was quite self-possessed however, and not-with-standing the "enthoosemoosy" (*enthusiasm), which was very startling, as cool as a cucumber. I wish to God you had been there, as it is impossible for the "distinguished guest" to describe the scene. It beat all natur'…'

A youthful portrait of Charles Dickens, aged twenty seven,
by Maclise exhibited at the Royal Academy.
Two years later *The Old Curiosity Shop* was selling one
hundred thousand copies weekly.

'We start next Sunday (that's tomorrow week). A hundred thanks for your letter. I read it this morning with the greatest pleasure and delight. Where shall I begin – about my darlings? I delighted with Charley's precocity. He takes arter his father he does. God bless them, you can't imagine how much I long to see them. It makes me quite sorrowful to think of them.'

'Yesterday the Lord Provost, council, and magistrates voted me by acclamation the freedom of the City, in testimony (I quote the letter from James Forrest, Lord Provost) "of the sense entertained by them of your distinguished abilities as an author." I acknowledged this morning in appropriate terms the honour they had done me, and through me the pursuit to which I was devoted. It *is* handsome, is it not? '

The parchment scroll of the City Freedom, recording the grounds on which it was voted, hung framed in his study to the last, and was one of his most valued possessions.

Normally quite extroverted and sociable, Dickens began to tire of the hectic round of engagements. He also began to miss his home and friends, as the letter to Forster shows.

'You will like to know how we are living. Here's a list of engagements past and present. Wednesday we dined at home, and went incog. to the theatre at night to Murray's box, the pieces admirably done, and M'Ian in the *Two Drovers* quite wonderful and most affecting. Thursday, to Lord Murray's: dinner and evening party. Friday, *the* dinner. Saturday to Jeffrey's, a beautiful place about three miles off, stop there all night, dine on Sunday and home at eleven. Monday, dine at Dr Alison's four miles off. Tuesday, dinner and evening party at Allan's.

Wednesday, breakfast with Napier, dine with Blackwoods seven miles off, evening party at the Treasurer's of the town council with all the artists (!!).Thursday, lunch at the Solicitor General's, dine at Lord Gillies's, evening party at Joseph Gordon's. Friday, dinner and evening party at Robertson's. Saturday, dine again at Jeffrey's, back to the theatre at half-past nine to the moment for public appearance.

Sunday off at seven o'clock in the morning for Stirling and then to Callender a stage further; next day, to Loch Earn and pull up there for three days to rest and work.

The moral of all this is, that there is no place like home; and I thank God for having given me a quiet spirit, and a heart that won't hold many people. I sigh for Devonshire Terrace and Broadstairs.

On Sunday evening, the 17th of July I shall revisit my household gods, please heaven. I wish the day were here. For God's sake be in waiting. I wish you and Mac would dine in Devonshire Terrace that day with Fred. He has the key of the cellar. I must leave off sharp, to get dressed and off upon the seven mile dinner trip. Kate's affectionate regards.'

Exhausted with the social round and endless parties, they both set off on a Highland tour, with some relief.

'We left Edinburgh yesterday morning at half-past seven, and travelled, with Fletcher for our guide, to a place called Stewart's Hotel nine miles further than Callender.

We had neglected to order rooms and were obliged to make a sitting room of our bed chamber; in which my genius for stowing furniture away was of the very greatest service. Fletcher slept in a kennel with three panes of glass in it, which formed part and parcel of a window; the other three panes whereof belonged to a man who slept on the other side of the partition. He told me this morning that he had had a nightmare all night, and had screamed horribly, he knew. The stranger as you may suppose, hired a gig and went off at full gallop with the first glimpse of daylight. Being very tired (for we had not had more than three hours' sleep on the previous night) we lay till ten this morning; and at half-past eleven went through the Trossachs to Loch Katrine, where I walked from the hotel after tea last night. It is impossible to say what a glorious scene it was. It rained as it never does rain anywhere but here. We conveyed Kate up a rocky pass to go and see the island of the Lady of the Lake, but she gave in after the first five minutes, and we left her, very picturesque and uncomfortable with Tom (the servant from Devonshire Terrace) holding an umbrella over her head, while we climbed on. When we came back, she had gone into the carriage. We were wet through to the skin, and came on in that state four and twenty miles.'

The bedrooms are of a size which renders it impossible for you to move, after you have taken your boots off, without chipping pieces out of your legs.

There isn't a basin in the Highlands which will hold my face, nor a drawer which will open after you have put your clothes in it; nor a water-bottle capacious enough to wet your tooth brush.

The food "not bad": oatcake, mutton, hotch potch, trout from the loch, small beer bottled, marmalade, and whisky. Of the last named article I have taken about a pint today.'

This is a wonderful region.

The way the mists were stalking about today; and the clouds lying down upon the hills; the deep glens, the high rocks, the rushing waterfalls, and the roaring rivers down in deep gulfs below; were all stupendous.

On the ninth of July 1841, Dickens was eager to tell Forster about the Pass of Glencoe; his friend had wanted join them on the tour but was otherwise engaged. This was one place they had thought about and discussed.

Glencoe which fascinated and alarmed Charles and Kate

Today we have had a journey of between fifty and sixty miles through the bleakest and most desolate part of Scotland, where the hills tops are still covered with patches of snow, and the road winds over steep mountain passes, and on the brink of deep brooks and precipices.

The cold all day has been *intense*, and the rain sometimes most violent. It has been impossible to keep warm, by any means; even whisky failed. One stage of ten miles, over a place called the Black Mount, took us two hours and a half to do; and when we came to a lone public (*house) called The King's House, at the entrance to Glencoe – this was about three o'clock – we were well nigh frozen.

We got a fire directly, and in twenty minutes they served us up some famous kippered salmon, broiled; a broiled fowl; hot mutton ham and poached eggs; pancakes; oatcake; wheaten bread, butter; bottled porter; hot water; lump sugar, and whisky; of which we made a hearty meal.

All the way, the road had been among moors and mountains with huge masses of rock, which fell down God knows where, sprinkling the ground in every direction, and giving it the aspect of the burial place of a race of giants.

Now and then we passed a hut or two, with neither window nor chimney, and the smoke of the peat fire rolling out at the door.

But there were not six of these dwellings in a dozen miles; and anything so bleak and wild, and mighty in its loneliness, as the whole country, it is impossible to conceive.

Glencoe itself is perfectly terrible. The pass is an awful place. It is shut in on each side by enormous rocks from which great torrents come rushing down in all directions. In amongst these rocks on one side of the pass there are scores of glens, high up, which form such haunts as you might imagine yourself wandering in, in the very height and madness of a fever. They will live in my dreams for years.

They stayed in a house on the banks of Loch Leven.

'They speak Gaelic here and understand very little English. I rang the girl upstairs, and gave elaborate instructions for a pint of sherry to be made into boiling negus; mentioning all the ingredients one by one, and particularly nutmeg. When I had finished, seeing her obviously bewildered, I said, with great gravity, "now you know what you're going to order?" "Oh yes, sure!" "What" – a pause- "just" –another pause- "just plenty of nutbergs!"

Charles and Kate had not finished with The Pass of Glencoe because they had to cross it once more, and in violent weather. An adventure awaited them there.

'To get to Ballyhoolish (as I am obliged to spell it) to Oban, it is necessary to cross two ferries, one of which is an arm of the sea, eight to ten miles broad.

Into this ferry boat, passengers, carriages, horses, and all, get bodily, and are got across by hook or by crook if the weather be reasonably fine. Yesterday morning, however, it blew such a strong gale that the landlord of the inn, where we had paid for horses all the way to Oban (thirty miles) honestly came upstairs just as we were starting, with the money in his hand , and told us it would be impossible to cross.

There was nothing to be done but to come back five and thirty miles, through Glencoe.

Accordingly we turned back, and in a great storm of wind and rain began to retrace the dreary road we had come the day before...I was not at all pleased to have to come again through that awful Glencoe.

If it had been tremendous on the previous day, it was perfectly horrific. It had rained all night. Through the whole Glen, which is twelve miles long, torrents were boiling and foaming, and sending up in every direction spray like the smoke of great fires. They were rushing down every hill and mountain side, and tearing like devils across the path, and down into depths of the rocks.

Some of the hills looked as if they were full of silver, and had cracked in a hundred places. Others as if they were frightened, and had broken out into a deadly sweat. In others there was no compromise or division of streams, but one great torrent came rushing down with a deafening noise, and a rushing of water that was quite appalling.

The post-boy was not at all at his ease, and the horses were very much frightened by the perpetual raging and roaring; one of them started as we came down a steep place, and we were within that much --- of tumbling over a precipice; just then, too, the drag broke, and we obliged to go on as best we could without it; getting out every now and then, and hanging on at the back of the carriage to prevent its rolling down too fast, and going Heaven knows where.

Well, in this pleasant state of things we came to King's House again, having been four hours doing the sixteen miles. The horses that were to take us on, were out on the hills somewhere within ten miles round; and three or four bare-legged fellows went out to look for 'em, while we sat by the fire and tried to dry ourselves.

At last we got off again (without the drag and with a broken spring, no smith living within ten miles), and went limping on to Inverouran. In the first three miles we were in a ditch and out again, and lost a horse's shoe.

All this time it never once left off raining; and was very windy, very cold, very misty, and most intensely dismal. So we crossed the Black Mount, and came to a place we had passed the day before, where a rapid river runs over a bed of broken rock.

Now, this river had a bridge last winter, but the bridge broke down when the thaw came, and has never since been mended; so travellers cross upon a little platform, made of rough deal planks, stretching from rock to rock; and carriages and horses ford the water at a certain point. As the platform is the reverse of steady, it is very slippery, and affords anything but a pleasant footing, Kate decided to remain in the carriage, and trust herself to the wheels rather than to her feet.

I advised her, as I had done several times before, to come with us; for I saw the water was very high, the current being greatly swollen by the rain and that the post-boy had been eyeing it in a very disconcerted manner for the last half hour. This decided her to come out and Fletcher, she, Tom and I began to cross, while the carriage went about a quarter of a mile down the bank in search of a shallow place. The platform shook so much that we could only come across two at a time, and then it felt as if it were hung on springs.

When we got safely to the opposite bank, there came riding up a wild highlander, in a great plaid, whom we recognised as the landlord of the inn, who without taking the least notice of us went dashing on - with the plaid he was wrapped in, streaming in the wind - screeching in Gaelic to the post-boy on the opposite bank and making the most frantic gestures you ever saw, which he was joined by some other wild man on foot, who had come across by a short-cut, knee deep in mire and water.

As we began to see what this meant, Fletcher and I scrambled on after them, while the boy, horses, and carriage were plunging in the water, which only left the horses' heads and the boy's body visible.

It made me quite sick to think how I should have felt if Kate had been inside.

The carriage went round and round like a great stone, the boy was as pale as death, the horses were struggling and plashing and snorting like sea-animals, and we were all roaring to the driver to throw himself off and let them and the coach go to the devil, when suddenly it came all right (having got into shallow water), and, all tumbling and dripping and jogging from side to side, climbed up onto dry land.

It seemed that the man on horseback had been looking at us through a telescope as we came to the track, and knowing that the place was very dangerous and seeing that we meant to bring the carriage, had come at a great gallop to show the driver the only place he could cross.

By the time he came up, the man had taken the water at a wrong place, and in a word was as nearly drowned (with carriage, horses, luggage, and all) as ever man was.

We went to the inn and there we dined on eggs and bacon, oat-cake and whisky; and changed and dried ourselves.

The place was a mere knot of little outhouses, and in one of these were fifty highlanders *all drunk*...they were lying about in all directions; on forms, on the ground, about a loft overhead, round the turf fire wrapped in plaids, on the tables and under them.

We paid our bill, thanked our host very heartily, gave some money to his children, and after an hour's rest came on again.'

Kate and Charles were now impatient to go home, they were missing their children.

They had enjoyed their visit to Scotland, and Dickens, on his return decided to take an extended rest from writing. Sales had fallen with the final episodes of *Barnaby Rudge* and he decided to close the *Clock*. He wanted to produce a new work monthly, in twenty numbers.

In early September 1841, Forster, acting on his behalf, contacted Chapman and Hall.

They were delighted, only to be left speechless when Forster stated that the book would not begin for a year. However, "the best of publishers", had little option but to agree.

So Chapman and Hall, whatever they felt, acquiesced, and plans were made by Charles and Kate for an adventure farther a-field, namely a tour in the United States of America.

Chapter 14

Dickens had an almost insatiable need to travel, born out of interest for new people and places, the social problems therein, and also (following his trip to Scotland) the desire for the adulation he engendered and received. It was a heady mix; and nowhere was he more adored than in the United States of America. Washington Irving had written a congratulatory letter about Little Nell and many more arrived from all walks of life. Macready, who had visited the United States and greatly enjoyed it, was very encouraging.

Macready – a keen advocate of
the trip to America.

However, there was the family to consider.

He now had his grand house, furnished in the style he felt befitting of his status and worthy of entertaining his friends. Kate was a doting mother and also engaged in whatever festivities her husband brought her way. His practical jokes and impromptu joviality showed itself in numerous guises, none more bizarre than when he feigned despair over the impending marriage of Queen Victoria to Albert. "What on earth does it all mean?" wrote a puzzled Landor having received an epistle that stated "I have fallen hopelessly in love with the Queen, and wander up and down with vague and dismal thoughts." He kept up the joke for a few days, and then it came down like a damp squib. However, Kate did not criticise and her attitude of calm tolerance was shown (for example) when, on a holiday at Broadstairs, Dickens jokingly picked up a friend, and held the young lady above the rising tide, using the cry, "Beloved of my soul" while she yelled "Mrs Dickens, help me! Make Mr Dickens let me go."

"Charles, how can you be so silly?" replied the phlegmatic Kate, "You'll spoil the poor girl's silk dress." It was all taken 'in good fun', although when the same lady and her mother visited Devonshire Terrace some months later, Dickens was busy writing and somewhat cooler, intent on getting on with his work.

However, when the subject of leaving the family for a six month's trip to the United States was raised, Kate was less than forthcoming. The last few months of 1841 had been a great strain on her emotions.

The preparations for the trip were interrupted by an abscess Dickens developed. It made him very ill and required surgery. Then her younger brother died with the same suddenness as Mary; this event following closely on the death of her grandmother.

The grandmother's wish was to be buried next to her granddaughter, Mary, and the potential opening of the grave caused great anguish to Dickens, whose one overriding desire was to be buried next to Mary.

'I cannot bear the thought of being excluded from her dust; and yet I feel that her brothers and sisters, and her mother, have a better right than I to be placed next to her. It is but an idea. I neither think nor hope (God forbid) that our spirits would ever mingle there. I ought to get the better of it, but it is very hard. I never contemplated this – and coming so suddenly, and after being ill, it disturbs me more than it ought. It seems like losing her a second time.'

Kate had to contend with her depressed husband staying in his rooms for several days. However, by late November, Charles and Kate, plus Georgina, spent some days with Forster at the White Hart in Windsor, and according to his friend, "in the ordinary state he was wont to pride himself, a deep sleeper, a hearty eater and a good laugher."

Macready had wrung a reluctant consent from Kate. At first, Dickens wanted to take the four children with them, but his friends persuaded them against it. Mr and Mrs Macready said that they would look after the family and Maclise sketched the children, so that Charles and Kate would have a keep-sake during the long period away.

'Kate is quite reconciled. Anne (her maid) goes, and is amazingly cheerful and light of heart upon it. And I think, at present, that it's a greater trial to me than anybody. Macready's note to Kate was received and acted upon with a perfect response. She talks about it quite gaily, and is satisfied to have nobody in the house but Fred, of whom they are quite fond.'

Kate had early misgivings about the USA trip

'I shall never forget the one-fourth serious and three-fourths comical astonishment with which, on the morning of the third of January 1842, I opened the door of, and put my head into, a "state-room" on board the Britannia steam packet, twelve hundred tons, bound for Halifax and Boston.'

The room was so small that it would 'not hold more than two enormous portmanteaus' which 'could no more be got in at the door, not to say stowed away, than a giraffe could be persuaded or forced into a flower pot.'

Katey, Walter, Charley and Mamie by Maclise draw at Kate's request for the trip to the United States of America. The raven is included.

On January the fourth 1842 they set sail in the steamship 'Britannia' belonging to the Cunard Line.

As soon as they left Liverpool, a storm began and was to get progressively worse as they crossed the Atlantic. The seas raged and a hurricane blew. The gales were so furious and unrelenting that the funnel had to be lashed down, several lifeboats were smashed and the wooden casing of the paddle-wheel ripped off. The Chief Engineer stated he had never seen such weather and the Captain said later 'that nothing but a steamer of that strength could have stood out against it and made the journey'.

S.S Britannia by Stanfield

The trip was certainly worse than Kate had ever imagined, and worse than Dickens's vivid imagination could ever have conceived.

'It is the third morning. I am awakened out of my sleep by a dismal shriek from my wife, who demands to know whether there's any danger. I rouse myself and look out of bed. The water-jug is plunging and leaping like a lively dolphin; all the smaller articles are afloat, except my shoes, which are stranded on a carpet-bag, high and dry, like a couple of coal barges. Suddenly I see them spring into the air, and behold the looking glass, which is nailed to the wall, sticking fast upon the ceiling. At the same time the door entirely disappears, and a new one is opened in the floor. Then I begin to comprehend that the state room is standing on its head. (American Notes)

Dickens managed to avoid sea-sickness for one day and then went to bed, unable to eat for eight.

'I say nothing of what may be called the domestic noise of the ship: such as the breaking of glass and crockery; and the very remarkable and far from exhilarating sounds raised in their various staterooms by the seventy passengers who were too ill to get up to breakfast. I say nothing of them: for although I lay listening to this concert for three or four days, I don't think I heard it for more than a quarter of a minute, at the expiration of which term, I lay down again, excessively sick. Not sea-sick be it understood, in the ordinary sense of the word: I wish I had been: but in a form which I have never seen or heard described though I have no doubt it is very common.' (American Notes)

He then regained his cheerful manner, "determined to conquer a realm or two of fun every hour," as one person remarked.

'We have 86 passengers; and such a strange collection of beast never was got together upon the sea, since the days of the Ark. I have never been in the saloon since the first day; the noise, the smell, and the closeness being quite intolerable. I have only been on deck once, and then I was surprised and disappointed at the smallness of the panorama The sea, running as it does and has done, is very stupendous, and viewed from the air or some great height would be grand no doubt. But seen from the wet and rolling decks, in this weather and these circumstances, it only impresses one giddily and painfully.

I have established myself, from the first, in the ladies cabin. First for the occupants. Kate, and I, and Anne – when she is out of bed, which is not often. A queer little Scotch body, a Mrs P. whose husband is a silversmith in New York. He married her at Glasgow

193

193

three years ago, and bolted the day after the wedding; being (which he had not told her) heavily in debt. Since then she has been living with her mother; and she is now going out under the protection of a male cousin, to give him a year's trial. If she is not comfortable at the expiration of that time, she means to go back to Scotland again. A Mrs B., about 20 years old, whose husband is on board with her. He is a young Englishman domiciled in New York, and by trade (as well as I can make out) a woollen-draper. They have been married a fortnight. A Mr and Mrs C, marvellously fond of each other, complete the catalogue. Mrs C, I have settled, is a publican's daughter, and Mr C is running away with her, the till, the time-piece off the bar mantelpiece, the mother's gold watch from the pocket at the head of the bed, and other miscellaneous property. The women are all pretty; unusually pretty I never saw such good faces together, anywhere.'

Dickens passed some of the time playing cards.

'In playing whist we are obliged to put the tricks in our pockets, to keep them from disappearing altogether; and that five or six times in the course of every rubber, we are all flung from our seats, roll out at different doors, and keep on rolling until we are picked up by stewards. This has become such a matter of course, that we go through it with perfect gravity; and when we are bolstered up on our sofas again, resume our conversation or our game at the point where it was interrupted.

One man lost fourteen pounds at vingt-un in the saloon yesterday, another got drunk before dinner was over, another was blinded with lobster sauce spilt over him by the steward, another had a fall on deck and fainted. The ship's cook was drunk yesterday morning (having got at some salt-water-damaged whisky), and the captain ordered the boatswain to play upon him with the hose of the fire-engine until he roared for mercy – which he didn't get; for he was sentenced to look out, for four hours at a stretch for four nights running, without a great coat, and to have his grog stopped. Four dozen plates were broken at dinner. One steward fell down the cabin-stairs with a round of beef, and injured his foot severely. Another steward fell down after him, and cut his eye open. The baker's taken ill: so is the pastry cook. A new man, sick to death, has been required to fill the place of the latter officer, and has been dragged out of bed, and propped up in a little house upon the deck, between two casks, and ordered (the captain standing over him) to make and roll out pie-crust; which he protests with tears in his eyes. Twelve dozen of bottled porter have got loose upon deck; and the bottles are rolling about distractedly. Lord Mulgrave laid a wager with twenty-five other men last night, whose berths, like his, are in the fore-cabin, which can only be got at by crossing the deck, that he would reach his cabin first. Watches were set by the captain's, and they sallied forth, wrapped up in coats and storm caps. The sea broke over the ship so violently, that they were five and twenty minutes holding on by the handrail at the starboard paddle-box, drenched to the skin by every wave, and not daring to go on or come back, lest they should be washed overboard.'

The excitement was not over, and Kate's conviction of doom was further heightened as they approached land for the first time.

'We were running into Halifax harbour on Wednesday night with a little wind and a bright moon, had made the light at its outer entrance, and given the ship in charge to the pilot; were playing our rubber, all in good spirits, when suddenly the ship struck. A rush upon deck followed of course. The men (I mean the crew) were kicking off their shoes and throwing off their jackets preparatory to swimming ashore; the pilot was beside himself; the passengers dismayed; and everything in the most intolerable confusion and hurry. Breakers were roaring ahead; the land within a couple of hundred yards; and the vessel driving upon the surf, although her paddles were working backwards and everything done to stay her course. It is not the custom of steamers, it seems, to have an anchor ready. An accident occurred in getting ours over the side; and for half an hour we were throwing up rockets, burning blue lights, and firing signals of distress, all of which remained unanswered, though we were so close to the shore that we could see the waving branches of the trees. All this time, as we veered about, a man was heaving the lead every two minutes; the depths of water constantly decreasing; and nobody self-possessed but Captain Hewitt. They let go the anchor at last, got out a boat, and sent her ashore with the fourth officer, the pilot, and four men aboard, to try and find out where we were. The pilot had no idea; but Hewitt put his finger upon a certain part of the chart, and was as confidant of the exact spot (though he had never been there in his life) as if he had lived there from infancy. The boat's return about an hour afterwards proved him to be quite right. We had got into a place called Eastern Passage, in a sudden fog and through the pilot's folly. We had struck a mud-bank, and driven into a perfect little pond, surrounded by banks and rocks and shoals of all kinds; the only safe speck in the place. Eased by this report, and the assurance that the tide was past the ebb, we turned in at three o'clock in the morning, to lie there all night.'

The next morning the Speaker of the House of Assembly in Halifax, Nova Scotia (Canada) arrived and Dickens received his first triumphant welcome.

'Then comes a breathless man who has been already into the ship and out again, shouting my name as he tears along. I stop, arm in arm with the little doctor whom I have taken ashore for oysters. The breathless man introduces himself as the Speaker of the House of Assembly; *will* drag me away to his house; and *will* have a carriage and his wife sent down for Kate, who is laid up with a hideously swollen face. Then he drags me up to the Governor's House (Lord Falkland) and then Heaven knows where; concluding with both Houses of Parliament...the crowds cheering the inimitable (*his old master's epithet)...the judges, law-officers, bishops, and law makers welcoming the inimitable,' Dickens wrote, tongue in cheek, to Forster.

'The indescribable interest with which I strained my eyes, as the first patches of America soil peeped like molehills from the green sea, and followed them, as they swelled, by low and almost imperceptible degrees, into a continuous line of coast, can hardly be exaggerated. A sharp keen wind blew dead against us; a hard frost prevailed on shore; and the cold was most severe. Yet the air was so intensely clear and dry, and bright, that the temperature was not only endurable, but delicious.'

'I was standing in full fig on the paddle-box beside the captain, staring about me, when suddenly long before we were moored to the wharf, a dozen men came leaping on board at the peril of their lives, with great bundles of newspapers under their arms; worsted comforters very much the worse for wear round their necks; and so forth. And what do you think of their tearing violently up to me and beginning to shake hands like madmen? Oh! If you could have seen how I wrung their wrists! And if you could but know how I hated one man in very dirty gaiters, and with very protruding upper teeth, who said to all comers after him, "So you've been introduced to our friend Dickens, eh?"'

They were editors determined to be the first to meet the great writer. After an introduction, one of the men ran two miles and ordered dinner and before long Kate, Charles and Lord Mulgrave (who was going to Montreal to join his regiment) sat down 'to a very handsome dinner.'

The welcome he had in Halifax was nothing to what he was about to receive - beginning in Boston, where they arrived on the 22nd of January. After dinner on the first night there, he was able to go out for a walk with Lord Mulgrave, stretching his sea-legs by running in the snow. It was the only respite, for the rest of the time in America was hectic. The crowds that pressed around him were unrelenting in their enthusiasm. Two artists sketched continually, his face was measured with callipers (even as he ate breakfast) for a bust that was being commissioned, letters poured in and autographs poured out, throngs thrust their heads into the carriages in which they travelled or pressed against their hotel door; often they locked themselves in for a welcome rest. Otherwise they did not have a moment to themselves.

The first known photograph of Charles Dickens, USA 1843

He wrote to Forster: 'How can I tell what has happened since the first day? How can I give you the faintest notion of my reception here; of the crowds that pour in and out the whole day; of the people that line the streets when I go out; of the cheering when I went to the theatre; of the copies of verses, letters of congratulation, welcome of all kinds, balls, dinners, assemblies without end? There is to be a public dinner to me here in Boston, next Tuesday, and great dissatisfaction has been given to many by the high price (three pounds sterling each) of the tickets. There is to be a ball next Monday week at New York.

But what can I tell you about any of these things which will give you the slightest notion of the enthusiastic greeting they give me, or the cry that runs through the whole country! I have had deputations from the far west, who have come from more than two thousand miles distance; from the lakes, the rivers, from the back woods, the log-house, the cities, the factories, villages and towns. Authorities from nearly all the States have written to me. I have heard from the universities, Congress, Senate, and bodies, public and private of every kind. "It is no nonsense and no common feeling," wrote Dr Canning to me yesterday, "It is all heart. There never was, and never will be, such a triumph."

We leave here next Sunday. We go to a place called Worcester, about seventy five miles off, to the house of the Governor of this place; On Monday we go by railroad to a town called Springfield where I am met by a reception committee from Hartford. On Wednesday I have a public dinner there. On Friday evening I am obliged to present myself at Newhaven thirty miles further.

On Saturday evening I hope to be in New York and there I shall stay ten days or a fortnight.

I have a secretary (* George Putnam) whom I take on with me. He boards and lodges at my expense when we travel; and his salary is ten dollars a month. There will be dinners and balls at Washington, Philadelphia, Baltimore, and I believe everywhere. In Canada I have promised to *play* at the theatre with the officers, for the benefit of a charity.

The women are very beautiful, but they soon fade; the general breeding is neither stiff nor forward; the good nature, universal.

If you ask the way to a place – of some waterside man who don't know you from Adam – he turns and goes with you. Universal deference is paid to ladies; and they walk about at all seasons, wholly unprotected.

The hotel is a trifle smaller than Finsbury Square; and is made so infernally hot by means of a furnace with pipes running through the passage ways so that we can hardly bear it. There are no curtains to the beds, or the bedroom windows. I am told there never are, hardly, all through America. The bedrooms are indeed very bare of furniture.

Of course you will not see in the papers any true account of our voyage, for they keep the dangers of the passage, when there are any, very quiet. On the night of the storm, I was wondering within myself where we should be, if the chimney were blown over-board; in which case the vessel must be instantly on fire from stem to stern. When I went on deck the next day, I saw that it was held up by a perfect forest of chains and ropes, which had been rigged in the night.

Hewitt told me (when we were on shore and not before) that they had men lashed, hoisted up, and swinging there, all through the gale, getting these stays about it.

The American poor, the American factories, the institutions of all kinds – I have a book, already. There is no man in this town, or in this State of New England, who has not a blazing fire and a meat dinner every day of his life. A flaming sword in the air would not attract so much attention as a beggar in the streets. There are no charity uniforms, no wearisome repetition of the same dull ugly dress in the blind school. All are attired after their own taste, and every boy and girl has his or her individuality as distinct and unimpaired as you would find it in their own homes. At the theatres all the ladies sit in front of the boxes. The gallery are quiet as the dress circle at dear Drury Lane. A man with seven heads would be no sight at all, compared with one who couldn't read.'

Dickens ends his letter to Forster.

'I won't speak (I say "speak"! I wish I could) about the dear precious children, because I know how much we shall hear about them when we receive those letters.

While in Boston he went on a tour of institutions - for the blind, a school for deaf and dumb children, an orphanage, a hospital for the mentally sick, a prison, a reform school, the industrial mills of Lowell (where welfare levels for the workers were exceptional) and universities. But his itinerary was too hectic, and inevitably some invitations had to be turned down. This led to pockets of displeasure – how he combed his hair at the dinner table, dressed too flashily, and (on one occasion) his apology for not attending a superlative dinner prepared by one leading socialite was not received until after the dinner had ended. Unfairly, his manners were called into question.

Mount Tom and the Connecticut River in New England

'We left Boston on the fifth, and went away with the Governor of the City to stay till Monday at his house at Worcester. The village of Worcester is one of the prettiest in New England. On Monday morning at nine o'clock we started again by railroad and went to Springfield. Owing to the mildness of the weather, the Connecticut river was 'open', videlicet not frozen and they had a steamboat ready to carry us on to Hartford; thus saving a land journey of only twenty-five miles, but on such roads at this time of year that it takes nearly twelve hours to accomplish! The boat was very small, the river full of floating blocks of ice, and the depth where we went (to avoid the ice and the current) not more than a few inches. After two hours and a half we got to Hartford. There, there was quite an English inn; except in respect of the bedrooms which are always uncomfortable; and the best committee of management that has as yet presented itself. They kept us more quiet, and were more considerate and thoughtful, even to their own exclusion, than any I have yet to deal with. Kate's face being horribly bad, I determined to give her a rest here.

At both Hartford and Newhaven a regular bank was subscribed, by these committees, for *all* my expenses. No bill was to be got at the bar, and everything was paid for. But as I would on no account suffer this to be done, I stoutly and positively refused to budge an inch until Mr Q (*Putnam) should have received the bills from the landlord's own hands, and paid them to the last farthing. Finding it impossible to move me, they suffered me, most unwillingly, to carry the point.

On returning to New York there was a Ball in honour of Charles and Kate.

We were waited upon by David Colden and General George Morris. The General took Kate, Colden gave his arm to me, and we proceeded downstairs to a carriage at the door, which took us to the stage door of the theatre; greatly to the disappointment of an enormous crowd who were besetting the main door. The scene on our entrance was very striking. There were three thousand people present in full dress; from the roof to the floor the theatre was decorated magnificently; and the light, glitter, glare, show, noise, and cheering baffle my descriptive powers. We were walked in through the centre of the centre dress-box, the front whereof was taken out for the occasion; so to the back of the stage, where the Mayor and other dignitaries received us; and we were then paraded all round the enormous ballroom twice, for the gratification of the many-headed. That done, we began to dance – Heaven knows how we did it, for there was no room. And we continued dancing until, being no longer able even to stand, we slipped away quietly, and came back to the hotel.

After the New York Boz Ball (heavily oversubscribed) Dickens refused to participate in any further public spectacle of himself and Kate.

However, the minor blandishments which were talked about in certain venues were nothing to the ill-feeling felt in some quarters when he used a banquet in Boston, given in his honour, to rail against the iniquities of international copyright.

At that time there was no law to restrain the piracy of an author's work abroad; and no money was forthcoming. Dickens considered that of all writers, he and Sir Walter Scott were the greatest losers by it.

'I had no sooner made the second speech (*Hartford) than such an outcry began… assertions that I was no gentleman, but a mere mercenary scoundrel; coupled with the most monstrous misrepresentations relative to my design and purpose in visiting the United States; came pouring in on me every day,' he wrote to Forster, 'The dinner committee here were so dismayed, that they besought me not to pursue the subject *although every one agreed with me.* I answered that I would. That nothing should deter me.'

The press was hostile, accusing Dickens of 'insulting those who came to honour him and were, instead, lectured and reprimanded'.

It must be said, as Dickens had written, that many American authors sided with him, but surreptitiously. He was dismayed by their lack of public support. A few did, like Washington Irving (whose humour Dickens enjoyed), Cornelius Matthews who spoke up at a Dickens Dinner and Horace Greeley. The latter remarked that the publishers and booksellers had profited from the piracy offering 'only acres of inflated compliments soaked in hogsheads of champagne.' Dickens, however, was forging lifelong friends, like the poet Longfellow and the Harvard Professor of Greek, Felton. He was also captivated by Mrs David Cadwallader Colden (his friend, Lord Jeffrey's sister-in-law) .He wrote amusing and flirtatious letters to her for many years afterwards.

Thus despite hostility found and expressed in some quarters, nothing could affect his triumphant following in New York.

'I can do nothing that I want to do, go nowhere I want to go, and see nothing that I want to see. If I turn into a street, I am followed by a multitude. If I stay at home, the house becomes with callers, like a fair. If I visit a public institution, with only one friend, the directors come down incontinently, waylay me in the yard, and address me in a long speech. I go to a party in the evening, and am so enclosed and hemmed about by people, stand where I will, that I am exhausted for want of air. I dine out, and have to talk about everything, to everybody. I go to church for quiet, and there is a violent rush to the neighbourhood of the pew I sit in, and the clergyman preaches *at* me. I take my seat in the railroad car, and the very conductor won't leave me alone. I get out at a station, and can't drink a glass of water, without having a hundred people looking down my throat when I open my mouth to swallow.'

However, Dickens's warmth and admiration for the citizens of the United States were tempered by several factors. The first, and most over-ridding, was slavery, which he abhorred. He saw in it the potential for civil war (as was to happen twenty years later).

'The upholders of slavery in America –of the atrocities of the system- may be divided into three great classes. First are those more moderate and rational owners of human cattle, who have come into the possession of them as so many coins in their trading capital, but who admit the frightful nature of the institution in the abstract.

The second consists of all those owners, breeders, users, buyers and sellers of slaves, who will, until the bloody chapter has a bloody end, own, breed, use, buy, and sell them at all hazards; who doggedly deny the horrors of the system, in the teeth of such mass of evidence as never was brought to on any other subject...who would at this or any other moment gladly involve America in a war, civil or foreign, provided that it had for its sole end and object the assertion of their right to perpetuate slavery, and to whip and work and torture slaves.

The third and not the least numerous or influential, is composed of all that delicate gentility which cannot bear a superior and cannot brook an equal…whose pride, in a land where voluntary servitude is shunned as a disgrace,…must be ministered to by slaves.'(American Notes)

A prison visit was obligatory for Dickens, and he did just that in New York, going to a place called the "Tombs". He was, as usual, appalled by the rat-run, cramped conditions. He spoke out strongly in *American Notes*.

'A long narrow lofty building, stove heated as usual, with four galleries, one above the other. On each tier, are two opposite rows of small iron doors. They look like furnace doors, but are cold and black.' One is 'a small bare cell, into which the light enters through a high chink in the wall. There is a rude means of washing, a table and a bedstead. Upon the latter, sits a man of sixty, reading. He looks up for a moment: gives an impatient dogged shake; and fixes his eyes upon his book again. This man has murdered his wife, and will probably be hanged.'

Whenever he diplomatically asked questions he received cool, non-committal replies, as for example from the jailer who was showing him round. He sees in the adjacent cells a lonely child of ten or twelve years old.

'For what offence can that boy be shut up here?" Dickens asks.

"Oh! That boy? He is the son of the prisoner we saw just now; is a witness against his father; and is detained here for safe keeping, until the trial, that's all."

"But it is a dreadful place for a child to pass the long days and nights in. This is rather hard treatment for a young witness, is it not?"

"Well, it ain't a very rowdy life, and *that's* a fact."

Dickens also condemned the lack of air and exercise for the prisoners.

The institutions at Boston and Hartford are most admirable. But this is not so at New York; where there is an ill-managed lunatic asylum, a bad jail, a dismal workhouse, and a perfectly intolerable place of police-imprisonment. A man is found drunk in the streets, and is thrown into a cell below the surface of the earth; profoundly dark; so full of noisome vapours that when you enter it with a candle you see a ring about the light, like that which surrounds the moon in wet and cloudy weather; and so offensive and disgusting in its filthy odours, that you *cannot bear* its stench. He is shut up with an iron door, in a series of vaulted passages where no one stays; has no drop of water, or ray of light, or visitor, or help of any kind; and there he remains until the magistrate's arrival. If he dies (as one man did not long ago) he is half eaten by rats in an hour's time (as this man was).

As Kate and Charles awaited post from England their fears of the perilous trans-Atlantic journey to come, were awaken.

There begins to be great consternation here, in reference to the Cunard packet which (we suppose) left Liverpool on the fourth. She has not yet arrived. I have really had serious thoughts of going back to Boston, alone, to be neared news. God grant she may not have gone down: but every ship brings intelligence of a terrible gale. (*The Caledonia did not arrive but went down somewhere in the Atlantic).

Dickens wrote: 'It would be difficult to tell you what an impression this has made upon our minds, or with what intense anxiety and suspense we have been waiting.'

They were delayed in leaving New York.

We were to have quitted last Tuesday, but have been detained there all the week by Kate having so bad a sore throat that she was obliged to keep to her bed.

After Baltimore they travelled to Washington to meet the President of the United States. Charles and Kate were used to smoking in their presence, for most men of income puffed away on cigars, and Dickens was not adverse to one himself. But, being in the company of men who chewed tobacco, they hated.

'I visited both houses (Congress and Senate) nearly every day during my stay in Washington. Both houses are handsomely carpeted, but the state to which these carpets are reduced by the universal regard to the spittoon with which every honourable member is accommodated, and the extraordinary improvements on the pattern which are squirted and dabbled upon in every direction, do not admit of being described. I will merely observe, that I strongly recommend to all strangers not to look at the floor; and if they happen to drop anything, though it be their purse, not to pick it up with an ungloved hand on any account. It is strange enough too, to see an honourable gentleman leaning back in his tilted chair with his legs on the desk before him, shaping a convenient "plug" with his pen knife, and when it is quite ready for use, shooting the old one from his mouth, as from a popgun, and clapping the new one in its place. I was surprised that even steady old chewers of great experience are not always good marksmen, which has rather inclined me to doubt that general proficiency with the rifle, of which we have heard so much in England. Several gentlemen called upon me who, in the course of the conversation, frequently missed the spittoon at five paces; and one (but he was certainly short-sighted) mistook the closed sash for the open window at three. On another occasion, when I dined out, and was sitting with two ladies and some gentlemen round a fire before dinner, one of the company fell short of the fire-place, six distinct times.

In the courts of law, the judge has his spittoon on the bench, the counsel have theirs, the witness has his, the prisoner his and the crier his. The jury are accommodated at the rate of three men to a spittoon.'

Poor Kate was not exempt from the disgusting shower; when they were travelling 'the flashes of saliva flew so perpetually and incessantly out of the window all the way' that they were both covered and he had to wipe off the half-dried flakes with his handkerchief.

An invitation came from President Tyler, who was eager to meet the young author.

'The President's mansion is more like an English club house.

We entered a large hall, and having twice or thrice rung a bell which nobody answered, walked without any further ceremony through the rooms on the ground floor, as divers other gentlemen (most with their hats on and their hands in their pockets) were doing very leisurely Some of these had ladies with them to whom they were showing the premises; others were lounging on the chairs and sofas; others, in a perfect state of exhaustion from listlessness, were yawning drearily.

We went upstairs into another chamber, where were certain visitors, waiting for audiences.

We had not waited in this room many minutes before the messenger returned, and conducted us into another of smaller dimensions, where, at a business-like table covered with papers, sat the President himself. He looked somewhat worn and anxious, as well he might; being at war with everybody – but the expression of his face was mild and pleasant and his manner was remarkably unaffected, gentlemanly and agreeable. I thought that in his whole carriage and demeanour, he became his station singularly well.'(American Notes)

A contemporary account of President Tyler's meeting with the thirty year old author says: "The President rose, and said, "Is *this* Mr Dickens? "Sir, it is." "I am astonished to see so young a man, Sir," said the President. Dickens smiled, and thought of returning the compliment, but the President looked so worn and jaded, 'that it stuck in my throat like Macbeth's amen.' "I am happy to join with my fellow citizens, warmly, in welcoming you to this country," said the President.

The two men shook hands. Then they sat and looked at each other until Dickens rose, observing doubtless the President's time was fully occupied and that he had better go."

"The President rose, and
said, "I am astonished
to see so young a man."
(Maclise)

They received a further invitation from President Tyler. It was to visit the President, one evening at ten, for a general assembly which was called a "Levee."

'In the smaller drawing room, the centre of a circle of company, were the President and his daughter-in-law, who acted as the lady of the mansion: and a very interesting, graceful and accomplished lady too.'

Dickens had noted to Forster; 'The ladies of America are decidedly and unquestionably beautiful. Their complexions are not as good as those of Englishwomen; their beauty does not last long; and their figures are inferior. But they are most beautiful.'

Throughout the long and arduous schedule, Kate proved to be 'a most admirable traveller' and 'proved herself perfectly game.' Although very homesick, she was dutiful. Wherever they stayed, the first thing to be unpacked and set up was the watercolour portrait of the children. One feature of the trip which upset them, at first, was the fact that they did not receive mail until they reached Washington. This delay was due to the severe Atlantic weather. When it finally arrived Dickens was engaged with a dinner and Kate, considerately and nobly, waited until he returned so that they could open the mail together.

Dickens wrote to Forster: 'Last night your letters reached us. I was dining with a club and Kate sent me a note about nine o'clock to say they were here. But she didn't open them – which I consider heroic – until I came home. That was about half past ten; and we read them until nearly two in the morning.'

Dickens was also aware of Kate missing the children, and having purchased an accordion, regularly played to her at night to cheer her up; always ending with the tune 'Home, Sweet Home.'

From Washington, they went to Virginia; then by steam boat to St Louis. It was on the boat one morning, while washing himself in his cabin with Kate in bed, he saw, to his amazement, a party of men watching them through the window, 'transfixed'.

They visited the town of Cincinnati, amongst many, where he met 'at least one hundred and fifty first-rate bores.' To keep fit he jogged alongside the coach for miles, unable to tolerate the oppressive heat within and the closed company, 'as to having a window open, that's not to be thought of.'

The journey from Cincinnati to Columbus took 'three and twenty hours', travelling overnight.

From Columbus to Sandusky the road had been surface cross-ways with logs that gave the impression of 'going up a steep flight of stairs in an omnibus.' But, for once, they were alone and had a thoroughly enjoyable day 'with no spittle, or eternal prosy conversation about dollars and politics.' They had a picnic and toasted 'our darlings and friends at home'. However, they did not like the country people in Lower Sandusky and the surrounding area, 'I am quite serious when I say that I have not heard hearty laughter these six weeks but my own. Lounging listlessly about; idling in bar-rooms; smoking; spitting; and lolling on the pavements in rocking-chairs outside the shop doors; are the only recreations.'

Dickens records the trials and tribulations of his secretary and general manager, at Sandusky. Putnam was driven out of his room by a swarm of bedbugs and slept in the coach. The next morning he was besieged by pigs who 'looking upon the coach as a kind of pie with some manner of meat inside, grunted round it so hideously that he was afraid to come out again, and lay there shivering, til morning.'

Putnam, who greatly admired Dickens's cheerfulness and high spirits, records that when Dickens was writing letters 'his face would be convulsed with laughter at his own fun.'

They went on to Niagara Falls by railroad.

'I never in my life was in such a state of excitement. I looked out for the spray, and listened for the roar, as far beyond the bounds of possibility. At last when the train stopped, I saw two great white clouds rising up from the depths of the earth – nothing more. They rose up slowly, majestically, into the air. I dragged Kate down a deep and slippery path leading to the ferry boat; bullied poor Anne for not coming fast enough; perspired at every pore; and felt, it is impossible to say how, as the sound grew louder and louder in my ears, and yet nothing could be seen for the mist.

He took Kate to see Horse Shoe Falls.

'I went down alone into the very basin. It would be hard for a man to stand nearer God than he does there. There was a bright rainbow at my feet; and from that I looked up to – great Heaven! to *what* a fall of bright green water.'

Niagara Falls 1840

He wrote to Forster:

'I can shudder at the recollection of Glencoe but when I think of Niagara, I shall think of beauty. If you could hear the roar that is in my ears as I write, both falls are under our window. From our sitting room and bedroom we look down straight upon them. There is not a soul in the house but ourselves. What would I give if you and Mac were here, to share the sensations of this time! I was going to add, what would I give if the dear girl whose ashes lie in Kensal Green, had lived to come so far along with us – but she has been here many times, I doubt not, since her sweet face fade from my earthly sight.'

Charles and Kate by Millais

So on to Canada, where at Montreal, he fulfilled a promise to Lord Mulgrave to act in a special performance for the Coldstream Guards.

It was a particularly happy occasion for Dickens, and also for Kate, because it was the first time she had acted with her husband – who was particularly proud, recording that 'she played devilishly well.'

On the 7th of June 1842 they embarked from New York to England on a comfortable steam-packet, with two staterooms for their accommodation. Kate had been excellent throughout, and so had Anne, her maid who had maintained a stoical English demeanour, refused to be impressed by anything (including Niagara which in her romanticism was "nothing but water") and had been haunted by the conviction that they would be scalped by hostile Indians, which amused Charles and Kate.

They arrived home just after the children had been put to bed, but they were got up and there was an ecstatic reunion. A family holiday followed at Broadstairs.

The record of the journey appeared as *American Notes*, it received vindictive reviews in the United States; and sales were poor at home.

On the bright side, Dickens received one thousand pounds towards the cost of the trip.

It has been said that the American acrimony towards Dickens after his tour was from certain sectors of the press and publishing world, who were annoyed by his constant and heated reference to the need for an international copyright law to protect authors, whose works were being issued with little or no recompense.

But many issues, especially slavery, were harshly criticised in *American Notes* and Dickens chose to conclude the book:

'I have little reason to believe, from certain warnings I have had, since I returned to England, that it will be tenderly or favourably received by the American people; and as I have written the Truth…I have no desire to court, by any adventitious means, the popular applause.'

Chapter 15

Charles Dickens, still in his early thirties, had become the supreme author of his day.

Older and more distinguished artists and writers were pleased to visit and hear him read extracts from his books, which he willingly did in the drawing room of his house; and Charles and Kate entertained their guests lavishly.

No expense was spared. Dickens was always in good humour and resplendent in the latest fashion, with Kate, good natured, laughing.

But with all the parties, dinners and social comings and goings, plus the period away, Dickens found it hard to settle down to his new book.

It seemed the year off had taken its toll. He was devoid of inspiration, describing how 'he paced his room for days, sullen and horribly cross.' The new book was to have one theme, that of selfishness, and he called it *Martin Chuzzlewit.*

Once he got going, he felt it was immeasurably his best book so far. As in the past with *Master Humphrey's Clock* there was an initial rush, followed by a slump in sales. Only twenty thousand copies were being sold a month. *The Old Curiosity Shop* had achieved five times that figure, weekly.

Chapman and Hall began to wonder if the year away had been beneficial to his talents. But Dickens, as always, aware of his public, decided to change direction and send his hero to the United States.

He buckled down to the task and, as ever, was punctual and tidy – his desk neatly arranged, his hours regular. He worked in the morning; disciplined and meticulous in his composition and rewriting, as Frederick Chapman (the publisher) noted, even carrying out extensive revisions at the proof stage. He loved order in the house and would inspect the children's room daily for neatness - a folded note would be left in an offending room. That's not to say that he did not shower affection on his family, he did; but there were the periods (as daughter Mary wrote later) when "he would come in, take something to eat in mechanical way, and return to his study to finish the work he had left, scarcely having spoken a word. Our talking at these times did not seem to disturb him, though any sudden sound, as the dropping of a spoon or the clinking of a glass, would send a spasm of pain across his face."

However, these preoccupied moments were rare. His children were to write in adulthood of Dickens's 'tenderness and care; of his sympathies with childhood terrors, when he would sit beside the cot of one who had been startled and hold a hand until the child was asleep; or the singing of comic songs and the amusing games, dances and funny theatricals. "He never was too busy to interest himself in his children's occupations, lessons, amusements and general welfare," Mamie records.

While in the United States Georgina Hogarth, Kate's fifteen year-old sister, had helped with the care of her nephews and nieces; although the young family were living with the Macready's. So pleased were Charles and Kate, on their return, that they asked Georgina to come to live with them - just as Mary had, at the same age. Dickens thought back to that happy time with Mary, as he looked at Georgina sitting by the fireside or at the table.

'When she and Kate and I are sitting together, I seem to think that what has happened is a melancholy dream from which I am just awakening.

He worked enthusiastically on his new book, determined to make it a success.

Martin Chuzzlewit is the story of young Martin Chuzzlewit (his grandfather is the old Martin) who loves a young orphan the old man has brought up, Mary Graham. Young Martin's selfish character leads him to being dismissed as a pupil to the architect, Pecksniff, and so he goes to America to work (unknowingly) for a fraudulent firm, Eden Land Corporation. He looses his money, catches a fever and nearly dies. Old Martin exposes Pecksniff as a hypocrite and a bully (towards Mary whom the architect wants to marry), befriends his grandson once more and gives him Mary's hand.

There is the usual villain, Jonas Chuzzlewit (son of old Martin's brother) who is a compound of Dickens's other villains. Jonas attempts patricide, murders the director of a bogus insurance company who had swindled him and is consistently brutal to his wife before taking poison.

Still a young family: Charles, Kate and Georgina – her sister, who lived with the Dickens's family (by Maclise).

The most popular character in the story is Mrs Sarah (Sairey) Gamp. She is the drunken, disreputable and dirty old nurse who is content in the neglect of her patients; she provides some acidic comic relief.

'She was a fat old woman, with a husky voice and a moist eye, which she had a remarkable power of turning up, and only showing the white of it. Having very little neck, it cost her some trouble to look over herself, if one may say so, at those to whom she talked. She wore a very rusty black gown, rather the worse for snuff, and a shawl and bonnet to correspond. The face of Mrs Gamp – the nose in particular – was somewhat red and swollen, and it was difficult to enjoy her society without becoming conscious of a smell of spirit. Like most persons who have attained to great eminence in their profession, she took to hers very kindly, that setting aside her natural predilections as a woman, she went to a lying-in or a laying-out with equal zest and relish. (Martin Chuzzlewit)

Mrs Gamp has a best friend, Mrs Harris. For once, however, there is no description. Because Mrs Harris does not exist, except in the mind of Mrs Gamp. Mrs Harris is her confidant and her alter-ego. All Mrs Gamps friends are curious about the mysterious Mrs Harris, including Betsey Prig.

"I have know'd that sweetest and best of women," said Mrs Gamp, shaking her head and shedding tears, "ever since afore her First, which Mr Harris who was dreadful timid went and stopped his ears in an empty dog kennel, and never took his hands away or come out once till he was showed the baby, wen bein' took with fits, the doctor collared him and laid him on his back upon the airy stones, and she was told to ease her mind, his owls were organs.

Mrs Gamp proposes a toast with Betsey Prig.

And I have know'd her wen he has hurt her feelin' 'art by saying of his Ninth that it was one too many, if not two*, while that dear innocent was cooin' in his face, which thrive it did through brandy.' (Martin Chuzzlewit)

(*Dickens at his most prophetic. He said the same thing when the seventh or eighth arrived, putting the blame fairly and squarely on Kate)

The American scenes partially revived the circulation, and Mrs Gamp became a popular figure, said by many critics (almost a century later) to be one of his finest creations. Mr Pecksniff's hypocrisy and the general tone of the book had a harshness which readers did not warm to.

In the United States, when it became evident the people and places were ridiculed and misrepresented, the book died. There it was savaged by the critics and public alike, for extracts like the following:

'Several of the gentlemen got up, one by one, and walked off as they swallowed their last morsel; pausing generally by the stove for a minute or so to refresh themselves at the brass spittoons. A few sedentary characters, however, remained at table full a quarter of an hour, and did not rise until the ladies got up.

"Is there no dessert, or other interval of conversation?" asked Martin who was disposed to enjoy himself after his long voyage.

"We are busy people here, sir, and have no time for that," was the reply.

So the ladies passed out in single file: Mr Jefferson Brick and such other married gentlemen as were left, acknowledging the departure to their other halves by a nod; and that was the end of *them*. Martin thought this an uncomfortable custom, but he kept his opinion to himself for the present, being anxious to hear and inform himself by, the conversation of the busy gentlemen, who now lounged about the stove, as if a great weight had been taken off their minds by the withdrawal of the other sex; and who made a plentiful use of the spittoons and their tooth-picks.

It was rather barren of interest, to say the truth; and the greater part of it may be summed up in one word – dollars. All their cares, hopes, joys, affections, virtues and associations, seemed to be melted down into dollars. Whatever the chance contributions that fell into the slow cauldron of their talk, they made the gruel thick and slab with dollars. Men were weighed by their dollars, measures gauged by their dollars; life was auctioneered, appraised, put up, and knocked down for its dollars. (Martin Chuzzlewit)

Dickens was unrepentant, saying his writings had driven them 'stark raving mad across the water.' However, he discreetly refused to accompany his friend Macready to Liverpool, for fear of jeopardising the actor's tour of the United States.

Critics have generally been very favourable to *Martin Chuzzlewit*, some even describing it as a very great book. But the public has, in general, remained 'lukewarm'. Even at its peak only twenty three thousand copies were sold monthly.

Dickens, it must be remembered at this stage, had never finished a book before it was published, keeping the interest of the public in mind, rather like the 'soap operas' of today.

So the plot rarely develops as a whole, and some degree of harmony becomes lost amongst a rash of characterisations. The Chuzzlewits are all selfish and self-absorbed; and America is a health-risk and the average American preoccupied with the mighty dollar by what ever means it can be acquired.

It is still puzzling why Dickens adopted this approach to a country where he had been very generously received, although in later years he was to apologise, at least in part.

His well-known hasty temper was to surface one day, when William Hall rashly pointed out that there was a clause in Dickens's contract which would reduce the monthly salary from £200 to £150 if the sales of *Chuzzlewit* were below average. 'I am so irritated, so rubbed in the tenderest part of my eyelids with bay-salt, by what I told you yesterday that a wrong kind of fire is burning in my head, and I don't think I can write,' he wrote to Forster, 'I am bent upon paying Chapman and Hall *down*.'

In total fairness to Dickens, Chapman and Hall had made a huge sum of money – indeed almost all their prosperity – from him. They just accepted the fact in the usual publisher's way. Theirs was simply a business venture, and although they valued Dickens (as well they might!) they saw nothing untoward in the arrangement.

Dickens, of course, did not agree. He felt the injustice badly. He decided to find a new publisher as soon as he could. He took holidays in Yorkshire and Broadstairs; then completed a round of public duties and speeches including helping Angela Burdett-Coutts to assist a Ragged School in Holborn, as well as becoming chairman of the Society of Authors.

However, it was in Manchester while addressing the Athenaeum Institute that 'the bright eyes and beaming faces' of the children made him consider a cheerful, heart-warming short story – his most popular ever, it was:

IN PROSE.

BEING

A Ghost Story of Christmas.

He started writing it in October 1843 and completed in November.

'Marley was dead to begin with. There is no doubt whatever about that. The register of his burial was signed by the clergyman, the clerk, the undertaker and the chief mourner. Scrooge signed it. And Scrooge's name was good upon the 'Change, for anything he put his hand to.'

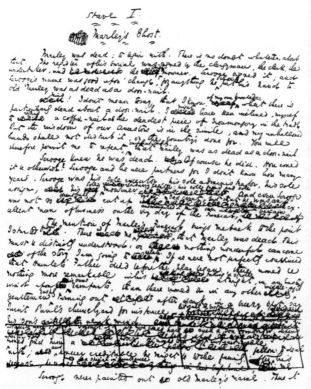

Dickens made extensive revisions at all stages of the manuscript as seen in *A Christmas Carol*

So begins *A Christmas Carol*. All of Dickens's gifts seem to coalesce into this little gem – the humour, the moral, the poetic kindness and the pathos are all present and in the right proportions; while the characters and scenes are memorable – the Cratchits including Tiny Tim; the party given by Scrooge's nephew and niece; the visions of his early and lonely school days and, of course the three ghosts of Past, Present and Future.

But Scrooge is the greatest masterpiece and unforgettable – the tight fisted hand at the grindstone, a squeezing, wrenching, grasping, scraping, clutching, covetous old sinner- has his own views on the Festive Season.

'A Merry Christmas, uncle. God save you!' cried a cheerful voice. It was the voice of Scrooge's nephew.

"Bah!" said Scrooge, "Humbug!"

"Christmas a humbug uncle," said Scrooge's nephew." You don't mean that, I am sure?"

"I do," said Scrooge. "Merry Christmas! What right have you to be merry? What reason have you to be merry? You're poor enough."

"Come then," returned the nephew gaily. "What right have you to be dismal? What reason have you to be morose? You're rich enough."

Scrooge, having no better answer ready on the spur of the moment, said "Bah!" again; and followed it up with "Humbug!"

"Don't be cross uncle!" said the nephew.

"What else can I be," returned the uncle, "when I live in such a world of fools as this? Merry Christmas! Out upon Merry Christmas! What's Christmas time to you but a time for paying bills without money; a time for finding yourself a year older, and not an hour richer; a time for balancing your books and having every item in 'em through a round dozen of months presented dead against you? If I could work my will," said Scrooge indignantly, "every idiot who goes about with 'Merry Christmas' on his lips, should be boiled with his own pudding, and buried with a stake of holly through his heart."(A Christmas Carol)

The Ghost of Christmas Present

Christmas at Devonshire Terrace was a favourite time for family and friends and the party held that year was more boisterous than usual due to the phenomenal success of *A Christmas Carol*. The first edition of six thousand copies was sold on the day of publication.

'Such dinings, such dancing, such conjuring (*Dickens's hobby), such blind-man's-buffing, such theatre goings, such kissings out of old years and such kissings-in of new ones never took place in these parts before. Forster and I conjured bravely, that a plum-pudding was produced from an empty sauce-pan, held over a blazing fire kindled in Stanfield's hat without damage to the lining; that a box of bran was changed into a live guinea pig, which ran between my godchild's feet, and was the cause of such a shrill uproar and clapping of hands.'

At this party Jane Carlyle, the admired wife of the famous historian, recorded that "he was the best conjuror she had ever seen. The gigantic Thackeray and everyone else capered madly," she recorded, "when we were all madder than ever with the pulling of crackers, the drinking of champagne, and the making of speeches, a universal country dance was proposed and Forster, seizing me round the waist, whirled me into the thick of it. By midnight the party was something not unlike the rape of the Sabines. I doubt that there was as much witty speech uttered in all the aristocratic, conventional drawing rooms throughout London that night as amongst us little knot of blackguardist literary people who felt ourselves above all rules, and independent of the universe!"

Mr Fezziwigg's Ball (*Christmas Carol*)

Sales continued over the ensuing month but Dickens greeted the accounts in February with horror and anger.

'Such a night as I have passed, I really believed I should never get up again, until I had passed through all the horrors of a fever. I found the *Carol* account awaiting me, and they were the cause of it. The first six thousand copies show a profit of £230!

I had set my heart and soul upon a Thousand clear. What a wonderful thing it is, that such a great success should occasion me such intolerable anxiety and disappointment. My year's bills, unpaid, are so terrific, that all the energy and determination I can possible exert will be required to clear me before I go abroad; which, if next June comes and finds me alive, I shall do.

I was so utterly knocked down last night, that I came up bold this morning. If I can let the house for this season, I will be off to some seaside place as soon as a tenant offers.

Chapman and Hall, he believed were 'preposterously ignorant of all the essentials of their business.' He felt that they had not advertised the book enough; however, the expensive production he had insisted on, in a beautifully produced edition with four colour plates, was completely forgotten, 'I have not the least doubt that they have run up expenses purposely to bring me back.'

He opened up negotiations with Bradbury and Evans and they offered to advance him £2800 in return for a twenty-five per cent in all his work for eight years to come.

He had also had enough of piracy. It had affected the *Carol's* sales. He instructed Thomas Talfour to represent him in an injunction against another publisher's piracy, and he won; despite threats from dark strangers sent to menace him and by the firm's flight into bankruptcy.

Once again his bills mounted and he was seriously short of money. In January 1844 a fifth baby, Francis, was born. And he still supported his parents and Frederick. Dickens felt he had to reduce his expenses at Devonshire Terrace including the cost of the servants, the endless dinners and the relentless social rounds, and the not infrequent financial demands from the rest of his family.

He decided, in his restlessness, to take the family to Italy as soon as circumstances allowed and rent the house.

An unusual event occurred at a meeting in Liverpool in February 1844. There he introduced "a young lady whom I have some difficulty and tenderness in announcing- Miss Weller."

Dickens was suddenly aware of the audience's laughter and conscious that the young girl was trying to hide her embarrassment. He was so enthralled by her piano playing that he invited her to lunch the next day with her father. Over the ensuing days he began to reproach himself for the 'incredible feeling I have for that girl.'

Dickens introduces Christiana Weller, at the piano, in Liverpool

He decided to confide in a friend, Thompson, but found to his dismay that his friend was in love with Christiana Weller. He asked Dickens for advice and was told not to hesitate. Dickens attended their wedding; but it was not long after, that his opinion of

Christiana changed, describing her as 'a devil of a whispering, pouting temper, a mere spoiled child.' Later brother Fred married Christiana's sister.

Dickens had many friendships and an admiring following amongst the women of the day.

Lady Blessington, a friend of Dickens

Sydney Smith wrote to him describing 'the anxieties of some ladies of his (*Smith's) acquaintance about meeting him'. "My friends have not the smallest objection to be put into a number (*instalment), but on the contrary would be proud of the distinction: and Lady Charlotte, in particular, (he joked) you may marry to Newman Noggs."

Dickens always had a susceptibility towards banter and flirtation with the opposite sex but this was the first time he had shown any loss of interest, albeit temporary, in Kate.

Chapter 16

So they set off for Genoa, Italy. It was a mammoth undertaking in an old coach, 'as for comfort about the size of a library, with night lamps and day lamps; it was marked at £60s,' he wrote, but he got it for forty-five.

The cumbersome contrivance trundled along pulled by four stout horses. Inside were Charles, Kate, five children, Georgina, Anne (maid), a cook, two nurses for the children, and a French courier called Roche.

Also in the party was Timber, a white spaniel that Dickens adored and who travelled with them extensively. He had an attraction for Italian fleas. 'Timber has had every hair upon his body cut off because of the fleas, and he looks like the ghost...it is awful to see him slide into a room. He knows the change upon him, and is always turning round and round to look for himself.'

They crossed to Boulogne, onwards to Paris, Burgundy and Lyons, took a steamer down the Rhone to Avignon, rolled onto Aix-en-Provence to Marseille, where they arrived on the 14th July 1844, and thence (with the carriage on a steam ship) they sailed on to Genoa.

Crowds followed and besieged the hotels, applause greeted them everywhere, and was made even more tumultuous by the appearance of the baby. Dickens was pleased to be away and seemingly relaxed in the warmth and sunshine.

The children had not cried, the carriage had gone lightly over abominable roads and the courier had been excellent. Dickens said, 'Surrounded by strange and perfect novel circumstances, I feel as if I had a new head on side by side with my old one.'

He felt no urge to go back home to a "society" 'the more I see of its extraordinary conceit and its stupendous ignorance of what is passing out of doors, the more certain I am that it is approaching the period when, being incapable of reforming itself, it will have to submit to be reformed by others off the face of the earth.'

On landing he went to the bank

The journey had been expensive (costing about £200), and having given a laborious address in French as to how much money was needed, listened to patiently by the clerk, Dickens was surprised by the Lombard Street reply, in perfect English, "How would you like to take it, Sir?" He took it, as everyone had to at that time, in five-franc pieces. It was such a tiny denomination that he had to carry it everywhere in two small, heavy sacs, regularly taking it into his head that he had mislaid one, somewhere, and irksomely searching frantically until it was found.

The evening of the 16th of July 1844 saw them at Albaro on the outskirts of Genoa.

At first Genoa was a disappointment, considered shabby and dirty, the house they had been given, the Villa di Bella Vista in Albaro, they nicknamed 'the pink jail. It is the most perfectly lonely, rusty, stagnant old staggerer of a domain that you can possibly imagine...the stable so full of vermin and swarmers that I always expected to see the carriage going out bodily, with a legion of industrious fleas harnessed to it and drawing it off, on their own account.'

From late July into early August there were many cloudy days, 'I am most disappointed, I think, in the evenings, which are as commonplace as need be: for there is no twilight, and as to the stars giving more light here than elsewhere, that is humbug.

The story goes that it is in autumn and winter, when other countries are dark and foggy, that the beauty and clearness of this area are most observable. I hope it may prove so, for I have postponed going round the hills which encircle the city, or seeing any of the sights, until the weather is more favourable.'

But the sunshine came and revived all their spirits beneath a clear blue sky. He wrote: 'O Mac (*Maclise), if you ever have occasion to paint the Mediterranean, let is be exactly of that colour. It lies before me now, as deeply and intensely blue. Such greens, as flutters in the vineyards down below the windows, that I never saw; nor yet such lilac and such purple as float between me and the distant hills.

Everything is in extremes. There is an insect here that chirps all day. There is one outside the window now. The chirp is very loud. The creature is born to chirp; to progress in chirping; to chirp louder, louder, louder; till it gives one tremendous chirp and bursts itself. The day gets brighter, brighter, brighter, till it's night The summer gets hotter, hotter, hotter, till it explodes. The fruit gets riper, riper, riper, until it tumbles down.'

Being near the sea, when the Sirocco blew, the heat became excessive.

'One feels it most, on first getting up. Then it is really so oppressive that a strong determination is necessary to enable one to go on dressing; one's tendency being to tumble down anywhere and lie there.'

Once accustomed to the heat, Dickens was off exploring the countryside, the sea shore and the city. He quickly became fluent in Italian (as he had in French), and 'as bold as a lion.' He remarked, 'the audacity with which one begins to speak when there is no help for it, is quite astonishing.'

They quickly made friends, and one evening, having been to the Marquis de Negri's grotto villa, Dickens had to race home before the city gates were locked at twelve.

'I barely had time to reach the gate before midnight; and was running as hard as I could go, downhill, over uneven ground, along a new street called the strada Sevra, when I came to a pole fastened straight across the street, nearly breast high, without any light or watchman – quite in the Italian style. I went over it, headlong, with such force that I rolled myself completely white in the dust, but although I tore my clothes to shreds, I hardly scratched myself except in one place on the knee. I had no time to think of it then, for I was up directly and off again to save the gate: but when I got outside the wall, and saw the state I was in, I wondered I had not broken my neck. I "took it easy" after this and walked home, by lonely ways enough without meeting a single soul. But there is nothing to be feared, I believe, from midnight walks in this part of Italy.'

However, the kidney pains returned and he rested for a few days until he could go swimming once more 'in the little blue bay just below the house here, like a fish in high spirits.'

There was one sea-episode that terrified Dickens.

He had gone to Marseille to meet Fred, who was joining them for two weeks. They stayed at a hotel where 'the fleas were of elephantine dimensions were gambolling in the dirty beds; and the mosquitoes! We had scarcely any sleep, and rose up with hands and arms hardly human.'

In his first day at the villa Fred swam too far out in the bay and got into difficulties having to be rescued by a fishing boat that happened to be passing. 'It was a world of horror and anguish crowded into four or five minutes of dreadful agitation; and to complete the terror of it Georgy (Georgina), Charlotte (the nurse) and the children were on a rock in full view of it all, crying, as you may suppose, like mad creatures.'

They changed to a sumptuous house, the largest to let in the area; it was rented from the end of September, and they took a floor in Palazzo Peschiere, which contained frescoes by Michelangelo, 'frescos three hundred years old as fresh as if the colours had been laid on yesterday.' There were lemon and orange trees surrounding fountains; and a magnificent view across the sweep of Genoa harbour to the Alps beyond. As he admitted, to work in such idyllic surroundings was difficult.

'Never did I so stagger upon a threshold before.'

His back caused sleepless nights and he began dreaming about Mary, seeing a vision draped in blue like a Madonna. He called out and it shrunk back. He asked as to what was the true religion; was any true, was Roman Catholicism the best? The vision replied, "For you it is the best," and departed. He awoke with tears running down his cheeks.

The sumptuous Palazzo Peschiere flanked by antique sculptured figures and seven fountains playing in the garden.

Resting and enjoying the sun and suddenly inspired by the very sounds that interrupted his concentration – the bells of Genoa; he would call his next Christmas story *The Chimes*. It was to be a blow on behalf of the poor and oppressed, told through the down-at-heel Toby Veck, a porter and runner of errands, who has a vision under the influence of the goblins who descend from the church bells. Dickens's premise was that the poor were to labour all the joyless days of their lives and be grateful for subsistence wages or the system would collapse. The people who benefited were the 'dupes', eventually to see the system fall with riots.

It is worth noting that as Dickens wrote this story Marx and Engel were in contact about their theories on the political economy of the British, which they felt had greed as the motive behind a system of private property, which was destroying the British people. As in the case of the American Civil War,

Dickens was reading the mood of the people at that time, especially the working class. He felt the book would be 'a great blow for the poor'.

The Spirit of the Bells for *The Chimes* by Maclise

He was up at seven and after a cold bath and breakfast he settled down in his punctual way until three.

Everyone knew that he had not to be disturbed. When the local governor called and Dickens politely made his excuse for not being able to come down, the Governor left stating "excuses, I wouldn't interfere with such an occupation for all the world. Pray tell him that my house is open to the honour of his presence when it is perfectly convenient to him; but not otherwise. And let no gentleman," said the Governor a-surweyin' of his suite with a majestic eye, "call upon Signor Dickens till he is understood to be disengaged." Determined to finish the book within a month he would not be distracted. 'My cheeks , which were beginning to fill out, have sunk again; my hair is very lank; my eyes have grown immensely large; and the head inside the hair is hot and giddy...I have undergone as much sorrow and agitation as if the thing were real; and have wakened up with it at night.. However, he still liked to walk even when the weather was bad, 'in pure determination to get the better of it, I walked twelve miles in the mountain rain.'

Apart from such brief spurts of writing, Dickens travelled widely in Italy, including Parma, Modena, Bologna, Venice, Verona, and Milan, and he was enchanted with Venice. 'Milan being within reasonable journey from here, Kate and Georgy will come to meet me when I arrive there on my way towards England.' He met Kate and Georgina and was delighted to hear recent news of the family, and especially Charley's French and writing skills. He also asked Kate to be patient with Macready's youngest sister (who was an irritating guest at their Palazzo);

then with Roche he crossed into Switzerland and on towards London.

Nine days later Maclise and Forster were there to greet him, and he was, once more, amongst his circle of friends.

Forster gave his customary advice; *The Chimes* was revised where necessary and within days had been given to Bradbury and Evans. His friends considered the story a triumph when he read it to them. Everyone was moved. He wrote to Kate, 'if you had seen Macready last night, undisguisedly sobbing, and crying on the sofa as I read, you would have felt, as I did, what a thing it is to have power.'

Dickens reading *The Chimes* to his friends (Maclise)

The book was a great success, but its appeal has diminished in time. Although not an attack on private property (the trappings of which, Dickens and his friends greatly enjoyed) it lifted the novelist in Marx's esteem to one of a great social reformers; where he remains, by repute, in Eastern Europe today.

Chapter 17

Dickens only stayed a week.

He had time, however, to arrange assistance for the bereaved family of John Overs, who although a carpenter by trade, he had befriended and encouraged to write. Then, he was off to Genoa for Christmas. The brevity of his visit must have puzzled some, if not all, of his friends, knowing his love of London and his warmth towards them; because he wrote to them regularly and took an unflagging interest in their affairs while abroad.

He stopped in Paris to see Macready, who was engaged there with an English Company of Actors.

He went to the theatre to see Dumas' *Christine*, played by Madame St George, who was 'once Napoleon's mistress; now of an immense size, from dropsy I suppose; and with little weak legs which she can't stand upon. Her age, withal, somewhere about 80 or 90. I never in my life beheld such a sight. Every stage-conventionality she ever picked up (and she has them all) has got the dropsy too, and is swollen and bloated hideously. The other actors never looked at one another, but delivered all their dialogues to the pit, in a manner so egregiously unnatural and preposterous that I couldn't make up my mind whether to take it as a joke or an outrage.'

He left Paris on the 13th of December 1844. The travelling was in atrocious conditions and on horrible roads, which he had to endure for three days and three nights before reaching Marseille. Then, confused as to which ship he had to take, he held up the right one for more than an hour. On stepping on board he was heartily hailed by five Americans, one shouting, "I am blarmed if it ain't Dickens!"

This speaker, who was their leader, was overjoyed having met Dickens in New York. Despite the stormy passage, they all enjoyed themselves immensely. One member of this group had the translation dictionary, but was sea-sick in his cabin and could not help. So Dickens was regaled with requests – "I say, what's French for pillow?" or "Is there an Italian phrase for a lump of sugar?" "What the devil does echo mean? The garcon says echo to everything". The questions were incessant, they wanted to know the population of every little town and village on the Cornice, and if Dickens did not know, then the Italian steward was asked – and when he hazarded the vaguest of guesses the leader burst forth with "Non possible!" (almost the only phrase he knew) and the steward doubled or trebled the figure which then satisfied their curiosity.

On the 22nd of December 1844 he reached Genoa and an enthusiastic welcome from Kate, Georgina and the family.

'Miss Coutts has sent Charley a Twelfth Night cake weighing ninety pounds magnificently decorated'.

However, Dickens was saddened by the news of the death of John Forster's brother and wrote a touching letter.

'I feel the distance between us now, indeed. I would to Heaven, my dearest friend, that I could remind you in a manner more lively and affectionate than this dull sheet of paper can put on, that you have a brother left. One bound to you by ties as strong as Nature even forged...The day when he visited us in our old house is as fresh to me as if it had been yesterday. I remember him as well as I remember you...I have many things to say, but cannot say them now.'

On the 20th of January 1845 he set off on a trip south with Kate, stopping first at Pisa and then on to Rome by the 30th. His first impressions were one of disappointment - dull, cold rain, and endless muddy streets sent him to bed in 'an indifferent humour.' Many buildings, however, especially the Coliseum profoundly moved him. At Naples he thought the Bay inferior to Genoa, and generally disliked the city.

In Naples he was horrified to note that in the burial place for the poor there were three hundred and sixty five pits, covered by flagstones.

'One of these pits is opened every night in the year; the bodies of the pauper dead are collected in the city; brought out in a cart; and flung in, uncoffined. Some lime is then cast down into the pit, and it is sealed up until a year is past, and its turn again comes round.'

Here Georgina joined them. After touring Sorrento and Pompeii, Dickens led the sisters up Vesuvius on a winter night, with ice, snow and volcanic fire as the backdrop. Dickens walked with a stick and the ladies were carried in sedan chairs. Showers of cinders and sulphurous smoke were everywhere and Dickens inched forward and 'looked down into the flaming bowels of the mountain and came back again, alight in half a dozen places, and burnt from head to foot.'

Someone's boot shot from beneath him and he carried two others off, shrieking into the darkness and then silence. They were pleased to get back and Dickens was proud of Kate and Georgina's expedition.

'My ladies are the wonder of Naples, and everyone is open mouthed.'

Florence, he linked with Venice and Genoa. He thought these three the greatest of all Italian cities.

'Florence – in a sun-lighted valley, bright with winding Arno, and shut in by swelling hills.' (Pictures from Italy)

'Magnificently stern and sombre are the streets of beautiful Florence; and the strong old piles of buildings make such heaps of shadow, on the ground and in the river, that there is another and a different city of rich forms and fancies, always lying at our feet . In the midst of the city – in the Piazza of the Grand Duke, adorned with beautiful statues and the Fountain of Neptune – rises the Palazzo Vecchio, with its enormous overhanging battlements, and the Great Tower that watches over the whole town.

The chapel of Medici, the Good and Bad Angels, of Florence; the church of Santa Croce where Michelangelo lies buried; and where every stone in the cloisters is eloquent on great men's deaths.

Here, open to all comers, in their beautiful and calm retreats, the ancient Sculptors are immortal, side by side with Michelangelo, Canova, Titian, Rembrandt, Poets, Historians Philosophers – those illustrious men of history, beside whom its crowned heads and harnessed warriors show so poor and small, and are so soon forgotten.' (Pictures of Italy)

However, the trip was not without its tensions.

They had met the de la Rues. Madame de la Rue was the pretty English wife of a Swiss banker in Genoa. She suffered from a nervous tic and Dickens offered to help in his own inimitable manner. For several years he had been interested in mesmerism (hypnosis) and had seen demonstrations on stage in London. Acquainting himself with an exponent, Dr Elliotson, he had tried it out on Kate in America and banished her headaches. Now he would put his expertise to the test on Madame de la Rue. However, her attacks were not subject to any periodicity but occurred at all hours, day and night. Thus Dickens was often summoned, even in the middle of the night. Increasingly Kate became fed up and jealous; and ill-feeling spilled over. In Rome it was Carnival week and they met up to have fun. But Madame de la Rue was the damp squib, demanding more and more of Dickens's attention. So he continued his therapeutic mesmerism, to Kate's great annoyance. By now she was not speaking to Madame, and the air was frosty. In turn, he felt humiliated. But his annoyance was short lived. For he had made plans for a delightful surprise – Devonshire Terrace was to be completely redecorated. *The Chimes* had brought in £2500.

In May, a couple of English travellers rented another portion of the Palazzo Peschiere. They had a meek English footman, made to do everything in the hot climate, even cooking, wearing thick crimson breeches and a smart, traditional outfit. His master 'locks him up at night, in a basement room with iron bars to the window. Between which our servants poke wine in, at midnight.'

The Dickens family left Genoa in mid-June on the homeward journey. Before departing Dickens went to see the de la Rues to teach M. de la Rue how to mesmerise his wife. However, Kate's cook did not go with them; she had decided to marry a French cook and open a restaurant in Genoa. Dickens was doubtful about the project but he made provision to get her back to England if the business failed.

'The man hasn't a penny. If there were an opening for a nice clean restaurant in Genoa – which I don't believe there is, for the Genoese have a natural enjoyment of dirt, garlic and oil- it would still be a very hazardous venture, as the priests will certainly damage the man, if they can, for marrying a Protestant woman.'

They had all thoroughly enjoyed their time in Italy- 'the beautiful Italian manners, the sweet language, the quick recognition of a pleasant look or a cheerful word; the captivating expression of a desire to oblige in everything; these are left behind in the Alps.'

The travelled home via the Great St Gothard Pass into Switzerland.

'We came over the St Gothard, which has been open only eight days. The road is cut through snow, and the carriage winds along a narrow path between two massive snow walls, twenty feet high or more.

I look upon coming down from the Great St Gothard with a carriage and four horses and only one postilion, as the most dangerous thing that a carriage and horses can do. The road is like a geometrical staircase, with horrible depths beneath it; and at every turn it is a toss-up or seems to be, whether the leaders shall go round or over. The lives of the whole party may depend upon a strap in the harness; and if we broke our rotten harness once yesterday, we broke it at least a dozen times. The difficulty of keeping the horses together in the continual and steep circle is immense. They slip and slide, and get their legs over the traces, and are dragged up against the rocks; carriage, horses, harness and all in a confused heap.'

Dickens was impressed, 'what a beautiful country it is!'

At Brussels, Maclise, Jerrold and Forster were waiting for them and they all spent a week there as an excited, cheerful group. They finally arrived home by the end of June 1845.

Domesticity as seen by Leech, for *The Cricket on the Hearth.*

His next thoughts were about the traditional Christmas story and he decided to make 'a cricket a little household god – silent in the wrong and sorrow of the tale; and loud again when all went well and happy.'

He called the book *The Cricket on the Hearth* when it was published at the end of the year.

Its success was immediate, the sales being more than double the previous two. Forster told Macready that he had misgivings about the book; but Dickens was jubilant – its sales had proved him right.

Getting back to writing had proved difficult, and the second half of 1845 was given over to his favourite diversion, acting.

Charles Dickens – the actor- in *Every Man in his Humour*. His love of acting competed with his love of writing. Such was the success of the Ben Jonson's play in September 1845 that 'it turned our little enterprise into one of the small sensations of the day', as fellow actor Forster noted.

He had choosing Ben Jonson's *Every Man In His Humour*, which played to an appreciative audience on September 21st.

Forster played Kitely and Dickens was Captain Bobadil (one of Jonson's most famous creations); most of their friends (Leech, Jerrold, Cruikshank, Lemon, Cattermole etc as well as his brother Fred) also had parts.

The same love of the theatre: John Forster in *Every Man in his Humour* (drawn by Maclise). They often reminisced about this happy time, even at their last meeting.

On the first occasion there was an invited audience. Macready pronounced "that several of the actors were fine amateurs". But on the second occasion, with Prince Albert, Prince George and Wellington present, among others, Lord Melbourne remarked in the interval, "I knew the play would be dull, but that is should be so damnably dull as this I did not suppose." What Melbourne's attractive confidant, the Hon Mrs Caroline Norton, said, is not retained for posterity. However, there was a bonus for Melbourne and others, for the audience was spared the huge form of Thackeray giving one of his 'inimitable' renditions of the popular songs of the day. Thackeray said "he was wounded when his offer was declined".

There was another bonus. The play realised a good sum for charity. So at New Year the company rose to another benefit performance of *The Elder Brother.*

On the 28th of October the patient Kate gave birth to a sixth child (and fourth son) He was named Alfred D'Orsay Tennyson after his godfathers D'Orsay and Tennyson.

Then his second pet raven died three days later, having acquired the same illicit taste for paint and putty which was fatal to his predecessor. He died unexpectedly before the kitchen fire.

'He kept his eye to the last upon the meat as it roasted, and suddenly turned over on his back with a sepulchral cry of "Cuckoo!"

However, Dickens began to feel unwell and wrote to Forster one morning:

'I have been so very unwell this morning, with giddiness, and headache, and botheration of one sort or other, that I didn't get up till noon; and shunning Fleet Street am now going for a county walk, in the course of which you will find me, if you feel disposed to come away in the carriage which goes to you with this.

There is much I would like to discuss, if you can manage it. It's the loss of my walks, I suppose; but I am as giddy as if I were drunk, and can hardly see'

He had agreed to take on the editor's job, at a top salary of £1000 – which he decided to double - of a new paper, the *Daily News*. It was to have liberal views and represent all walks of society and to be produced by Bradbury and Evans. Forster was against him being involved and, for a time, Dickens wavered. He assembled a first-class team of writers and reporters. Then his fears returned, because he was convinced that a collapse of the enterprise was imminent because several advertisers and brokers suddenly went bust. Bradbury and Evans disagreed. They were right but he was never happy and gave up after four months; compiling *Pictures of Italy* instead. For a while there was the possibility of him becoming appointed to the paid magistracy of London. He also continued his charity work and became a trustee of the General Theatrical Fund.

They decided he needed a break.

Chapter 18

Kate and Charles made up their minds. Once again the family were going to live abroad, in Switzerland. Kate had flatly refused to meet up with the de la Rues. Their house was rented to Sir James Duke for twelve months and he kept strictly to the agreement. On the 31st of May 1846 they departed.

It is generally inferred that Dickens's restless spirit was the cause of their travelling far more widely than the vast majority of even rich people journeyed in those days. It has also been inferred that this restlessness was due to an increasing dissatisfaction with Kate. If this was the case, it would seem curious that he would distance himself from his close friends, social engagements and writings, to spend more time with Kate and the family. Kate, in turn, had to move a family of six plus servants and effects in what were then time-consuming journeys, and over vast distances by cumbersome coaches on hazardous roads. But Dickens had been writing flat-out for a decade and his health often caused concern. He probably realised that the purity of Swiss air would be beneficial for them all – at that time London was often cloaked in an acrid fog during the damper months.

They settled in Lausanne, which always 'seemed to be coming down the hill with its steeples and towers, not able to stop itself.' They rented a residence called 'Rosemont', which was quite a doll's house, with two pretty little salons, a dining-room, hall and kitchen, on the ground floor; and with just enough bedrooms for the family to leave one spare. It was beautifully situated on a hill that rose from the Lake.

Rosemont at Lausanne 1846

'The country is delightful in the extreme – as leafy, green and shady, as England; full of deep glens and branchy places, and bright with all sorts of flowers in profusion. It abounds in singing birds besides – very pleasant after Italy; and the moonlight on the lake is noble. Prodigious mountains rise up from its opposite shore (it is eight or nine miles across at this point), and the Simplon, the St Gothard, Mont Blanc and Alpine wonders are piled there, in tremendous grandeur.'

Dickens spoke no German but was reassured by a man from Worms, "that needn't trouble you, for even in so small a town as ours, where we have few travellers, I could make a party of at least forty people who understand and speak English."

In July 1846 Dickens noted: 'While we were sitting at dinner, one of the prettiest girls in Lausanne was drowned in the lake. She was bathing in one of the nooks set apart for women, and seems somehow to have entangled her feet in the skirts of her dress. She was an accomplished swimmer. Three or four friends who were with her ran away, screaming. Our children's governess was on the lake in a boat with Dr Verdeil and his family. They ran inshore immediately, and M.Verdeil with three or four other doctors laboured for some hours to restore animation…She was obliged to be borne to her father's house. She was his only child and but 17 years old.'

Dickens was as famous in Europe as elsewhere, although social engagements were not as pressing as in England, Scotland and the United States. His work as a social reformer compelled him in several directions, with children always a priority. Handicapped children disturbed him; so he took a great interest in the Blind Institution. There, new techniques, especially the teaching of speech to those individuals who were also deaf and dumb, were being used with success. He records a girl of ten years old, born deaf and dumb and blind who, when left alone, 'instantly crouches down with her hands up to her ears, in exactly the position of a child before its birth.'

A month later on visiting the Blind Institution, he found:

'They have got her out of that strange, crouching position; dressed her neatly; and accustomed to have a pleasure in society. She laughs frequently, and also claps her hands and jumps; having, God knows how, some inward satisfaction. I never saw a more tremendous thing in its way, in my life, than when they stood her, the other day, in the centre of a group of blind children who sang a chorus to the piano; and brought her hand, and kept it, in contact with the instrument. A shudder pervaded her whole being, her breathing quickened, her colour deepened, - and I can compare it to nothing but returning animation in a person nearly dead.'

Two books were now being considered.

The first a novel called *Dombey and Son* and the fourth Christmas story, *The Battle of Life*.

He was having difficulty with his composition.

'Invention thank God, seems the easiest thing in the world, and I seem to have such a preposterous sense of the ridiculous, after this long rest, as to be constantly requiring to restrain myself from launching into extravagances in the height of my enjoyment.

But the difficulty of going at what I call a rapid pace is prodigious: it is almost an impossibility. I suppose this is partly the effect of two year's ease, and partly of the absence of streets.'

Maclise's 'The Sisters' – Marion and Grace –whose
initials were the same as Mary and Georgina.
(The younger sister Marion sacrifices her own affection
to give happiness to the elder Grace). (*The Battle of Life*)

Dickens was relying more than usual on the
expert advice and criticism of Forster.

'Do you think such a proceeding as I suggest
would weaken number one very much? I wish you
would tell, as soon as you can after receiving this,

what your opinion is on the point. If you thought it would weaken the first number, beyond the counterbalancing advantage of strengthening the second, I would cut down somehow or other, and let it go. I shall be anxious to hear your opinion.' 'I have no doubt you are right…in case more cutting is wanted, I must ask you to try your hand. I shall agree to whatever you propose.'

In September 1846, Dickens arrived to holiday in Geneva he had 'a bloodshot eye; and my head was so bad with a pain across the brow, that I thought I must have got cupped.'

'Georgy has come over from Lausanne and joins with Kate. My head remains greatly better. My eye is recovering its old hue of beautiful white, tinged with celestial blue' he joked.

It could have been shingles but there are no further notes on the matter.

He had been fearful of 'wearing myself out if I go on' and at one stage said, 'that they may be no Christmas book.'

He had not lost his sense of humour, however. He reports the following amusing encounter with two very 'un-Victorian' ladies:

'In our hotel there were a mother and daughter Lady A and Lady B... I knew them to be rather odd. "You smoke, don't you?" said the younger lady. "Yes, I generally take a cigar after dinner when I am alone." "I'll give you a good 'un,' said she 'when we go up stairs.

There we were joined by an American lady residing in the same hotel, who looked like what we call in old England "a regular Bunter" – fluffy face (rouged), considerable development of the figure; one groggy eye; blue satin dress made low with short sleeves, and shoes of the same. Also a daughter; face likewise fluffy; figure likewise developed; dress likewise low, with short sleeves and shoes of the same; and one eye not yet actually groggy but going to be. American lady married at sixteen; daughter sixteen now, often mistaken for sisters &. &. &. When that was over, Lady B brought out a cigar box, gave me a cigar which she said would quell an elephant in six whiffs. She lighted hers…leaned against the mantelpiece, in conversation with me; put out her stomach, folded her arms, and with her pretty face cocked up sideways and her cigarette smoking away like a Manchester cotton mill, laughed and talked and smoked in the most gentlemanly manner I ever beheld. Lady A immediately lighted her cigar; the American lady immediately lighted hers; and in five minutes the room was a cloud of smoke. Lady B sat down to whist with a cigar continually in her mouth. She certainly smoked six or eight.'

In October his health had improved and he wrote at Rosemont, 'I have been greatly better at Geneva, though I still am made uneasy by occasional giddiness and headache. Dickens, once again, made light of a problem that was insidious in its onset.

The family now decided to stay in Paris, which they reached on the evening of Friday 20th November 1846. 'We have been thoroughly good humoured and agreeable together, and I'll always give a hurrah for the Swiss and Switzerland.'

Forster noted at the time, 'No man enjoyed brief residence in a hotel more than Dickens, but 'several tons of luggage, other tons of servants, and other tons of children' are not desirable accompaniments to this kind of life; and his first day in Paris did not close before he had made an offer for an eligible mansion. That same Saturday night he took a 'colossal' walk around the City.

Within two days their happiness was shattered. John Dickens had written concerned about the health of his eldest daughter. 'I was going to the theatre but hadn't the heart to leave home after my father's letter and sent Georgy and Kate by themselves. There seems to be no doubt whatever that Fanny is in consumption (*tuberculosis).'

She had broken down while trying to sing at a gathering in Manchester, and Sir Charles Bell's nephew was present and made the diagnosis.

He confided in Forster: 'He advised that neither she nor Burnett (*her husband) should be told the truth, and my father has not disclosed it. You remember my fears about her when she was in London the time of Alfred's marriage, and that I said she looked to me as if she was in decline? Kate took her to Elliotson, who said that her lungs were certainly not affected then. And she cried for joy. Don't you think it would be better for her to be brought up, if possible, to see Elliotson again? I am deeply, deeply grieved about it.'

Dickens came to London for eight days in December, pleased to launch a cheap edition of his earlier books that he felt everyone could afford. They were to be issued weekly in a three-halfpenny number.

On his return to Paris 'the cold intense. The water in the bedroom jugs freezes into solid masses from top to bottom, bursts the jugs with reports like small cannon, and rolls out on the tables and wash-stands, hard as granite. I stick to the shower-bath, but have been most hopelessly out of sorts – writing sorts, that's all. Couldn't begin...took a violent dislike to my study…fell into black contemplation…sat six hours at a stretch, and wrote as many lines.'

He returned with Kate to London in February 1847. His eldest son who had travelled back from Paris with Forster to go to King's College School, Eton (Miss Coutts had offered to pay for him) caught scarlet fever (*then a very serious disease that could affect the heart and kidneys) and had to go into isolation. After a month Dickens managed to see him in the grandmother's (Mrs Hogarth) house. Dickens was amused when an elderly charwoman said, "Lawk ma'am. Is the young gentleman upstairs the son of the man that put *Dombey* together?"

Evidently she lodged at a snuff-shop where on the first Monday of the month there was a special tea where one of the lodgers, who had the benefit of reading, rang out the next issue to the others. "Lawk ma'am! I thought that three or four men must have put together *Dombey*."

Dickens said how much he enjoyed the compliment.

The book was proposed in shilling numbers.
Phiz was the illustrator and Dickens, as ever, carefully scrutinised each drawing.

Dombey and Son slowly progressed. It is a story about pride, shown by a rich father's aspirations regarding his shipping business, in terms of his son Paul – a sickly child whose mother dies at his birth. The cold, although caring, father sends him to Dr Blimber's school where under the strenuous discipline, he sickens and eventually dies. Dombey has little love for his devoted daughter, Florence.

"I think Paul very good indeed."
(preliminary drawing, letter to Phiz)

"Florence is too old, particularly about
the mouth.(preliminary drawing, letter to Phiz)

Preliminary drawings for Mr Dombey
by Phiz, Dickens's preferences are shown

He marries the proud but penniless Edith, but his arrogance drives them apart and Edith into the arms of the manager Carker. They flee to France, but when pursued by Dombey, Carker falls in front of a train and is killed. The business fails and Florence, who has been driven from home, marries Walter Gay, an unfairly treated, ex-employee. He has survived a ship wreck.

The death of Paul Dombey affected the nation almost as much as Little Nell, and many critics later thought it immeasurably better as a scene. Sales of around thirty thousand began to decline after Paul's passing.

But many characters are well written. Often it is difficult to put a face, a distinguishing mark, on a villain; but in Carker, Dickens succeeds.

'Thirty-eight or forty years old, of a florid complexion, and with two unbroken rows of glistening teeth, whose regularity and whiteness were quite distressing. It was impossible to escape the observation of them, for he showed them whenever he spoke; and bore so wide a smile upon his countenance (a smile, however, very rarely, indeed, extending beyond his mouth), that there was something in it like the snarl of a cat.' (Dombey and Son)

One amusing character is Captain Cuttle 'a gentleman in a wide suit of blue, with a hook instead of a hand attached to his right wrist; very bushy black eyebrows; and a thick stick in his left hand, covered all over (like his nose) with nobs.'

Another is the parody of military pomposity - the gouty, bronchitic, retired major, Joe Bagstock who refers to himself in the third person.

A wooden-featured, blue-faced major, with his eyes starting out of his head.

"Joey B., sir," the major would say, with a flourish of his walking stick, "is worth a dozen of you. If you had a few more of the Bagstock breed among you, sir, you'd be none the worse for it. Old Joe, sir, needn't look far for a wife even now, if he was on the look-out; but he's hard-hearted, sir, is Joe – he's tough, sir, tough, and de-vilish sly." After such a declaration wheezing sounds would be heard; and the major's blue would deepen into purple, while his eyes strained and started convulsively. (Dombey and Son)

Florence is the gentle but ignored daughter who contrasts with the aloof and opportunist Edith, the second wife.

Mr Dombey introduces his daughter Florence to his future-wife

Devonshire Terrace was still rented-off when they returned to London in February 1847 and they resided for a time at Chester Place, Regent's Park where their fifth son, Sydney Smith Haldimand was born in April. Dickens was deeply saddened by the death of William Hall who had done so much to encourage him in his early days.

It has been said that Dickens had no particular sentiment of locality, nor any special regard for the houses he lived in. However, in August, he was pleased to be ensconced in Devonshire Terrace once more.

'Here we are in the noble old premises; and very nice they look all things considered. My portmanteau fell off a cab last night somewhere between London Bridge and here. Thank God the MS of the chapter wasn't in it. Whenever I travel, and have anything of that valuable article, I always carry it in my pocket.'

They had the usual welcoming breaks in the 'old watering hole', Broadstairs. But Dickens was becoming disillusioned with the town, as he noted in September.

'I fear Broadstairs and I must part company in time to come. Unless it pours with rain, I cannot write half and hour without the most excruciating organs, fiddles, bells or glee singers. There is a violin of the most torturing kind under the window now (time, ten in the morning) and an Italian box of music on the steps – both in full blast.' (Although he was to regularly visit until 1851, the vagrant music stopped the regular migration to one of his favourite haunts).

He felt he had to produce another Christmas book; then changed his mind to concentrate on *Dombey*. They visited Edinburgh where Kate had a miscarriage. The old restlessness still prevailed; he was 'at a great loss for means of blowing my superfluous steam off...but that is my misfortune.' So he arranged to produce a play to help purchase Shakespeare's house in Stratford-upon-Avon. There was total disagreement between the actors as to which play should be produced and, annoyed, he withdrew from the project. *Dombey and Son* was finally finished at Brighton in March 1848. He was pleased with the initial payment of £2220. For the first time in his life Dickens was saving money and he never had to struggle financially again.

But there was another blow imminent in July 1848. The faint hope the Doctor had given had completely broken down, and the cherished memories of trotting about with his elder sister in the small back garden came flooding back.

'A change took place in poor Fanny about the middle of the day. Her cough suddenly ceased almost, and, strange to say, she immediately became aware of her hopeless state; to which she resigned herself, after an hour's unrest and struggle, with extraordinary sweetness and constancy. I had a long interview with her to-day alone; and when she had expressed some wishes about the funeral and her being buried in unconsecrated ground (*the Burnett family were dissenters), I asked her if she had any care or anxiety in the world. She said No, none. It was hard to die at such a time of life, but she had no alarm whatever in the prospect of the change; felt sure we should meet again in a better world; and although they had said she might rally for a time, did not really wish it. Burnett had always been very good to her; they had never quarrelled; she was sorry to think of his going back to such a lonely home; and was distressed about her children. She showed me how thin and worn she was; spoke about an invention she had heard of that she would have liked to have tried for the deformed child's back; called to my remembrance all our sister Letitia's patience and steadiness; and though she shed tears sometimes, clearly impressed upon me that her mind was made up and at rest.

I asked her very often if she could recall anything that she could leave to my doing, to put it down or to mention it to somebody if I was not there; and she said she would, but she firmly believed there was nothing - nothing.

Her husband being young and her children infants, she could not help thinking sometimes, that it would be very long in the course of nature before they were united; but she knew that was a mere human fancy, and could have no reality after she was dead.

I don't know why I write this before going to bed. I only know that in the very pity and grief of my heart, I feel as if it were doing 'something.'

She died a few weeks later and the little child with the deformed spine died soon after (* he was the inspiration for both Tiny Tim and Paul Dombey).

Dickens was crushed with grief.

Fanny had been the closest person to him in his childhood, and someone he always admired and loved.

Chapter 19

Few people, if any, have heard of Thomas Mag – the younger.

Forster thought the name unsatisfactory and the title Mag's Diversions even worse. Kate and Georgina gave their opinion.

At first Thomas became David Mag, the younger, of Copperfield House and his great aunt was called Margaret.

Charles Dickens then subconsciously reversed his own initials, and David Copperfield was born.

Forster records, "that he was much startled when I pointed this out and it was just in keeping with the fates and chances that were always befalling him." The full title he concluded should be 'The Personal History, Adventures, Experiences and Observation of David Copperfield the Younger, of Blunderstone Rookery.' Dickens found it difficult to get started, planning and working between February and April 1849. Forster had also suggested that a new novel should be written in the first person, by way of a change, and that seemed to catalyse his desire to blend fact with fiction.

'My hand is out in the matter of *Copperfield* . Today and yesterday I have done nothing. Though I know what I want to do, I am lumbering on like a stage-wagon.'

Although the new novel had occupied his thoughts during the latter part of 1848, he had produced another, and final, Christmas book, *The Haunted Man or The Ghost's Bargain* which had an immediate sale of twenty thousand.

The haunted man is a chemist (Redlaw), haunted by recollections of a great wrong done to him in early life, and the consequent sorrow it brought. He is visited by a ghost who, in turn, is the dark presentiment of himself. Redlaw, despite his success, attempts to cherish the memories from the past, including an unhappy childhood, lost love, negligent parents and a dead sister.

The gloomy and wintry scenes, the boy who is an outcast on the streets, the kind staff in the college, the saviour ghost - are drawn together in a series of inconsistencies. In all, it has not stood the test of time.

Redlaw and the Phantom seem uninspired
by the plot as found in *The Haunted Man*
(drawing by Leech)

However, this obvious self-analysis had stirred
his inner-turmoil and he made a brief attempt at an
autobiography, although some parts of childhood and
his romance with Maria Beadnell thwarted the project.
He needed a different approach through symbolism
and vivid characterisation. He had already settled on
Forster to be his biographer. One small episode points
to this fact. His daughters had taught him how to do
the polka for Charley's Twelfth Night birthday party.
The night before, he suddenly feared he had forgotten
the steps. Leaping out of bed, he began a final
practice. 'Remember that for my biography,' he joked
to his friend.

However, despite his continued popularity, the last chapters of *Dombey* and the recent Christmas books had caused some critics to wonder if the great era of Dickens had passed, although they still admired his technical skills.

They were to be proved wrong.

The simple-minded Mr Dick, lodger and "sagacious" friend of David's great aunt – Betsey Trotwood - finds that he is being spoken to by King Charles's head.

He uses a kite to release these thoughts as written words into the atmosphere. Mr Dick is writing 'A Memorial' about his life and David found that 'Mr Dick had been for upwards of ten years endeavouring to keep King Charles the First out of the Memorial; but he had been constantly getting into it.'

Charles Dick-ens was to do the "same" by this semi-autobiography; which is arguably his greatest work and one of the greatest works in English literature. Once started the story bore him irresistibly along. He hesitated over David's child-wife Dora, basing her on Maria Beadnell.

Dickens instilled his own sense of the ridiculous into the character of Mr Dick.

"Do you recollect the date," said Mr Dick, looking earnestly at me, and taking up his pen to note it down, "when that bull got into the china warehouse and did so much mischief." I was very much surprised by the inquiry but remembering a song about such an occurrence that was once popular at Salem House, and thinking he might want to quote it, replied that I believed it was on St Patrick's Day. "Yes, I know," said Mr Dick – "in the morning, but what year?"

David Copperfield begins with David's birth at Blunderstone, soon after the death of his father. His gentle mother marries Mr Murdstone.

'He had that kind of shallow black eye – I want a better word to express an eye that has no depth in it to be looked into – which, when it is abstracted, seems, from some peculiarity of light, to be disfigured, for a moment at a time, by a cast.'

Abetted by his sister, Murdstone drives his new wife to an early grave.

The severe and reprimanding Miss Murdstone is 'a gloomy lady with very heavy eyebrows, nearly meeting over her large nose, as if, being disabled by the wrongs of her sex, from wearing whiskers; she had carried them to that account'

The kindly maid Clara Peggotty tries to mother David, but she is finally driven out of the household and married Mr Barkis, the carrier.

'The carrier had a way of keeping his head down, like his horse, and of drooping sleepily forward as he drove, with one of his arms on each of his knees. I say 'drove', but it struck me that the cart would have gone to Yarmouth quite as well without him, for the horse did all that: and as to conversation, he had no idea of it but whistling.

"So she makes," said Mr Barkis, after a long interval of reflection, "all the apple parsties, and does all the cooking, do she? P'raps you might be writin' to her? Well! If you was writin' to her, p'raps you'd recollect to say that Barkis was willin', would you?"

"That Barkis was willing," I repeated innocently. "Is that all the message?"

"Ye-es," he said, considering. "Ye-es. Barkis is willin'."

David is beaten by Murdstone and sent to the sadistic Creakle's school, where he is saved from punishment by an elder boy - Steerforth, whom David admires, and another pupil Traddles, who also befriends him.

David, still a child, is given a menial and degrading employment in London in the wine merchants 'Murdstone and Grinby' He finds lodgings with Mr and Mrs Micawber, and their large family, forever in debt. They are a kind family and warmly welcome him. Mr Micawber moved optimistically from one financial crisis to another, but the family retain a staunch friendship with David.

Eventually the young David runs away from the firm and walks penniless to Dover, where he asks his great-aunt Betsey Trotwood for help. She had lost all interest in him at birth, because she was certain he was going to be a girl. Reconciled, David is allowed to stay with her and the amiable lodger, Mr Dick.

'Her features were rather handsome than otherwise, though unbending and austere. I particularly noticed that she had a very quick, bright eye.'

The Murdstones call to reclaim David and take him away. Miss Murdstone rides her donkey over the garden grass. They are summarily dismissed.

"Miss Trotwood," rejoined Mr Murdstone, shrugging his shoulders as he rose, "if you were a gentleman –".

"Bah! Stuff and nonsense!" said my aunt. "Don't talk to me!"

"How exquisitely polite!" exclaimed Miss Murdstone, rising. "Over-powering really!"

"Do you think I don't know," said my aunt, turning a deaf ear to the sister, and continuing to address the brother, and to shake her head at him with infinite expression, "what kind of life you must have led that poor, unhappy misdirected baby (*her niece)? Do you think I don't know what a woeful day it was for the soft little creature when *you* first came in her way – smirking and making great eyes at her, I'll be bound, as if you couldn't say boh! to a goose!"

"I've never heard anything so elegant!" said Miss Murdstone.

Do you think I can't understand you as well as if I had seen you," pursued my aunt, "now that I *do* see and hear you – which I tell you candidly, is anything but a pleasure to me? Oh, yes, bless us! Who so smooth and silky as Mr Murdstone at first! The poor, benighted innocent had never seen such a man. He was made of sweetness. He worshiped her. He doted on her boy- tenderly doted on him! He was to be another father to him, and they were all to live together in a garden of roses, weren't they? Ugh! Get along with you do! Good day to you sir," said my aunt, "and good-bye! Good day to you too, ma'am," said my aunt turning suddenly upon his sister. "Let me see you ride a donkey over *my* green again, and as sure as you have a head upon your shoulders, I'll knock your bonnet off, and tread upon it!"

David trains in the legal profession and is articled to Mr Spenlow and marries his daughter Dora – a simple and kind child-bride, but who is unable to cope with married life.

Steerforth is introduced to the Peggotty's family at Yarmouth and runs away with Emily, who is engaged to the caring Ham. After a while, Steerforth deserts Emily and is ship-wrecked and drowned. Ham also perishes trying to save him.

Miss Trotwood's lawyer is duped by the cunning clerk (and later partner) Uriah Heep. 'Hardly any eyebrows, and no eyelashes, and eyes of a red-brown, so unsheltered and unshaded, that I remember wondering how he went to sleep. He had long, lank skeleton hands, I observed; for he frequently ground the palms against each other as if to squeeze them dry and warm besides; often wiping them, in a stealthy way, on his pocket-handkerchief. "Be 'umble, Uriah," says father to me, "and you'll get on".

Heep aspires to marry Wickfield's daughter Agnes; however, she secretly loves David. Micawber and Traddles (now a barrister) expose Heep's forgery and theft and he is sent to prison.

Dora dies and after travelling widely and becoming an author, David returns, and marries Agnes. Mr Micawber goes to Australia and prospers as a colonial magistrate, to the delight of Mrs Micawber and the family.

Dickens said, 'I like this the best'. Although sales were around twenty five thousand monthly, which did not reach his expectations, it went on to become the public's all time favourite.

In January 1849 their eighth son, Henry Fielding was born. It was a difficult birth. It was ascribed, rightly or wrongly, to Kate having been thrown around in a chaise with a bolting pony the summer before. Dickens insisted on chloroform being used (Victoria had been an advocate) although 'the doctors were dead against it. It spared her all pain and saved the child all mutilation.' He was to become their most successful child in every way.

Instead of ringing the bell, Miss Betsey Trotwood came
and looked in at the window, pressing the end of her nose
against the glass. (David Copperfield)

From the first instalment in May 1849, *David
Copperfield* was a popular success. As the chapters
were written they moved with him - Broadstairs, Isle of
Wight, Brighton, London, Paris and back to
Broadstairs. He wrote to the admiring Macready, 'May

it be as good a book as I hope it will be for your children's children to read.'

It is curious why Phiz represents the Peggotty's home of a boat as inverted, Dickens made no textual reference and it's hard to believe he overlooked it. (In later years, Browne claimed that his drawings often inspired the characters, especially Fagin, but the author repudiated this claim.)

His eldest son was at Eton and Dickens had dined a few days before with the Prime Minister, Lord John Russell and was in good spirits when he received the sad news of Lord Jeffrey's death (his Scottish friend and admirer).

'Poor dear Jeffrey, I bought a *Times* (January 1850) at the station and was so stunned…I had a letter from him in extraordinary good spirits within this week or two. I say nothing of his wonderful abilities and great career, but he was a most affectionate and devoted friend to me…I am very, very deeply grieved for his loss.'

However, the writing of David Copperfield was going well and his enthusiasm for the new book revived his spirits. He wrote to Forster:

I am wonderfully in harness and nothing galls or frets after two day's very hard work indeed; and I think a smashing number. Am eschewing all sorts of things that present themselves to my fancy – coming in such crowds. I feel the story to its minutest point.

Mrs Micawber (*Kate who was close to having another baby) is still (August 15th 1850), I regret to say *in stau quo*. Ever yours, Wilkins Micawber. (*Charles).

A girl was born the next day and called Dora Annie.

However, the child and Kate were both ill and both continued to be so until the beginning of 1851. 'Little Dora is getting on bravely, thank God,' he recorded in February.

Kate was suffering from a nervous breakdown, probably a form of post-natal depression. Dickens decided to take Kate for a complete rest at Great Malvern Spa in March 1851. Georgina came to help but the children stayed behind in London.

'O Heaven, to meet the Cold Waterers (as I did this morning when I went out for a shower bath) dashing down the hills, with severe expressions on their countenances, like men doing matches and not exactly winning! Then, a young lady in a grey polka going *up* the hills, regardless of legs; and meeting a young gentleman (a bad case, I should say) with a light black silk cap on under his hat, and the pimples of I don't know how many douches under that. Likewise an old man who ran over a milk-child, rather than stop - with no neckcloth, on principle; and with his mouth wide open, to catch the morning air.'

But a fresh sorrow interrupted their holiday, and alarmed, he hurried to Devonshire Terrace.

On the 31st March 1851 the distressed Dickens sought solace from Forster.

'My poor father died this morning. They sent for me. I arrived at eleven last night. But he did not know me, nor anyone. I remained there until he died – O so quietly. I am going up to Highgate to get the ground. Perhaps you may like to go, and I should like it if you do.'

Forster was to help once more in his hour of need, and within fifteen days. Dickens had travelled up from Malvern to chair the meeting of the General Theatrical Fund, a fund to give generously to all actors – great or small. Forster listened in anguish as Dickens said "how often is it with all of us, that in our several spheres we have to do violence to our feelings, and to hide our hearts?"

Forster had learned that baby Dora had just died, but he did not have the heart to tell Dickens before the speech began.

Chapter 20

The 1850s proved to be a successful period, although critical acclaim did not generally come until years later. *Bleak House* outsold *David Copperfield*, for example; and the writing became more technically accomplished.

The plots were generally better although complex (often said to be due to the influence of his new friend Wilkie Collins). The social themes became more diverse.

Charles Dickens aged forty nine (from the painting by Frith).

He began a magazine *Household Words* in March 1850 and it continued until it was absorbed by *All the Year Round* in May 1859; the essays he wrote for the magazine were published in 1858 as *Reprinted Pieces* by Chapman and Hall.

He also wrote *A Child's History of England*, begun in October 1850 and finished in September 1853. It was finally published by Bradbury and Evans, having been a serial in *Household Words*.

Acting and directing proved a continual diversion with, for example, a performance of *Animal Magnetism* and *Used Up* given at Rockingham Castle in January 1851. Bulwer-Lytton wrote a costume drama, *Not so Bad as We Seem,* and it was to be performed at Devonshire House, Piccadilly, London (the home of the Duke of Devonshire) in May, before Queen Victoria and Prince Albert. This play allowed Dickens, the producer, to act with the Hon. Mary Boyle. He enjoyed her vivacious company and had danced, flirted and acted a few dramatic scenes with her when staying at Rockingham Castle. She had been unable to join the acting group in 1850 when they were playing at Knebworth but in 1851 she was the star of the show. In an earlier performance Kate had been a member of the cast but had managed to fall through a trapdoor and sprain her ankle (Dickens was sometimes amused and at other times exasperated by Kate's clumsiness – on this occasion he laughed); while Georgina, in the play too, had 'covered herself in glory. 'Acting ,' recounted Dickens, 'has charms for me - I hardly know for how many wild reasons – so delightful, that I feel a loss of, oh!, I can't say what exquisite foolery, when I loose the chance of being someone in voice etc, not at all like myself.'

Around this time Dickens and Kate decided to move to a larger house. They chose Tavistock House, Bloomsbury; and moved there, with Georgina, in November 1851. Coincidently Kate published her only work, a cookery book *What Shall We Have for*

Dinner? (written under the pseudonym of Lady Maria Clutterbuck).

Tavistock House – their home 1851-1860

On March 13th 1852 Edward Bulwer Lytton Dickens was born. Only four months later Kate and Georgina accompany him on an extensive tour round England in *Not So Bad as We Seem* and other plays.

There were packed houses; although sometimes the venues were smaller than expected.

Into the room at Newcastle they squeezed six hundred people into a space reasonably capable of holding three hundred

But at Sunderland, late August 1852, Dickens had an anxious time.

'Last night, in a hall built like a theatre, we had about twelve hundred – I dare say more. But what I suffered from a dreadful anxiety, I can never describe. When we got here at noon, it appeared that the hall was a perfectly new one, and had only had the slates put upon the roof by torchlight overnight. Further, that the proprietors of some opposition rooms had declared the building to be unsafe, and there was a panic in the town about it…I didn't know what to do. The horrible responsibility of risking an accident of that awful nature seemed to rest wholly upon me. I asked W. what *he* thought, and he consolingly observed that his digestion was so bad that death had no terrors for him. I went and looked at the place; at the rafters, walls, pillars, and so forth: and fretted myself into a belief that they really were slight. To crown all, there was an arched iron roof without any brackets or pillars, on a new principle!

I took the builder aside. He told me there wasn't a stronger building in the world; and that, to allay the apprehension, they had opened it on Thursday night, to thousands and induced them to sing and beat their feet and make every possible trial of the vibration…I was in such a dread, however, lest a false alarm should spring up among the audience and occasion a rush, that I kept Catherine and Georgina out of the front.

When the curtain went up and I saw the great sea of faces rolling up to the roof, I looked here and looked there, and thought I saw the gallery out of the perpendicular, and fancied the lights in the ceiling were not straight. Rounds of applause were perfect agony to me, I was so afraid of their effect upon the building. I was ready all night to rush on in case of an alarm – a false alarm was my main dread – and implore the people for God's sake to sit still. I had our great farce-bell rung to startle 'Sir Geoffrey' instead of throwing down a piece of wood… I had a palpitation of the heart, if any of our people stumbled up or down a stair. I am sure I never acted better, but the anxiety of my mind was so intense, and the relief at last so great, that I am half-dead today, and have not yet been able to eat or drink anything or to stir out of my room.'

Georgina, painted by Augustus Egg, circa 1850. She was aged about 25 in this painting. She was to refuse Egg's offer of marriage.

Following the exhausting tour, and bearing in mind his writing and editorial duties, they holidayed in Boulogne.

Dickens had also begun working on *Bleak House*. The novel was to illustrate the evils caused by long drawn out suits in the Court of Chancery and to point out the terrible conditions of the uneducated, as shown by Jo, the crossing sweeper. One of the initial titles was *The Ruined (? House, Building, Factory, Mill) that got into Chancery and never got out.* Dickens felt it summed up the mood of the novel, but he opted for *Bleak House*.

The book is full of allegorical details, such as the all pervading London fog that represents the miasma surrounding the victims of Chancery and the terrible London slums. It is a satire on the abuses of the old court of Chancery which brought untold misery and ruin to its suitors.

It is also Dickens's first full-length novel which has a woman narrating, Esther Summerson.

Attorney and Client, Fortitude and Impatience (Bleak House)

*Bleak House was published in monthly parts 1852-1853: In it the case of Jarndyce and Jarndyce has dragged on for years in the High Court of Chancery and has used up much of the money for the edification of the lawyers engaged.

287

Ester is illegitimate and brought up by her stern aunt; unaware that she is the daughter of Captain Hawdon and (the future) Lady Dedlock - who accidentally sees the Captain's handwriting in a legal document. The writing warns her of his existence; for she had been told that he had perished at sea. However, she finds out that he has recently died. Lady Dedlock enlists the aid of a poor, wretched crossing-sweeper called Jo, who takes her to a cemetery, where her former lover has been buried.

Jo takes Lady Dedlock to the cemetery where her former lover is buried. (Bleak House)

The Dedlock's cunning lawyer, Tulkinghorn, discovers the truth about her illegitimate child and informs Lady Dedlock that he is about to expose her. However, the lawyer is fortuitously murdered by a former French maid. When Sir Leicester Dedlock learns of the secret, Lady Dedlock flees and dies in the cemetery where her lover is buried.

Ester loves a young doctor Woodcourt but, conscious of the devoted help by John Jarndyce, accepts Jarndyce's proposal of marriage. However, on learning her secret, he decides that she can go to Dr Woodcourt after all.

Many of his contemporaries thought it marked a decline in his reputation although later critics felt it was the high point of his achievement. Minor characters - like the whimsically mad old Miss Flite, also a victim of Chancery; Mrs Jellyby, who neglects her family and devotes all her time and energy to the cause of African natives; and the drunken landlord, Krook, an eccentric old rag-and–bottle merchant, - are humorously etched.

Harold Skimpole ('he was a little bright creature, with a rather large head) was so like Leigh Hunt, that the writer was not at all pleased with Skimpole's personality - especially the irresponsibility and dishonesty in money matters. Dickens wrote to assure him that his intentions were not meant to be offensive, but Leigh Hunt remained lukewarm to him forever afterwards. Dickens was saddened by the rift and when the writer died in 1859, Dickens wrote a fulsome and kind obituary, praising Hunt highly and denying any intention of ever hurting him.

Today, however, many feel that *Bleak House* marks the end of Dickens's great comic invention.

He completed the novel in August 1853, having gone to Boulogne in June, with the extended family. Dickens felt he needed a change and a short period of complete rest. He had felt under great nervous strain for some months.

This break in Boulogne was followed by a tour of Switzerland and Italy with Wilkie Collins and Augustus Egg. One purpose was to visit the Blind Institution to see how the work was progressing there.

The three travellers arrived in Switzerland in October. They visited the Mer de Glace (a glacier near Geneva) and not for the first time Dickens courted danger.

'We were a train of four mules and two guides, going along an immense height like a chimney piece, with a sheer precipice below, when there came rolling from above, with fearful velocity, a block of stone about the size of one of the fountains in Trafalgar Square, which Egg, the last of the party, had preceded by not a yard, when it swept over the ledge, breaking away a tree, and rolled and tumbled down into the valley.'

In Genoa "Signor Carlo" was greeted enthusiastically by everyone and he was thrilled to be back although joking: The beastly gate and guardhouse in the Albaro Road are still in their dear old beastly state; and the whole of the road is just as it was. The man without legs is still in the Strada Nuova; but the beggars in general are cleared off'

The Peschiere, his favourite abode, he found converted into a girl's college; and was amazed to see all the paintings of gods and goddesses canvassed over, and the garden gone to ruin, 'but oh! What a wonderful place' in 'near brilliant old Genoa.'

The de la Rues still lived in Genoa but Madame declined any further mesmeric treatment despite still suffering from her nervous affliction.

The voyage to Naples was full of the usual humour and incident that Dickens always seemed to conjure up. Their steamer was full

'The scene on board beggars description. Ladies on tables; gentlemen under tables…ladies and gentlemen lying indiscriminately on the open deck, arranged like spoons in a sideboard. No mattresses, no blankets, nothing. Towards midnight attempts were made by means of awning and flags, to make this latter scene remotely an Australian encampment; and we three (Collins, Egg and self) lay together on the bare planks covered with our coats. We were all gradually dozing off, when a perfectly tropical rain fell, and in a moment drowned the whole ship. The rest of the night we passed upon the stairs, with an immense jumble of men and women. When anybody came up for any purpose we all fell down, and when anybody came down we all fell up again. Still, the good-humour in the English part of the passengers was quite extraordinary.' (Knowing Dickens's capacity for laughter, no doubt it was!)

Rome was facing a malaria crisis but Dickens was, as usual, undaunted.

'Isn't it very extraordinary to think of its encroaching and encroaching on the Eternal City as if it were commissioned to swallow it up? This year it has been extremely bad, and had long outstayed its usual time. Rome has been very unhealthy, and it not free now. Few people care to be out at the bad times of sunset and sunrise, and the streets are like a desert at night.'

Venice

Venice was a delight with 'the Grand Canal before the two front windows, and this wild little street at the corner window; into which too, our three bedrooms look. The gondoliers have old customs...it is a point of honour with them, while they are engaged, to be always at your disposal. Hence it is no use telling them they may go home for an hour or two – for they won't go. They roll themselves in shaggy capuccins, great coats with hoods, and lie down on the stone or marble pavements until they are wanted again...there are pictures by Tintoretto in Venice more delightful and masterly than it is possible to express.'

After visiting Turin on the 5th of December, they returned home.

December 27th 1853 was a landmark occasion. It was the first reading from his work; an idea that had occurred to him in Switzerland.

In front of a packed audience in Birmingham Town Hall Dickens stood up and gave his one man show – a reading from *A Christmas Carol* followed by *The Cricket on the Hearth* the next day, and the *Carol* once more on the 30th.

It was the beginning of an era which was to utilise much of his energies at the cost of his health.

Chapter 21

January 1854 saw his amateur theatricals on Twelfth Night (6th January), and he was joined by a professional in Mark Lemon. The actor so outshone him that the following year, in the spirit of fun, 'uncle Mark' had his performance muted by a quantity of sherry being slipped into his drink, which rendered Lemon to 'helpless imbecility', which greatly amused Dickens.

Also in January 1854 Dickens began *Hard Times* and completed it within six months. It is the shortest of all his novels and had to be compressed into the limited space of *Household Words*. Its success doubled the magazine sales which had been in decline.

'The difficulty of the space is *crushing*. Nobody can have an idea of it who has not had an experience of patient fiction-writing with some elbow-room always, and open places in perspective.' Dickens believed it would 'be a satire on those who see figures and averages, and nothing else.'

Charles Dickens at his desk

* *Hard Times* has a classic opening by the Headmaster Gradgrind, a man of realities.

"Now, what I want is, Facts. Teach these boys and girls nothing but Facts. Facts alone are wanted in life. Plant nothing else, and root out everything else. You can only form the minds of reasoning animals upon Facts: nothing else will ever be of any service to them. This is the principle on which I bring up my own children, and this is the principle on which I bring up these children. Stick to Facts, sir!"

The desolation of an Industrial Landscape; Coketown in *Hard Times* represented such places. …'miles of cinder paths, and blazing furnaces, and roaring steam engines, and such a mass of dirt, gloom and misery, as I never before witnessed'. (Dickens, on his journey North).

Thomas Gradgrind's family is ruled by Facts, as is the school in Coketown, a grim, northern, industrial town.

Gradgrind's children, Louisa and Tom, steal away to watch Sleary's Circus; they are caught and reprimanded by their father, who also decides that Sissy Jupe (a clown's daughter) would benefit from living with their family, since her father has run away. Gradgrind's friend is Josiah Bounderby - a boastful, bloated, self-made-man who owns the coke mills and bank. He always exaggerates and lies about his childhood.

"My mother left me to my grandmother…if I got a little pair of shoes by any chance, she would take 'em off and sell 'em for drink. Why, I have known that grandmother of mine lie in her bed and drink her fourteen glasses of liquor before breakfast...and as soon as I was big enough to run away, of course I ran away. Then I became a young vagabond; and instead of one old woman knocking me about and starving me, everybody of all ages knocked me about and starved me. They were right; they had no business to do anything else. I was a nuisance, an encumbrance, and a pest. I know that very well." His pride in having at any time of his life achieved such a great social distinction as to be a nuisance, an encumbrance and a pest was only to be satisfied by three sonorous repetitions of the boast.(Hard Times)

Stephen Blackpool, a worker in the mill, is ostracised for failing to join the union and leaves Coketown against the wishes of Rachael. She loves him but cannot marry him because he is married to a dissolute wife. Blackpool consults Bounderby about a divorce, and is told that divorce is impossible under existing laws.

Louisa marries Bounderby, whom she despises, and falls for a languid man of the world, James Harthouse. Tom steals from the bank and Stephen Blackpool, who has had to leave Coketown to get employment, is suspected. Before he can clear his name Blackpool falls down a disused mine shaft and dies. Bitzer, who works for the bank, tries to get Tom arrested; but Tom is smuggled away as a circus clown.

Louisa leaves Bounderby, whose neglected childhood is exposed as a total fabrication by his snobbish housekeeper Mrs Sparsit. She has discovered his kindly mother in a nearby town.

"It appears to me ma'am, I say, that a different sort of establishment altogether would bring out a lady of *your* powers. Such an establishment as your relation, Lady Scadgers's, now. Don't you think you might find some affairs there, ma'am to interfere with?"

"It never occurred to me before, sir," returned Mrs Sparsit, "but now you mention it, I should think it highly probable."

"Then suppose you try, ma'am," said Bounderby, laying an envelope with a cheque in it, in her little basket. "you can take your own time for going ma'am; but perhaps in the meanwhile, it will be more agreeable to a lady of your powers of mind to eat her meals by herself, and not to be intruded upon. I ought really to apologise to you- being only Josiah Bounderby of Coketown – for having stood in your light so long."

"Pray don't name it sir," returned Mrs Sparsit. "If that portrait could speak sir – but it has the advantage over the original of not possessing the power of committing itself and disgusting others – it would testify that a long period has elapsed since I habitually addressed it as the picture of a Noodle. Nothing that a Noodle does can awaken surprise or indignation; the proceedings of a Noodle can only inspire contempt." (Hard Times)

Gradgrind repents of his attitude to his children and his slavery to Fact which has precipitated their unhappiness.

Some critics were quite harsh about *Hard Times*. One called the book 'a romance which is a summary of all the rest…attacking all education based on statistic figures and facts; heaping sorrow and ridicule on the practical mercantile people…cursing the manufacturing towns for imprisoning bodies in smoke and mud…and searches out poor workmen, jugglers, foundlings and circus people, for types of good sense, sweetness of disposition, generosity, delicacy and courage.'

Indeed, it has been remarked that Dickens's novels generally eschew credible intellectuals, and skim over the great themes of human existence such as science, religion, politics and art. But in many respects this feature was accepted as part of his universal appeal; his books spoke to the underprivileged and carried a simple moral (e.g. being poor and illegitimate carried no stigma – Oliver, Arthur Clennam and Ester Summerson are illegitimate – in an era when such children were often looked down upon).

Dickens had based his knowledge on a hurried visit to Preston in January 1854 when a strike was in progress. He hoped to assess the mood of the workmen and women.

'I am afraid I shall not get much here. Except the crowds at the street corners reading the placards pro and con; and the cold absence of smoke from the mill chimneys; there is very little in the streets to make the tone remarkable. I am told that the people 'sit at home and mope'…At the theatre last night I saw *Hamlet* and should have done better to 'sit at home and mope' like the idle workmen.'

Because of its brevity *Hard Times* does not have Dickens at his most fluent best, with little humour or sentimentally. The poor dialect (as in the Yorkshire sequences of *Nicholas Nickleby*) adds to the general disquiet; but it remains an eminently forceful book, of its type, popular in Socialist and later Russian circles. Yet it is readable and overall, a satisfying novel with some good minor characters including Sleary – the circus owner (with a voice like the efforts of a broken old pair of bellows) and the sneak Bitzer (whose skin was so unwholesomely deficient in the natural tinge, that he looked as though, if he were cut, he would bleed white).

Boulogne became a favourite haunt for the Dickens family beginning in June 1853 and they stayed until September; they were to return for the summers of 1854 and 1856; holidaying in 1854 from June until late October. He wrote the final parts of *Hard Times* there.

He loved the French countryside, the friendly local people, and was amused by their quaint ways, especially the weekly pig-market held in Boulogne.

'Among the other sights of the place, there is a pig market every Saturday, perfectly insupportable in its absurdity. An excited French peasant, male or female, with a determined young pig, is the most amazing spectacle. I saw - a pretty young woman with short petticoats and trim blue stockings, riding a donkey with two baskets and a pig in each; an ancient farmer in a blouse, driving four pigs, his four in hand, with an enormous whip – and being drawn against walls and into smoking shops by any one of the four; a cart with an old pig looking out of it, and terrifying six hundred and fifty young pigs in the market by his terrific grunts.'

However, the quaintness of the area was interrupted in the summer of 1854 by the establishment of the huge Northern Military Camp. It began the week after he finished *Hard Times* and he watched its progress as it extended along the cliffs and interrupted his walking by ploughing up the fields with the heavy wagon wheels. His patience was also tried by trumpeters teaching newly-recruited men so that the strident sounds made the echoes hideous.

'The only thing new in this garden is that war is raging against two particular tigerish and fearful cats (from the mill, I suppose), which are always glaring in dark corners, after our wonderful little Dick (* the pet canary who was to live for sixteen years); keeping the house open at all points, it is impossible to shut them out, and they hide themselves in the most terrific manner, hanging themselves up behind draperies, like bats and tumbling out in the dead of night with frightful caterwaulings.'

However, he was on friendly terms with the soldiers and attended a play in the camp and congratulated the actors; the audience, he noted, consisted of officers apart from four women. He was very impressed by a conjuror whose slight of hand even perplexed Dickens, an expert himself.

The conjuror 'brought in some writing paper and wrote some words on half-sheets of paper. One of these he gave Kate to hold. Madame, he says aloud will you think of any class of objects? An animal! Of what animal? A lion! Will you think of another class of objects, Madame? Flowers! Of what class? The rose! Will you open the paper you hold in your hand? She opened it, and there was neatly and plainly written in pencil *The Lion and the Rose*. Nothing whatever has led up to these words, and they were the most distant conceivable from Kate's thought when she entered the room.'

Dickens interest in military matters culminated with a proposed visit to the area by the Prince Consort Albert and the Emperor of France. Dickens put up the French flag alongside the Union Jack, which he had permanently on a haystack in the field. After hoisting them every day he took the opportunity to fall asleep in the blazing sun, book in hand. Finally, one day while walking, he met Albert and Louis Napoleon riding on horseback along the Calais road.

'The Emperor is broader across the chest than in the old times when we used to see him so often at Gore House, and stoops more in the shoulder.'(In February 1856 he was to see him again in Paris. 'I suppose mortal man out of bed never looked so ill and worn as the Emperor does just now. Some English saluted him, and he lifted his hand to his hat as slowly, painfully and laboriously, as if his arm were made of lead.')

In 1855 he went to Paris with Wilkie Collins, and from October 1855 until April 1856 he and Kate lived there - with a wide circle of artistic friends, attending the theatre and visiting art exhibitions.

While Dickens was in Paris, Forster tells of an incident in early November. He had sallied out for one of his nightly walks one wintry, rainy evening and was amazed to see seven heaps of rags outside the door of a workhouse. 'Dumb, wet, silent; sphinxes set up against a wall'. He sent in his card to the Master of the Workhouse, but the wards were full. The rag-heaps were all girls and Dickens gave them a shilling each for food. One girl, 'twenty or so' had been without food for twenty four hours. 'Look at me,' she said clutching the shilling and without any thanks shuffled off. So did the rest; there was not a single 'thank you'; and the miserable crowd that had gathered and witnessed the money made room in silence for him to move on.

Another event stood out in the Paris trip. Emile Girardin gave a banquet in his honour. Dickens (who mentions eating and drinking some three hundred times in *Pickwick*) was ecstatic about the alcoholic beverages provided to mark the occasion of his being there. Glass jugs of peculiar construction, laden with champagne; port wine which would fetch two guineas a bottle with the third course; with the ice is issued brandy, buried for 100 years.

It was a festival time at New Year and on the Parisian Boulevards 'there is now a line of wooden stalls, three miles long, on each side of that immense thoroughfare. All sorts of objects from shoes and sabots, through porcelain and crystal, up to live fowls and rabbits are on sale. We have had wet weather here – and dark for these latitudes – and oceans of mud. Although numbers of men are perpetually scooping and sweeping it away in this thoroughfare, it accumulates under the windows so fast, and in such sludgy masses, that to get across the road is to get half over one's shoes in the first outset of a walk.'

In January 1856 Dickens, as enthusiastic as ever, was pleased to meet the celebrated writer George Sand and was amazed by what he found.

'I suppose it to be impossible to imagine anybody more unlike my preconceptions...chubby, matronly, swarthy and black-eyed. Nothing of the blue-stocking about her, except a little final way of settling all your opinions with hers.'

Some of the time he spent sitting for his portrait, which tried his patience and was not to his liking.

'The nightmare portrait is nearly done; and Scheffer promises that an interminable sitting next Saturday, beginning at ten o'clock in the morning, shall finish it. It is a fine spirited head...but it does not look to me at all like (me)...nor does it strike me that if I saw it in a gallery I should suppose myself to be the original. It is always possible that I don't know my own face.'

Returning to England for only a few weeks, he wrote to Forster:

'I have not seen Scheffer since I came back, but he told Catherine a few days ago that he was not satisfied with the likeness after all, and thought he must do more to it.'

While in Paris, he had a short diversion from his writing; being curious about events in a house on the Champs Elysees, just across the way.

'The murder over the way (the third or fourth event of that nature in the Champs Elysees since we have been here) seems to disclose the strangest state of things. The Duchess, who is murdered, lived alone in a great house which was always shut up and passed her time entirely in the dark. In a little lodge outside lived a coachman (the murderer) and there had been a long succession of coachmen who had been unable to stay there, and upon whom, whenever they asked for their wages, she plunged out with an immense knife, by way of an immediate settlement. The coachman never had anything to do, for the coach hadn't been driven for years; neither would she ever allow the horses to be taken out for exercise. Between the lodge and the house, is a miserable bit of garden, all overgrown with long rank grass, weeds and nettles; and in this, the horses used to be taken out to swim – in a dead green vegetable sea, up to their haunches. On the day of the murder, there was a great crowd, of course; and in the midst of it up comes the Duke her husband (from whom she was separated) and rings at the gate. The police open the grate. "C'est vrai donc ," says the Duke, "que Madame la Duchesse n'est plus?" (*Is it

303

really true that Madame is no more?) "C'est trop vrai, Monseigneur." (*very true.) "Tant mieux," (*so much the better) says the Duke, and walks off deliberately, to the satisfaction of the assemblage.

Dickens, never one to miss an opportunity for a character, would remember this lady when he wrote *Great Expectations*. In addition there was another droll set of neighbours with a 'brainwashed' wilful young girl.

'Tea or coffee never seen in the house, and very seldom water; beer champagne, and brandy, were the three drinkables. Breakfast: leg of mutton, champagne, beer and brandy. Lunch: shoulder of mutton, champagne beer and brandy. Dinner: every conceivable dish (Squire's income £7,000 a-year), champagne, beer and brandy. The Squire had married a woman of the town from whom he was now separated, but by whom he had a daughter. The mother, to spite the father, had bred the daughter in every conceivable vice. Daughter, then 13, came from school once a month. Intensely coarse in talk, and always drunk. As they drove about the country in two open carriages, the drunken mistress would be perpetually tumbling out of one, and the drunken daughter perpetually tumbling out of the other.'

After only a brief return to London and Dover, Dickens was back at Boulogne for the summer of 1856. He was busy. For interspersed with his writing were the preparations for the public performance of his readings. When the time eventually arrived and the series of readings began, each one was greeted by sell-out crowds. Dickens was elated. He was now spending more time with Wilkie Collins than with anyone else. He directed and acted in the play '*The Lighthouse*' written by Collins. Others in the cast included Lemon, Egg and Dickens's sister-in-law and eldest daughter.

Dickens used more and more of his time acting and directing as for example in *The Lighthouse* by his friend Wilkie Collins

Buoyed up by success they planned a new play for Christmas 1856 at Tavistock House. Once more it was written by Collins. He called it *The Frozen Deep*. No one realised that it was to have an unforeseen and overwhelming significance in Dickens's life

Dickens had written two short Christmas stories for *Household Words*, one (*The Holly Tree Inn*) being widely popular. However, he had plans for a new novel, the first part coming out at Christmas 1855 and being finished in April 1857. His theme was to be his life-long interest in prison conditions, which had always appalled him. The book was to portray the long term mental instability prolonged incarceration produced; with its crushing psychological effects, even when the prisoner was freed into normal society with all the trappings of wealth.

The enforced total silence in prison, some pick oakum, others work on a tread-wheel (background). Mental instability and suicides were common.

Little Dorrit was original called *Nobody's Fault* and was to be weaved around a man whose creed was "nobody was to blame you know!" However, this idea was abandoned to enlarge the story by bringing together fellow-travellers in a chance way. The book was to embody his bitterness about the decline of England and the nightmare of corrupt bureaucracy.

Dickens was, for once, undecided about the plot and made the central theme the Marshalsea prison, the scene of his childhood's grief and humiliation; the place where William Dorrit's face, after twenty years, bore 'the reflected marks of the prison bars'.

* In *Little Dorrit*: Arthur Clennam falls out with his mother, believing (as she doesn't) that his father has been guilty of dishonest business dealings. He meets the seamstress who sews for his mother, called Amy Dorrit (Little Dorrit). William Dorrit, her father, is incarcerated in prison, where Amy was born. Attempts to free William fail. Arthur meets Flora Finching, his early love who has grown fat, voluble and silly. Pancks, a rent collector, discovers that William Dorrit is heir to a great estate. He leaves prison and travels abroad, now arrogant and nouveau riche. However, he gradually becomes befuddled and dies, his mind reverting to his Marshalsea years.

Mr Dorrit becomes confused and embarrasses the company by welcoming them to the Marshalsea. (Phiz – *Little Dorrit*)

Meanwhile, Arthur's investments with the banker Merdle fail, the banker commits suicide and Arthur is imprisoned in the Marshalsea. His health deteriorates and he is nursed by Little Dorrit, but is afraid to ask her to marry him, feeling that she will think he is after her newly acquired fortune. However, Merdle has also wasted Amy's money and her loss removes any barrier to marriage. A French convict, Blandois (alias Rigaud) has found out that Arthur is adopted and that his family had once defrauded the Dorrits by suppressing a codicil in a will. Arthur and Amy marry, and Blandois is crushed to death by falling debris as the house, in which he is resting, disintegrates from rot and decay.

The satirising of the red tape bureaucracy of the Government's Circumlocution Office was popular at the time, as was the book

It is a gloomy novel, most of the characters are failures in life, and there are few light scenes. Although criticised at the time for its sombre tone and unduly complex plot, G B Shaw still felt it was 'a masterpiece among many masterpieces.'

The unhappiness of Dickens's home circumstances and no doubt the approbation of some of his friends (most would eventually side with him - being a man and, most of all, rich and famous) probably accounts for the dip in humour and the lack of his usual sense of the ridiculous in this book.

Yates wrote later, 'I have heard Dickens by those who knew him as aggressive, imperious, and intolerant, and I can comprehend the accusation. He was imperious in the sense that his life was conducted on the principal *sic volo sic jubeo* principle, and that everything gave way before him. The society in which he mixed, the hours which he kept, the opinions which he held, his likes and dislikes, his ideas of what should or should not be, were all settled by himself, not merely for himself, but for all those brought into connection with him, and it was never imagined they could be called into question. He had immense powers of will.'

However, this approbation can be considered to be at variance with the esteem and friendship in which Dickens was held by his circle of friends. However, there was a ring of truth to it, nonetheless.

Chapter 22

Dickens organised a performance of the *Frozen Deep*, a highly melodramatic play by Collins, which proved successful to the Victorian audience. It was based on an expedition to the Arctic in which all had perished. It was to be produced at Tavistock house; his family (but not Kate) and friends were to be involved.

He had first considered the play in the Spring of 1856, but the summer trip to Boulogne, cut short by an outbreak of cholera, plus the heavy schedule of *Little Dorrit* had led to a temporary postponement.

However the rehearsals were planned for late 1856 and went on twice weekly for two months. Once more, Dickens grew and sported his beard, which in some respects became his pictorial trademark, although the beards came and went over the years. His long walks around London, sometimes twenty miles, were punctuated by his shouting aloud his part. His house was packed with craftsmen and artists, including his regular set designer Stanfield plus another called Telbin, both of whom did not share each others secrets. Mary Boyle was one of the stars.

The play opened on Twelfth Night 1857 and had three repeat performances the following week.

Dickens assembled and entertained the huge cast of 'The Frozen Deep.' His melodramatic finale (a death scene) was said to bring tears and sobs from all present. Luckily, a small farce, as an encore, restored spirits.

Forster was now engaged to be married, which amazed everyone; but his influence and friendship were on the wane his place being taken by Collins. Dickens and Collins were having fun in various escapades around the theatres, as Dickens was only too pleased to go along with 'any mad proposal you please.'

A performance of *The Frozen Deep* was scheduled in a gallery in Regent Street, London. Arthur Smith, the manager, arranged everything, and felt Her Majesty should be invited. The Queen replied that she was eager to see the play and felt that perhaps it could be performed at Buckingham Palace. But Dickens hesitated with regard 'to the social position'. Her Majesty said she 'fully understood' and travelled to Regent Street with Prince Albert, the King of the Belgians, and numerous members of Court. They were all very impressed and she wavered the usual protocol and stayed late.

In Manchester, in July 1857, an important and defining event occurred. Dickens decided to strengthen the cast by hiring professional actresses including Mrs Ternan, and her daughters Maria and Ellen. Mrs Ternan and her husband had been solid, if not distinguished, actors and had spent some time in America. Added to his acting ability, Mr Ternan had at one stage simultaneously managed theatres in Newcastle upon Tyne and Doncaster. He was to die in Bethnal Green Lunatic Asylum of a general paralysis which, at the time, was usually the final stage (tertiary stage) of syphilis.

The three daughters, Fanny, Maria and Ellen, had stage careers, Ellen appearing first at the age of three; while Mrs Ternan had acted with Macready in several Shakespearian plays. She was strict and matronly in attitude, and full of Victorian idealism; Fanny was bright and became a writer and novelist later in life; Maria was cheerful and lively; and Ellen, as far as it is known, was quite quiet (called 'placid' by her friends) but firm in her convictions. Considered the least talented, she never rose above the ordinary in her acting. She had been born in Rochester (which would please Dickens, who liked coincidences) and she was the same age as Katey who described her as 'small, fair-haired and rather pretty;' although Ellen jokingly referred to herself as having 'a figure like an oak tree and a complexion like a copper saucepan.'

She was at times nervous, probably due to a lack of confidence in her own abilities compared to her sisters, and suffered migraines. She also had a mild skin condition, with a reddening and vesicular rash, which could have been due to an allergy (not recognised at that time) or have a psychosomatic basis.

It is quite probable that Dickens knew of, or had seen, the family acting. Thus he was pleased to hire the Ternans.

In the play the eighteen-year-old Ellen is the ward of an elderly gentleman (Dickens) who falls in love with her beauty.

Ellen Ternan

The play coincided with a period when he was beginning to question his marriage and his future.

'It is not only that she (*Kate) makes me uneasy and unhappy, but that I make her so too – and much more so. She is exactly what you know, in the way of being amiable and complying; but we are strangely ill-assorted for the bond there is between us. God knows she would have been a thousand times happier if she had married another kind of man, and that her avoidance of this destiny would have been at least equally good for us both. I am often cut to the heart by thinking what a pity it is, for her own sake, that I ever fell her way.'

The amiable Kate had more than once suggested they separate but Dickens believed they should stay together for the children's sake.

Dickens was desperate for a change of surroundings and set off on a tour with Wilkie Collins. Looking over a book called *The Beauties of England and Wales* before he left London, he made up his mind. Into the Lake District they went and the twelve day 'foray upon the fells of Cumberland' was later recorded (jointly) in *Household Words* as *The Lazy Tour of Two Idle Apprentices*. Dickens was taken by the exceptional beauty of the Lake District and wanted to expend his energy by climbing. He decided on Carrick Fell in Cumberland for one of his first forays.

'We came straight to it yesterday (9th of September)' he wrote to Forster, 'Nobody goes up. Guides have forgotten it. Master of a little inn, excellent, north-countryman, volunteered. Went up, in tremendous rain. CD beat Mr Porter (name of landlord) in a half a mile. Mr P done up in no time. Three nevertheless went on. Mr P again leading, CD and C (*Collins) following. Rain terrific, black mists, darkness of night. Mr P agitated, CD confident. C (a long way down in perspective) submissive. All wet through. No poles. Not so much as a walking stick in the party. Reach the summit, at about one in the day. Dead darkness as of night. Mr P (excellent fellow to the last) uneasy. CD produces compass from pocket. Mr P reassured. Farm-house where dog-cart was left N.N.W. Mr P complimentary. Descent commenced. CD with compass triumphant, until compass, with the heat and wet of CD's pocket, breaks. Mr P (who never had a compass),inconsolable, confesses he has not been on Carrick Fell for twenty years, and he don't know the way down. Darker and darker. Nobody discernable, two yards off, by the other two. Mr P makes suggestions, but no way. It becomes clear to CD and to C that Mr P is going round and round the mountain, and never coming down. Mr P sits on angular granite, and says he is "just fairly doon." CD revives Mr P with laughter, the only restorative in the company. Mr P again complimentary. Descent tried once more. Mr P worse and worse. Council of war. Proposals from CD to go "slap down". Seconded by C. Mr P objects, on account of precipice called The Black Arches, and terror of the country-side. More wandering. Mr P terror stricken, but game. Watercourse, thundering and roaring, reached. CD suggests that it must run to the river, and had best be followed, subject to all gymnastic hazards. Mr P opposes, but gives in. Watercourse followed accordingly. Leaps, splashes, and tumbles, for two hours. C lost. CD whoops. Cries for assistance from behind. C returns. C with horribly sprained ankle, lying in rivulet.

We got down at last in the wildest place, preposterously out of course; and propping up C against stones, sent Mr P to the other side of Cumberland for dog-cart, so got back to his inn, and changed. Shoe or stocking on the bad foot, out of question. Foot tumbled up in a flannel waistcoat. CD carrying C melodramatically everywhere, into and out of carriages; up and down stairs; to bed; every stop. And so to Wigton, got doctor, and he we are!'

They visited Maryport and on to the Ship Hotel at Allonby. This is a capital little homely inn, looking out upon the sea; with the coast of Scotland, mountainous and romantic over against the windows; and though I can just stand upright in my bedroom, we are really well lodged. Dickens was thrilled to meet the landlady who had lived at Greta Bridge when he stayed there, before *Nickleby*.

Behind Derwentwater lie the Northern Fells, Dickens enjoyed the Lake District.

He pondered on his recent 'rush' up Carrick Fell, the way his life was unfolding, and the dissatisfactions and misgivings. I have now no relief but in action. I am incapable of rest. I am quite confident I should rust, break, and die, if I spared myself. Much better to die, doing…I have always felt of myself that I must, please God, die in harness…it is much better to go on and fret, than to stop and fret. The old days – the old days! Shall I ever, I wonder, get the frame of mind back as it used to be then? Something of it perhaps – but never quite as it used to be. I find that the skeleton in my domestic closet is becoming a pretty big one.

On the way back he went to the St Leger at Doncaster and never having been before to the races, facetiously wrote down three names for three races, and each one won. But that night he heard a 'groaning phantom' in the hotel. The landlord apologised the next morning. The groaning man had lost nearly £2,000. Dickens felt that anybody with any good in them, with a desire to bet, and was brought to Doncaster races at an early age, it would cure them forever of that urge. He was not impressed by horse race meetings.

The meeting was, almost certainly, an excuse to visit Ellen who, with her family, were playing in the theatre in Doncaster. He was, however, annoyed when he was instantly recognised and the actors and audience gave 'three cheers for Mr Dickens.'

It is said that he left Doncaster suddenly and wrote that 'the Doncaster unhappiness remains so strong upon me that I can't write, and can't rest, one minute.'

There had been some problems with Ellen but, whatever they were, remains unclear. However, by early October, Dickens appears to have arranged for Ellen be placed under contract at the Theatre Royal, Haymarket, London, where she was to remain for most of the next two years.

The home atmosphere was bad. Kate had opened a parcel sent by a jeweller and found it to be a bracelet (some accounts say a brooch) which Dickens acknowledged, was a present for Ellen – following a similar incident in the plot of the play. Such tokens of gratitude were not unusual, however, often being given to members of the cast. Kate felt otherwise. She knew how Ellen had consistently sat on the arm of his chair whenever she could, eagerly pleasing him at rehearsals and joining him in duets at the piano. Kate felt slighted by the gift arriving at the house. Dickens was incensed that she should accuse him of such a thing in front of his own daughters and felt the best way for Kate to understand the situation was to meet Ellen, in all her innocence, at the Ternan's home.

Kate was very upset and Dickens tried to reassure her. Katey was furious when she heard that her mother was to do such a thing, and told her "she must not go". But Kate, dutiful as ever, went.

Chapter 23

Towards the close of 1855 Dickens had begun to realise a great childhood ambition.

Walking near Rochester with a friend (Wills) he pointed out Gad's Hill Place and recalled how his father had told him that if he grew up to be successful he might live in the house. That same night Wills was sitting next to Eliza Lynn (* a contributor to *Household Words*) and heard her remark that she had 'lived there as a child, was still the owner, and was considering selling it'. Wills was thrilled, immediately getting in touch with Dickens, telling him, "It is written that you were to have that house."

Dickens was both instantly elated and motivated. He began negotiations to buy Gad's Hill, something he had only dreamed of as a child.

'They wouldn't take £1700 for the Gad's Hill property (November 1855), but "finally" wanted £1800, I have finally offered £1750. It will require an expenditure of about £300.' (*It actually took almost a thousand). The transaction went through on a Friday to Dickens's delight (he always published and did most things of importance on a Friday).

He was also elated at the Shakespearean connection, recalling Sir John Falstaff's rally, "But, my

318

lads, my lads, to-morrow morning, by four o'clock, early at Gadshill."

Initially Dickens toyed with the idea of buying Gad's Hill as an investment and only living there in the summer. 'You will hardly know Gad's Hill again,' he wrote to Forster, 'I am improving it so much. – yet I have no interest in the place.'

Gad's Hill had its problems. The nearest spring was two miles away and 'we are still (6th of July 1856) boring for water here, at the rate of two pounds per day for wages.' And in September when the hop-picking season was in full flow in Kent, 'Hop-picking is going on, and people sleep in the garden, and breath in at the keyhole of the house door. I have been amazed, before this year, by the number of miserable lean wretches, hardly able to crawl, who go hop-picking.'

'Here are six men perpetually going up and down the well (I know that somebody will be killed) in the course of fitting the pump. By the time it is finished, the cost of this water will be something absolutely frightful. But of course it proportionally increases the value of the property, and that's my only comfort. The horse has gone lame from a sprain, the big dog has run a ten-penny nail into one of his hind feet, the bolts have all flown out of the basket-carriage, and the gardener says all the fruit trees want replacing with new ones. I have discovered that the seven miles between Maidstone and Rochester is one of the most beautiful walks in England.'

Cricket at Gad's Hill, Dickens encouraged matches which were played in aid of various charities. He is seen opening the bowling.

The more he improved the place the more he liked it, and he soon abandoned the idea of letting it. A new drawing room was built out from a smaller one, two extra bedrooms added on the third floor and on the ground floor a bedroom was transformed into a study which he lined with books; the drawing-room and dining room were hung with pictures and filled with fine furniture. The hall was embellished with prints by Hogarth which were eventually removed to his bedroom, being replaced by Stanfield's work. The breakfast room was changed into a retreat for smokers and a billiard table installed. 'As to the carpenters,' he wrote to his daughter, 'they are absolutely maddening. They are always at work yet never seem to do anything.'

Finally, in 1857, the whole family moved there, although he still retained the lease of Tavistock House.

He had obtained permission to partially clear a derelict shrubbery on the other side of the main road and to build an underground tunnel to reach his chalet from his front lawn. This work was completed in the summer of 1859.

The Chalet at Gad's Hill; his idyllic place for writing.

The Swiss chalet was given to him by the actor, Mr Fechter and arrived from Paris. The chalet was a great favourite and Dickens found it idyllic, doing much of his work there.

'I have put five mirrors in the chalet where I write,' he wrote to an American friend, 'and they reflect and refract, in all kinds of ways, the leaves that are quivering at the windows, and the great fields of waving corn, and the sail-dotted river. My room is up among the branches of the trees; and the birds and the butterflies fly in and out, and the green branches shoot in at the open windows, and the lights and shadows of the clouds come and go with the rest of the company.'

He would watch the birds all day and, especially, listen to the haunting nightingales in the summer months. He would take his friends and visitors for walks or rides along the Dover Road. Hans Andersen ('a bony bore') came for a fortnight and stayed for five weeks; but he was pleased to welcome Longfellow.

Work commenced in the morning, after inspecting the house, the stables and kitchen garden and – unless the weather was particularly bad – a walk, before settling at his desk. His dogs were a great enjoyment and went with him. It was said that 'his interest in these animals was "inexhaustible"'. There were nearly always two, usually large, and of the mastiff variety. His favourite was Turk, a noble animal full of affection and intelligence and a companion, Linda, a great St Bernard. Other dogs, including Irish and Newfoundland hounds, were acquired in time. One of the Newfoundlands, he called Bumble (after the parish beadle in *Oliver*) because of his 'peculiar pompous and over bearing manner he had of appearing to mount guard over the yard when he was an absolute infant.' Each dog was welcomed with the greatest pleasure. They also had a practical use, keeping the undesirable tramps and wayfarers out of his grounds.

However, he was finding life dull with such a divided household. The Twelfth Night, so often a time of great merriment and goodwill, was silent in 1858. Gone were the festivities; great was the contrast of the previous year when they had staged *The Frozen Deep*. To overcome his dejection, Dickens immersed himself in charity work, as before

The expense of renovating Gad's Hill led him to think about other ways of earning money. He suddenly decided to embark on a series of Readings, not just for charity as had always been the case, but to offset the out-going bills. He also felt 'that the mere physical effort and change of Readings would be good.'

He had confided his unhappiness and the difficulties of his marriage to Angela Burdett-Coutts. She was sympathetic and encouraged him to start the Readings again.

'What do you think of my paying for this place, by reviving that old idea of some readings from my books. I am strongly tempted. Think of it!'

Forster did, and thought the whole project 'vulgar'. But Dickens, forever his own man, went ahead. He used the excuse that he was not in the mood for writing, being depressed by his home circumstances. 'Nothing can put *them* right, until we are all dead and buried and risen. It is not, with me, a matter of will, or trial, or sufferance, or good humour, or making the best of it, or making the worst of it, any longer.'

He felt it would be an opportunity to travel and to communicate with an audience as never before. So on April 29th 1858, Dickens began his first paid readings from his books. The subjects were extracts from *Christmas Carol*, *The Chimes*, the trial in *Pickwick*, *Paul Dombey*, *Boots at the Holly Tree Inn*, *the Poor Traveller* and *Mrs Gamp*.

He gave sixteen performances at St Martin's Hall (London), the last on 22nd July, 1858 and there were plans for a further 87 in a provincial tour that embraced much of England and parts of Ireland and Scotland, concluding in late 1859.

Before the Readings were completed, matters at home came to a head in the summer of 1858.

It was triggered by Kate's family; the Hogarths who had already become (so Dickens believed) a pack of ungrateful jackals. He avoided them whenever he could; and was so annoyed on one occasion that he walked to Gad's Hill from Tavistock House (about thirty miles) through the night to avoid staying in their company. Any doubts Kate had, were resolved by her mother, who insisted she must leave. Kate followed the maternal advice, no doubt relieved that the decision had been finally made and the separation began.

There was, however, a family divide. Although Dickens had said that 'Mary was to be mistress of the house,' the role would fall, naturally to Georgina, if she decided to stay.

Georgina, who had refused Augustus Egg's proposal of marriage, thought quite differently about the split. She would stay on. She had been with the family for sixteen years and refused to be cajoled or shaken. One effect was to blunt the barbs aimed at Dickens by her parents.

Of course her mother and her sister immediately turned against her. Forster was brought in to negotiate a settlement and Dickens was willing to be generous. At first he procrastinated, feeling that Kate could have rooms of her own or shuttle independently between Tavistock House and Gad's Hill, thereby avoiding each other while ostensibly keeping up appearances.

Kate would have none of it.

She wanted a complete separation and her family agreed. Thus Kate got her own home and £600 per year. Charley (the eldest) bravely felt it was his duty to accompany his mother but was upset at leaving the father whom he loved and worshipped. Walter was in India and Frank, Alfred and Sydney were often at boarding school. Katey and Mary (Mamie) would look after the little ones with Georgina.

The Hogarths would not rest, however, and accused Ellen of being Dickens's mistress.

Katey said that it turned him 'into a madman. This affair brought out all that was worst – all that was weakest in him. He did not care a damn what happened to any of us.'

Dickens was furious, saying that unless the Hogarths publicly withdrew the accusation, Kate would not get a penny. They threatened a court action, and Dickens remained obdurate. 'Let them,' he replied.

Mrs Hogarth, whose anger knew no bounds, was determined to bring an action in the Divorce Court.

This was a major and serious development, since wives could only divorce their husbands on the grounds of incest, bigamy or cruelty – and it is certain that they had the last in mind, if not the first (i.e. incest with Georgina). Forster clarified the Divorce Act and had Georgina examined by a doctor to show that she was indeed virginal. The Hogarths' fury was appeased for the time being and they dropped the action. It takes little to imagine Georgina's fury at the slur. She cut herself off from her family.

Although people were bewildered, and in part not particularly interested outside of London, Dickens persisted, concerned that he was loosing his beloved public. A statement in *The Times* suggested that Dickens 'preferred his wife's sister to herself' sent Dickens, post haste, to seek legal advice as to whether the statement was libellous. He was advised to remain silent. The more dust he threw up, the more of a maelstrom it created.

The gossip that Dickens was having an affair with Georgina so angered Thackeray, that he thundered, 'It's with an actress!' believing it to be less scandalous. However, this public revelation was exactly what Dickens did not want. He wrote Thackeray a stinging letter. Another letter followed to Baroness Burdett-Coutts where the complaint against Kate was, 'She does not- and she never did – care for the children and the children do not – and they never did – care for her. The little play that is acted in your Drawing Room is not the truth.' Dickens was at his most vengeful and continued in the same exaggerated vein to Madame de la Rue. 'What we should do, or what the girls would do, without Georgy, I cannot imagine. She is the active spirit of the house and the children dote on her. We put the Skeleton away in the cupboard, and very few people, comparatively, know of its existence.'

Meanwhile Angela Burdett-Coutts was acting in a conciliatory manner, having been visited by Kate and her mother. She tried to bring Kate and Charles together once more. He replied, 'If you have seen Mrs Dickens in the company of her wicked mother, I cannot enter, not even with you – upon any question that was discussed in that woman's presence.' It has been said that the Baroness had sympathy for Kate and that there was a cooling relationship with Dickens after that gesture. There had never been a hint of romance between them and no suggestion, as far as it can be inferred, of jealousy on her part that the man whom she had admired (and had helped her in many worthy causes) had disregarded her for a much younger woman.

After two weeks 'the wickedest people I have loaded with benefits' (the Hogarths) signed a retraction. Dickens then went from bad to worse. Still feeling one statement was not enough, he published another in *Household Words*. He had sought advice from the editor of the Times, who said "go ahead"; while Kate, probably and rightly fed up, agreed.

'Some domestic trouble of mine, of long standing', has been brought to an arrangement satisfactory to all concerned, but, by some means, misrepresentations, most grossly false, most monstrous, and most cruel – involving, not only me, but innocent persons dear to my heart have been circulating. I most solemnly declare, and this I do both in my own name and in my wife's name – that all the lately whispered rumours touching the troubles at which I have glanced, are abominably false.'

The fat had been poured onto the fire, and, to add to the mess, he asked the papers to reprint the statement. His great friend, Mark Lemon refused to print it in *Punch*, making the excuse that it was inappropriate for a humorous magazine. Dickens cut him dead. So the repeated denials fuelled more gossip, which infuriated Dickens, and even his best friends kept quiet or distanced themselves for a time.

He then prepared a second statement, which he was advised to keep hidden but it leaked out, accusing Kate of 'throwing the children onto someone else, and through a mental disorder felt unfit for the life she had to lead as my wife.' He also felt annoyed that 'a young lady, virtuous and spotless, had been besmeared.' (* it is almost certain he meant Georgina and not Ellen.)

Another twist occurred when the letter purporting to Kate's incapacity as a mother reached the press, and one paper thundered 'that they considered it wantonly cruel' that she was thus maligned. Dickens response to the general outcry was to continue in his quest to justify himself. However, although Macready, Wills and Forster gave some support, there was a sense of uneasiness, a subliminal condemnation, for any miscreants who broke the sacredness of marriage. Several women including Mrs Gaskell (whom Dickens had championed), Harriet Martineau and Elizabeth Barrett Browning supported Kate and were withering in their criticism.

Katey, who was always full of spirit, said later that 'nothing could surpass the misery and unhappiness of our home.' Dickens had shown an uncharacteristic sense of cruelty in imagining and broadcasting the fact that Kate did not have the feelings for her children that he had. Katey summed him up with the remark, 'That my father did not understand women.' She later said that 'we were all wicked not to take her part...my mother never rebuked me. I never saw her in a temper.'

Perhaps cowed, and at the same time realising the futility of the situation, Kate and her mother signed the document prepared by Dickens on 29th May and later that day the pair left for Brighton, never to return to Tavistock House. He might have won, but the house was gloomy and the family divided. Dickens never regained his former happiness, and pondering on the circumstances around him, he concluded that 'it is all despairingly over.'

Forster, the indispensable mentor, had also fallen out of favour. He was also married -so not so accessible at all hours as he had been in the past. His place was largely taken by Wilkie Collins. However Collins, the man who was a master of book construction, clearly lost the plot in his own life. Never married, he lived with Caroline Graves, whom he first saw at a mysterious midnight encounter, which he used in *The Woman in White*. He stayed with her for many years. By Martha Rudd he had three illegitimate children. A sufferer from gout, he became addicted to opium from roughly 1860 onwards. He was often attacked by fellow writers for offending their notions of propriety.

Collins was not the best person to turn to for moral advice, but his opinions were sought by Dickens and often acted upon.

Dickens's standing with his friends, at that dark time, is difficult to determine. Clearly Forster and Dolby knew the facts but Ellen remains a shadowy figure and was almost completely ignored in their biographies.

Dickens had been a welcome friend and confident to many of the richest, most intelligent and beautiful women in Victorian Society. The divorce was one thing; the fact that his daughters elected to stay with an aunt and not their mother, was another. One letter between friends referred to the fact that Dickens's daughters '…are not received into Society. You would be excessively amused if you heard all the gigantic efforts the family make to keep their foot in the world…they have been treated with the most dire contempt.' Another family told of how, invited by the Dickens to Tavistock house, they told him…'that it was with Mrs Dickens they were acquainted'…and were 'very sorry', but they could not attend.

Also the Ternan's position was invidious, connected to one of the most famous men in the world. The strict moral code at that time castigated a woman living with a man to whom she was not married, as little more than a prostitute.

So the maelstrom continued for many months to come. There was no hope of reconciliation.

Clearly Dickens expected more from Kate, and Kate expected more from Charles; that was the simple equation.

For most biographers, however, Kate is portrayed as clumsy and dull and depressed; in this opinion they simply ape Dickens at his worst. John Forster (who wrote the best biography of Dickens, and the best that will ever be written) skirts over the marital problems. In this fact most readers believe that Forster wanted to keep his friend's character pristine and hallowed, but such adjectives may equally apply to Forster's attitude to Kate. No one outside the family knew her better. Over two decades the three of them celebrated, and enjoyed, the Dickens's wedding anniversaries together. There is no hint of anything wrong with Kate's temperament or friendship within the inner circle of friends. She had her failings, but so had Dickens.

Chapter 24

While all these domestic and marital problems were going on, Dickens continued his provincial Readings. Whatever the public thought there was no sourness, no acrimony against Dickens as he went on with the tour. Indeed the audiences were warmer and more enthusiastic than ever.

In Dublin (1858) the crowds were enormous.

'All the way from the hotel to the Rotunda (a mile), I had to contend against the stream of people who were turned away. When I got there they had broken the glass in the pay-boxes, and were offering £5 freely for a stall. Half the platform had been taken down, and people heaped in among the ruins. You never saw such a scene. Our men were flattened against walls and squeezed against beams. Ladies stood all night with their chins against my platform. Other ladies sat all night upon my steps. We turned away people enough to make immense houses for a week.

'In Belfast we turned away half the town,' he wrote to Georgina, 'I wish you and the dear girls could have seen the people look at me in thc strcct; or heard them ask me, as I hurried to the hotel after the reading last night to "do me the honour to shake hands, Misther Dickens and God bless you sir; not ounly for the light you've been in mee house sir (and God love your face!) this many a year."

He was asked to do another Irish tour soon.

'I have positively said No! The work is too hard. With a different place every night, and a different audience with its own peculiarity every night, it is a tremendous strain.'

In October 1858, on the journey home he wrote from York a letter that summed up his feelings for his public.

'I was brought very near to what I sometimes dream may be my fame when a lady whose face I had never seen, stopped me yesterday in the street, and said "Mr Dickens, *will you let me touch the hand that has filled my house with many friends*."

Crowds continued to come and thousands were turned away, for example in Manchester the audience numbered 2500 and as many could not gain admission; while in Hull Dickens's manager, Mr Smith, had to address and placate the crowds and arrange additional readings, as so many had come from the surrounding area.

Dickens reading from his novels; he became a sensation and theatres were packed. The audience laughed, wept, cheered and a few even fainted when he read the murder of Nancy. In his button-hole he wore a geranium, sent by Mary Boyle.

His notes show the effort involved in one day.

'On Friday we came from Shrewsbury to Chester; saw all right for the evening; and then went to Liverpool. Came back from Liverpool and read at Chester. Left Chester at 11 at night, after reading, and went to London. Got to Tavistock House at 5am on Saturday, left it at a quarter past 10 that morning, and came down here (Gad's Hill, 15th of August 1858)

In Edinburgh he was greeted as rapturously as ever. He was thrilled to have Mamie and Katey with him. 'I was so completely taken by storm, and carried in spite of itself. Travelling, dinner, reading, and everything else, come crowding together into this strange life. At Aberdeen we were crammed to the street, twice in one day. At Perth (where I thought when I arrived, there literally could be nobody to come) the gentlefolk came posting in from thirty miles round, and the whole town came besides, and filled an immense hall. At Glasgow, where I read three evenings and one morning, we took the prodigiously large sum of six hundred pounds!'

By the middle of November 1858 the eighty-seven Readings were completed – his public had remained loyal and he was £3000 better off. A relieved Dickens wrote, 'I consider it a remarkable instance of good fortune that it should have fallen out that I should, this autumn of all others, have come so face to face with so many multitudes.'

There were three Christmas readings in London, and five followed shortly afterwards.

In February 1859 Dickens was depressed, 'I have not had the heart to make any preparation for it,' he wrote to Collins about his forty-seventh birthday. He also considered renting Tavistock place to the

Ternans (Mother and Fanny had just returned from Italy) but Forster scotched the idea. However, the amiable Forster had commissioned a painting of Dickens by Frith, who described the novelist as 'delightful, talked all the while. No wonder people like him.' Frith thought it was of a man on the top rung of the ladder 'and was perfectly aware of his position.' Noting the expression of the portrait, Dickens was, as usual, more jocular, saying 'it is a little too much (to my way of thinking) as if my next-door neighbour were my deadly foe, uninsured, and I had just received tidings of his house being afire.'

Dickens was also frenetic on other fronts – he was deeply involved with many charities especially schooling, and continued writing articles for, and editing, *Household Words*. However, there was the inevitable 'falling out' with the backers of *Household Words* - Bradbury and Evans; so a bill was filed in Chancery. Fortunately, the matter was largely settled out of court and what was left of the magazine was not worth pursuing. So the publishers put their minority share up for auction. By one means or another, Dickens acquired the remaining shares, jubilant that it cost him no more than £500. Once again he had his critics but, undaunted, began another magazine called *All The Year Round*. He returned to the fold of Chapman and Hall, his first publishers. The first issue was in April 1859. Due to Dickens's benevolence and foresight, this magazine gave opportunities to a host of writers including Mrs Gaskell (*Cranford*) and Wilkie Collins (who achieved fame with the serials *Woman in White, No Name* and *Moonstone*).

Soon *All The Year Round* was selling three times the number of *Household Words* and was eventually to reach 300,000. Old and new contributors all listened to the 'Chief', who took pains to help everyone especially young writers of promise.

It was said that Dickens 'hates arguments... never talks for effect, his sympathies are the broadest, and his literary tastes appreciate all excellence.'

However, he had decided on a new and different novel for *All The Year Round*, based on France and the past events, therein. It was to be the corner stone of the magazine.

Wilkie Collins became a close friend and occasionally a co-author; his plots were admired by Dickens and his bohemian life style intrigued him.

In the summer of 1859, he had an offer to tour America and was tempted, but within a few months the Civil War began and that curtailed the tour for five years.

At home his family concerned him and he was torn by the break-up with Kate and how everyone was affected.

The unhappy Dickens found that the weekly - instalment form was as taxing as ever; but his new book was progressing well, and he took solace from that fact.

As for the past, he made a huge bonfire at Gad's Hill of all the thousands of letters he had received from the rich and famous. His sons 'roasted onions in the ashes of the great. Would to God every letter I had ever written was on that pile!' he wrote.

The most famous man in the Western World now felt he had expurgated part of his former life, but the memories of those happier days at Tavistock House remained.

These memories would be erased by selling the house; then nothing would be left, but a new future.

Chapter 22

In March 1859 Dickens began *A Tale of Two Cities*, which appeared as a serial in the first number of *All the Year Round*.

He had first considered such a historical novel when acting in *The Frozen Deep* during the summer of 1857. As he composed he scrupulously researched the details of the French Revolution (mostly from Thomas Carlyle).

A Tale of Two Cities opens in 1775: Dr Manette knows of the cruel treatment of a peasant family by the Marquis de St Evremonde, including murder of a boy. The marquis has had the doctor imprisoned for 18 years. Lucie Manette (French born although brought up in England) is told that her father Dr Manette is not dead, as she supposed, but a prisoner in the Bastille. She travels to France and is taken to a wine shop, run by M. Defarge, where her father once lodged and finds her aged, demented father sitting at a bench making shoes. He does not recognise her, but agrees to come to England. Five years later in a London court, a young Frenchman Charles Darnay (who has denounced his aristocratic ties, and incensed at the French nobility's cruelty to their subjects) is on trial accused of spying. Also in court is a dissolute, irresponsible, but brilliant lawyer called Sydney Carton, who looks uncannily like Darnay.

Everyone is surprised at the resemblance of the lawyer Carton and the defendant Darnay (*Dickens loved coincidences and this is his greatest). (Phiz)

337

Mr Stryver, the defence counsel, gets an acquittal on the grounds of any identification being unreliable, even as witnessed, for example, by the coincidence in this court. Meanwhile in Paris the revolution has broken out and Defarge leads the mob on the siege of the Bastille. Mrs Defarge, the leader of the women revolutionaries, has the prison governor beheaded. Although Carton loves Lucie, she marries Darnay, who returns to Paris to try and save a faithful servant.

Darnay is captured and jailed in La Force prison; he is condemned to the guillotine and Carton decides to help. Visiting Darnay in jail, he manages to get him smuggled out by the administration of a sleeping drug. Under the guise of being Darnay he is executed, fulfilling an earlier promise to Lucie (whom he loved dearly) that he would one day do something to justify her happiness.

Sydney Carton's final speech on the scaffold: "It is a far, far better thing that I do than I have ever done; it is a far, far better rest that I go to than I have ever known."

This rousing finale could also be the epitaph for the book. Without doubt it is totally humourless. The woman spectators, devoid of any pity, knitting assiduously while innocent people were guillotined, are a picture that remains once all other details are forgotten (apart, of course, the final, self-sacrificing speech).

Although at times technically brilliant, the plot is too coincidental and characters wooden. Beloved by examination boards, it must have dissuaded countless pupils from delving any further into Dickens's books.

Lucie falls for the aristocratic charms of Darnay
and not the careless and slovenly Carton .Dr Manette,
confused by his long imprisonment, looks on.

A Tale of Two Cities was to see the end of the Boz/Phiz partnership that had lasted 23 years. There had been disagreements, chiefly because Hablot Browne had a great tendency to exaggerate the characters and depict them differently from the text.

The artist was upset at "Dickens's strangely silent manner of breaking the connection. He probably thinks a new hand would give his old puppets a fresh look, or perhaps he does not like my illustrating Trollope neck-and-neck with him – though by Jingo, he need fear no rival *there*! Confound all authors and publishers, say I. There is no pleasing one or t'other. I wish I had never had anything to do with the lot."

The Sea Rises. (Dickens decided that he would dispense
with Phiz after this book. This drawing has verve but
on the whole they were tame and lacking in dramatic spirit).

Hablot Knight Browne, alias Phiz,
his last book was A *Tale of Two Cities*

Dickens also wrote a series of essays and
sketches from life, the first collection being published

in 1860 as *The Uncommercial Traveller*, updated until 1875 it is merely a collector's item today.

Dickens was concerned about his children, especially the two girls he adored. Mamie, twenty at the time of the separation, and Katey, a year younger, were affected quite differently. Mamie was devoted to her father and did not see her mother again for a decade. She almost got married, but believing her father to disapprove, stayed single and had a tendency to depression.

Katey matched her father's spirit, which he acknowledged. She did not care for, or particularly trust, Georgina and regularly reproached her aunt and her father for their behaviour to her mother; with whom, she continued to remain close. Katey particularly disliked the fact that Georgina never visited or spoke to her sister (*it was not until twenty-one years later, with Kate serious ill and dying, that Georgina went to see her.)

To escape the unhappy atmosphere of Gad's Hill, Katey defied her father and in the summer of 1860 she married Charles Alston Collins, twelve years older than herself. He had some talent as a writer and a pre-Raphaelite painter, and made a few contributions to *All The Year Round.* Dickens suspected that his favourite child had left the house for someone she did not love. Her mother was not invited to the wedding, which must have wounded her deeply.

It was late on the wedding day that Mary found her father sitting and weeping in Katey's room, repeating, "But for me, she would never have left home!"

Dickens at Gad's Hill with Katey, Mamie, HF Chorley,
Charles A Collins, Georgina

On the brighter side, Charley was pleasing
Dickens and doing well in business; while Walter had
proved himself as an officer in the army in India,
especially during the time of the Indian Mutiny. Frank,
who was shy and nervous, was given a job in the

magazine office, although hovering between medicine, the Foreign Office and colonial farming. Sydney and Alfred were at school, the former thinking about a career in the Navy, the latter in the Army. The two youngest boys (Henry and Edward) were at Rochester Grammar School.

The biggest thorns in his side were provided by John Dickens's impecunious genes that lived on in his children, Dickens's brothers.

Fred had turned up at a Reading in Belfast, his marriage to Anna Weller near collapse (as Dickens had foreseen). He was desperate and wanted money. He got some.

Augustus, having deserted his wife and now living in America, also needed money, and so, in turn, did his wife and family. Dickens, once more, handed it out.

His brother Alfred suddenly collapsed in Manchester. Dickens rushed there, but it was too late. He left a widow and five children. Dickens had to provide for them too.

Finally his mother was far from well and needed care.

'My mother, who was also left to me when my father died (I never had anything left to me but relations), is in the strangest state of mind from senile decay; and the impossibility of getting her to understand what is the matter, combined with her desire to be got up in sables like a female Hamlet, illumines the dreary scene with a ghastly absurdity that is the chief relief I can find in it.'

He called on his mother one day and she rallied. 'The instant she saw me, she plucked up spirit, and asked me "for a pound".'

There was one request denied. Maria Winter, whose parents had insisted she marry a young man of substance with a future and not Charles, wrote asking for money, her husband's business having failed. Dickens promptly referred her back to her father (who evidently refused to help!)

In October 1859, he ended with fourteen Readings in the provinces, making 125 over-subscribed and exhausting readings in just over fourteen months. Despite the stress involved, the remuneration Dickens received from the Readings was considerable; and - above all - he loved the adulation.

It was with some relief that Dickens sold Tavistock House and decided to concentrate on a new book. The highly successful *A Tale of Two Cities* had been followed by Collins's *The Woman in White* which was not proving to be so popular and sales of the magazine were declining. In December 1859 he began writing again. Mr Smith had arranged another series of Readings, but Dickens decided to delay the tour until he finished his latest novel.

Chapter 23

Just as the public, and his friends for that matter, were beginning to doubt his ability to produce a memorable novel, Dickens wrote one of his most memorable works, with a young hero who had faults and yet, at the same time, is totally believable. He has the sympathy of the reader from the very beginning.

'My father's name being Pirrip, and my Christian name Philip, my infant tongue could make of both names nothing longer or more explicit than Pip. So, I called myself Pip, and came to be called Pip.

I give Pirrip as my father's family name, on the authority of his tombstone and my sister – Mrs Joe Gargery, who married the blacksmith. As I never saw my father or my mother, and never saw any likeness of either of them (for their days were long before the days of photographs) my first fancies regarding what they were like, were unreasonably derived from their tombstones. The shape of the letters on my father's, gave me an odd idea that he was a square, stout, dark man, with curly black hair. From the character and turn of the inscription, "*Also Georgina Wife of the Above*" I drew a childish conclusion that my mother was freckly and sickly.'

Great Expectations first appeared in *All The Year Round* in 1860-61. Philip Pirrip (the narrator) is 'Pip', brought up by his sister and Joe Gargery, the blacksmith. The book begins (rarely noted however) on Christmas Eve, when Pip is visiting his parent's grave and is seized by the escaped convict Magwitch, for whom he steals food and a file. He is invited to the dusty, neglected house of Miss Havisham, a lady rendered half-crazed by being deserted on her wedding day. She has brought up a haughty young girl, called Estella, to despise and torture men with her beauty. Pip falls for her and, in consequence, has to endure her insults. Unexpectedly he is given money from a mysterious source and is groomed to be a gentleman, now embarrassed by his association with the humble blacksmith, Joe. Estella has married and is cruelly treated by Bentley Drummel. Pip finds the identity of his benefactor, and all his expectations perish as he becomes penniless and disillusioned. Eventually Pip and Estella get together; both having been taught a lesson which has changed their characters for the better.

Dickens had devised a less happy ending, but was persuaded to alter it by Bulwer-Lytton. It is the only weak spot in an excellent story. He had a clear, defined scheme for the work before it began and he read Copperfield to ensure there were no similarities. It is autobiographical in location more than events, yet portrays, in many respects, Dickens outlook on life.

Pip waits on Miss Havisham (by Marcus Stone)

The folly of pretended gentility and ease of manipulation of a human being (Miss Havisham/Estella) (Magwitch/Pip); the potential for money to corrupt, the gentlemanly simplicity of the honest workers (Joe Gargery) - are explored and exposed; while the lack of sub-plot and distracting comic characters all add to the special appeal of this work. Many consider it his finest.

The cold, aloof, tormenting Estella is loosely based, it is agreed, on Ellen Ternan; and probably describes the curious relationship that existed between them. The story closed in June 1861.

By this book, Dickens increased the circulation of *All The year Round* to almost treble that of his former magazine (*Household Words*); while there were other excellent contributor's novels, especially from Wilkie Collins, that strengthened the magazine's sales.

He was a popular editor being described as enjoying 'the fun of the thing'; although it was remarked that, on occasions, 'the very vehemence of his cheery good humour rather bore one down.'

Edmund Yates (son of the actor Frederick Yates) had a quarrel with Thackeray, who took umbrage about an article Yates had written, which was considered sneering in tone. All three were members of the Garrick Club and the Committee decided to examine the facts. Dickens supported Yates (while not approving of what he had done) since he had supported Dickens during the break up with Kate. Rightly or wrongly, Dickens offended Thackeray, who was so angered that he stopped speaking. He felt that Dickens was only orchestrating revenge after the comments on Ellen.

Dickens continued as benefactor to the Ternan family. For the first half of 1861 he had rented a house near Regent's Park to be close to the Ternan family. Although busy with *Great Expectations*, he spent many evenings at their house, playing cards and singing duets with Ellen. He also paid for the oldest sister to study music in Italy (her mother went with her) leaving Maria and Ellen to get occasional work on the stage. Once again, he was incensed when a policeman pestered them, strongly suspecting that the man had 'been suborned to find out details about their domesticity.'

Another tour was planned but Arthur Smith became ill and when Dickens visited him 'his wakings and wanderings so perpetually turn on his arrangements for the Readings, and he is so desperately unwilling to relinquish the idea of "going on with business" tomorrow and tomorrow and tomorrow, that I had not the heart to press him for the papers. He told me that he believed he had by him "seventy or eighty letters unanswered."

Dickens was due to start the Readings but he believed 'that with a sick man who has been so zealous and faithful, I feel bound to be very tender and patient.'

The manager died in October, and the day after the funeral, his brother-in-law, Henry Austin, who had been a wise counsellor on many public questions, also died. These deaths rekindled his depression.

There was a break from the sadness around him. In November 1861 the Readings commenced. But it was the same month that Charley married the daughter of Mr Evans, one half of the firm of Bradbury and Evans, his publisher and printer. Dickens did not approve, having quarrelled with Evans and thus there was further unhappiness heaped upon him.

However, the tour was the usual sell-out. It went from Brighton in the South to Berwick-upon-Tweed, Edinburgh and Glasgow in the North.

We turned away half of Dover and half of Hastings and half of Colchester; and we find 1000 stalls already taken here in Brighton., I left Colchester in a heavy snow storm (* early November) and at Dover they would not go but sat applauding like mad.

In Glasgow (December 1861) there was 'such a pouring of hundreds into a place already full to the throat, such indescribable confusion, such a rending and tearing of dresses, and yet such a scene of good humour on the whole...I read with the platform crammed with people. I got them to lie down upon it, and it was like some impossible tableau or gigantic picnic – one pretty girl, in a full dress, lying on her side all night, holding on to one of the legs of my table. It was the most extraordinary sight.'

One incident occurred in Newcastle-upon-Tyne.

'An extraordinary thing occurred on the second night. The room was tremendously crowded and my gas-apparatus fell down. There was a terrible wave among the people for an instant, and God knows what destruction of life a rush to the stairs would have caused. Fortunately a lady in the front of the stalls ran out towards me, exactly in a place where I knew that the whole hall could see her. So I addressed her, laughing, and half-asked and half-ordered her to sit down again; and, in a moment, it was all over. But the men in attendance had such a fearful sense of what might have happened (besides the real danger of Fire) that they positively shook the boards I stood on, with their trembling, when they came up to put things right.

I am proud to record that the gas-man's sentiment, as delivered afterwards, was "The more you want of the master, the more you'll find in him".

In January 1862 the tour continued in the South until June; Dickens was elated, he was off-setting his bills by up to £200 per night. He was even offered £10,000 to tour Australia. He eventually declined.

The family Christmas at Gad's Hill 1862 included his first grandchild called Mary, the daughter of his eldest son Charley and his wife Elizabeth. Katey and Charles Collins were also there. Mary Boyle, who shared the same sense of humour, found Dickens to be the font of laughter and good humour when "he invariably drew out what was best and most characteristic in others" rather than tell stories about himself. Afterwards there were the usual dances, charades, billiards and punch – which Dickens now took in small quantities because of his ill-health.

He did read abroad in January 1863, taking his daughter and Georgina to Paris for a double reading in the Embassy for the British Charitable Fund. He celebrated his birthday in Arras. He wrote to Forster a short, sad and lonely letter.

'You will remember me today I know. Thanks for it. An odd birthday but I am a little out of heart.'

In the Spring, he rented a house in London so that he could visit Ellen whenever he wished; she was provided with a family cottage in Slough. Georgina, curiously and bowing to the inevitable, made her welcome at Gad's Hill. Mamie and Katey were resigned to the situation but the latter was often distinctly unhappy about it; and Katey's outspokenness often caused an occasional emotional wave in her father.

She said that "Ellen flattered him – he was ever appreciative of praise – and though she was not a good actress, she had brains, which she used to educate herself, to bring her mind more on a level with his own. Who could blame her? He had the world at his feet. She was a young girl of eighteen, elated and proud to be noticed by him. I do not blame her. It is never one person's fault." Katey did state in later life that all was not well between her father and Ellen at times, and she believed that the relationship was 'more tragic and far-reaching in its effect' than the romance of Lord Nelson and Lady Hamilton.

In September 1863 his mother died after two years of ill-health. She never knew of the recent turmoil in her famous son's life. Then there was another blow. It was the sudden death of Thackeray on Christmas Eve, 1863. Katey had produced reconciliation between them just a few days earlier, when Thackeray declared, 'I love the man'. They had greeted each other warmly at their last meeting. Although never a person to be contrite and always slow to forgive, Dickens always enjoyed Thackeray's larger than life attitude, and admired his humour and literary skills. In earlier times they had regularly enjoyed each other's boisterous company. He was very upset.

But the worst blow was to come.

On his birthday in February 1864 he received news of Walter's death in the Military Hospital in Calcutta. Dickens had been proud of his second son and recalled, as he had written to his godfather Walter Savage Landor, 'Walter is a very good boy, and comes home from school with honourable commendations and a prize in the bargain. He never gets into trouble, for he is a great favourite with the whole house and one of the most amiable boys in the boy-world.'

Dickens must have felt his once-happy-world was falling apart around him. There was no other option but to immerse himself in a new book.

Chapter 25

Mamie and Katey at Gad's Hill in 1865. Often disappointed with his sons' progress in life, he adored the two girls.

Our Mutual Friend is essentially the last Dickens novel, written between May 1864 and November 1865. Once again his friends and readers found it forced, but it later gained critical acclaim. He had chosen the title and the plot, four years before he began.

Our Mutual Friend is a parable of failures and the corruption money can bring in a superficial society. John Harmon has returned from a separation with his rich, dustman father who has made his money out of mountains of ash piled up at Battle Bridge, North London. He will only give his son an inheritance providing he marries Bella Wilfer, but they do not know each other. Thus John conceals his identity to find out if he could love her. He confides in a ship's mate who tries to murder him, throwing his senseless body into the river. However, the mate is found dead and, with John's papers on him, is mistaken for Harmon. Under the assumed name of John Rokesmith he becomes the secretary of the greedy Mr Boffin, who has inherited the Harmon fortune.

Bella meets the secretary, John Rokesmith (really John Harmon) with his employer, Mr Boffin – the golden dustman

The Boffins have brought up Bella. She is beautiful, mercenary and arrogant in her wealth. 'Rokesmith' falls in love with her, nonetheless. Although dismissed by Boffin, Bella follows 'Rokesmith', realises she loves him and they marry. Then John reveals his true identity.

Parallel to this story is the love of Lizzie Hexham (the daughter of a boatman who trawls up the drowned) and Eugene Wrayburn, a lackadaisical young lawyer, whom a rival suitor attempts to murder. But he is saved from drowning by Lizzie.

The nouveau riche snobs - the Veneerings (brand new, like the furniture and carriages –shining with varnish); the Lammles who marry - each one believing the other has wealth; Rogue Riderhood - the waterside villain; Jenny Wren –the dolls' dressmaker who has psychic properties; and (for once) a refreshingly genuine heroine in Bella who has weaknesses, - are all on par with any previous Dickens characters.

Mr and Mrs Lammle – The Happy Pair (They have fooled each other, neither has any money).

The author had seen many dead bodies pulled from the Thames by men who made their living by

354

robbing corpses, and this horrendous trade is part of the central theme. The ash-heaps are the other. They were a strange, but valid, source of wealth at that time – which Dickens used in a dirt/money paradox

The View of a Dust Yard (from Mayhew's *London Labour and the London Poor*); men and women hunting for scraps while the proprietors grew wealthy.

Kate wrote to Chapman and Hall and asked them to send her the monthly instalments; a sad and touching indication as to how far their estrangement had progressed.

Sales and criticism were on the whole good, and Dickens was more than pleased with the new work. But there were dark shadows on the horizon. Insidiously at first, his health began to fail.

As always an optimist, and certainly never a neurotic, when he began to experience lameness in his left foot (which partially curtailed his walking) he felt it was but a passing phase. But this problem was never to leave him, although in France he wrote to Mamie, 'before I went away, I had certainly worked myself into a damaged state. But the moment I got away, I began, thank God, to get well.'

There was another major set-back; one which his close friends believe precipitated a sudden and serious decline in health.

On the 9th of June 1865 he was involved in a serious rail crash at Staplehurst.

He had boarded, with Ellen and her mother, the Folkestone to London train, having crossed the channel from Boulogne. The train approached a viaduct which was under repair and construction. Two of the rails had been lifted off and laid at the side of the track. It was a downhill gradient and the train had reached fifty miles per hour. The foreman in charge had looked incorrectly at the timetable and did not expect a train for two hours. The man with the red flag was thus unprepared, and although he hastily tried to stop the train, it was too late. The guard applied the brakes, but the engine jumped the gap and swerved, throwing the central and rear carriages from the bridge into the river below. Six of the seven first class carriages plummeted over the edge except the seventh, containing Dickens and the Ternans. Their carriage was angling over the side of the bridge. Everyone was thrown into the lowest corner. Dickens reassured the Ternans (Ellen was screaming and Mrs Ternan yelling "my God!") and told them to remain calm. He shouted for help and they were pulled out.

When Dickens saw the injured, however, he climbed in and retrieved his flask of brandy and his top hat. He used his hat to carry water from the river and bathe the injured, as well as administering brandy. Sadly one man died as he was being helped. Another passenger, a woman propped up against a tree, he tried to help, but she also died. An injured man asked Dickens about his new wife and had to be told the dreadful news that she had been killed.

In the midst of all the carnage, Dickens had forgotten about his manuscript. There was nothing for it. He had to risk climbing back in, when he had the chance, as the dangling carriage swayed to and fro. Despite the danger; he cautiously entered and retrieved the papers from his overcoat pocket.

'No imagination can conceive the ruin,' he wrote later, and although 'not in the least flustered at the time' as he retrieved his work, he 'felt quite shattered and broken up' when he got back to London. He was shaken 'not by the beating of the carriage, but by the work afterwards of getting out the dying and the dead.'

He requested not to be a witness at the inquest (to conceal his travelling companions) and wrote to the Charing Cross stationmaster to ask if a gold watch-chain and key, some charms and a seal engraved 'Ellen' had been found.

There are no contemporary accounts of her injuries although she did suffer left arm pain later in life and Dickens, initially, sent his servant to buy a basket of special delicacies 'for Miss Ellen'.

He also took an interest in the recovery of the injured, especially a young man named Dickenson, whom he not only visited at Charing Cross Hospital but invited to Gad's Hill when the man had recovered. The railway company sent Dickens an engraved plate in gratitude for his heroism and exemplary conduct.

The accident was to affect him permanently, both physically and mentally. By one of those strange quirks of fate, Turk, a mastiff and his favourite dog, was killed by a train shortly after the Staplehurst catastrophe. The dog dying in this way, only added to his grief. It cemented a deep seated fear of trains which was to torment him in his future travel.

Charles Dickens helps the injured at the Staplehurst railway accident, 9th June 1865.

In the autumn his left foot began to trouble him more and more, and he suffered what would be called to-day, flash-backs and post traumatic symptoms. Even in 1867 he wrote, 'I have sudden vague rushes of terror, even when riding in a hansom cab, which are perfectly unreasonable but quite insurmountable'

He must have known that further Readings would be injurious to his health. His life seemed relatively empty and he was driven to begin again. At the same time, he had to overcome the anxieties and apprehensions about travelling.

Dickens reading in his garden at Gad's Hill (it is believed to be taken circa 1866).

In February 1866 he confided in Forster, 'For some time I have been very unwell. Dr Beard wrote me word that with such a pulse as I described, an examination of the heart was absolutely necessary...Of course I am not so foolish as to suppose that all my work can have been achieved without *some* penalty, and I have noticed for some time a decided change in my buoyancy and, hopefulness – in other words in my usual "tone". But tonics have brought me round.' Forster must have blanched at the next statement, 'So I have accepted an offer from Chappell of Bond Street, of £50 a night for thirty nights to read in England, Ireland, Scotland, or Paris.'

In fairness to the firm, they had decided to employ people to arrange everything, so that all Dickens had to do was read. But the sheer distance by train and the fatigue involved, certainly worried Forster

Dickens, however, was up-beat.

'As to the readings,' he recorded on the 11th of March 1866, 'all I have to do is, to take in my book and read, at the appointed place and hour, and to come out again. For this they pay £1500 in three sums: £500 on beginning, £500 on the fifteenth Reading, £500 at the close.'

The tour was the brilliant success of old. 'The police reported officially,' he wrote to Mamie on the 14th of April from Liverpool, 'that three thousand people were turned away…Except that I cannot sleep. A dozen oysters and a little champagne between the parts every night seem to constitute the best restorative I have ever yet tried.' 'Such a prodigious demonstration last night at Manchester that I was obliged (contrary to my principle) to go back. I am very tired today.'

He confided in a letter to Georgina in May, 'It has been very heavy work, getting up at 6.30 each morning after a heavy night, and I am not at all well today.'

'We had a tremendous hall at Birmingham last night, £230 odd, 2100 people; and I made a most ridiculous mistake. Had *Nickleby* on my list to finish with, instead of *Trial* . Read *Nickleby* with great go, *and the people remained*. Went back again at 10 o'clock, and explained the accident; but said if they liked I would give them the *Trial (*Pickwick)*. They *did* like; - and I had another half hour of it, in that enormous place… I have so severe pain in the ball of my left eye that it makes it hard for me to do anything

360

after a hundred miles shaking (*rail) since breakfast. My cold is no better, nor my hand either.'

Another incident occurred when a hanging-wire supporting a gas lamp was burning through and threatened the stalls. Dolby, who was hidden behind a screen, whispered "How long shall you be?" "Not long!" Dickens, without pausing, had noticed the possible danger. With a rapid improvisation he concluded the reading, and no one was any the wiser as they safely left the Hall.

The company travelled as far north as Aberdeen, toured Scotland and had numerous English provincial engagements A valet accompanied him and, with Dolby, they attended to his every need, making the journeys 'as easy to me as it possibly can be.' But Dickens lay awake at night and tossed and turned, with only his determination keeping him going through the endless fatigue.

Whilst on tour Mrs Carlyle, one of his all time favourite woman, who amused him greatly by her wit, cheerfulness and charm, died. 'It was a terrible shock to me, and poor dear Carlyle has been on my mind ever since.'

Forster wrote 'that no one who knew Mrs Carlyle could replace her loss when she had passed away.'

The Readings ended in June. By now Dickens was utterly exhausted and the news of Stanfield's death saddened him more. He was elated by the tour's success but eager to spend some time at home.

'I came back last Sunday with my last country piece of work for this time done. Everywhere the success has been the same. I have only been able to get to Gad's Hill once since I left it, and that was the day before yesterday.'

Meanwhile Kate had been getting on with her own social life, visiting the children who still lived in England. However, Mamie still steadfastly refused to see her. Katey was the opposite. At her mother's request she agreed never to discuss her father; although on one occasion Kate produced an old photograph and asked her daughter, "Do you think he is sorry for me?"

Kate also kept in contact with many of her husband's former friends. She went to the theatre regularly, sometimes with those friends but usually with her sister Helen. On one unfortunate evening her estranged husband arrived and sat in a box opposite. She suddenly burst into tears and her grief provoked the friend who was with her to say, "That man is a brute!" After some thought and with mounting apprehension she plucked up courage to write and intimate that one day he might care to visit her. Without any thought on the matter, Dickens asked Georgina to reply and rebuff the suggestion – which Georgina willingly did.

Chappell pressed for more Readings and immediately accepted Dickens's offer of forty two nights for £2500. However, in September 1866, all was not well, I think there is some strange influence in the atmosphere. Twice last week I was seized in a most distressing manner – apparently in the heart; but I am persuaded, only in the nervous system.

I start on Wednesday afternoon (the 15th of January) for Liverpool, and then go on to Chester, Derby, Leicester and Wolverhampton. On Tuesday the 29th I read in London again, and in February I read at Manchester and then go on into Scotland.

The Readings were taxing his health although he would not admit it. The first alarming signs came in January 1867.

'On Friday night I quite astonished myself,' he informed a worried Forster; 'but I was taken so faint afterwards that they laid me on a sofa at the hall for half an hour. I attribute it to my distressing inability to sleep at night, and to nothing else.'

And so the exhausting tour went on all over England, with the daily complaint of being tired and unable to sleep. The travelling conditions were awful - in cold, damp, rattling trains. At Chester there was a blizzard of snow, 'I think it was the worst weather I ever saw'. At Wolverhampton the thaw set in and 'it rained furiously and I was again heavily beaten.' But he was so tired 'it was as much as I could do to hold out the journey. But I was not faint as at Liverpool. I was only exhausted.' To an invitation from Macready to dine at their house he wrote, 'I am very tired; cannot sleep; have been severely shaken on atrocious railways; read tonight and have to read at Leeds on Thursday. But I have settled with Dolby to put it off in the hope of coming to dine with you, and seeing our dear old friend. I say "in the hope" because if I should be a little more used up tomorrow than I am today, I should be constrained, in spite of myself, to take to the sofa and stick there.'

He wrote to Georgina. In February 1867 'I am not quite right within, but believe it to be an effect of the railway shaking. There is no doubt of the fact that, after the Staplehurst experience, it tells more and more (railway shaking, that is) instead of, as one might have expected, less and less.'

Forster did not accept the railway accident as the root of the problem. He felt that Dickens 'for a man of his sagacity...it was part of the too willing self-deception which he practised...that the continued excess of labour and excitement were doing him no harm.'

From Scotland (February), he returned via a Manchester Reading where the cheering was enormous. 'After a heavy week, it was rather stiff to start on this long journey at a quarter to two in the morning; but I got more sleep than I have ever got in a railway carriage before.'

He was off to Belfast and Dublin in March, and by May he had 'completed the 50th reading with great success.'

America, however, was beckoning. 'Every mail brings me proposals, and the number of Americans at St James's Hall has been surprising.

There was one problem, Ellen. He spent some time in the summer of 1867 searching for a new home for Ellen and her mother. Slough was inconvenient and he had a high profile there. So Dickens searched the neighbourhood near the Five Bells inn in New Cross where he often stayed. A house, Linden Grove, Peckham, was found within twenty minutes walk and he paid the rates for it under an assumed name of Charles Tringham. However, there is no evidence that he ever stayed there. He still believed that Ellen might accompany him, even as a companion to Mamie. His daughter was lukewarm about this proposal and it appears that Ellen's sister Fanny also had even greater misgivings for a variety of reasons, including the fact that she and her husband might be materially affected by the scandal if it leaked out (they lived in Florence at the time in a prosperous expatriate community).

Dolby sails to America on the 3rd August. It is impossible to come to any reasonable conclusion, without sending eyes and ears on the actual ground.

I am laid up with another attack in my foot, and was on the sofa all last night in torture. Henry Thompson says that there is no doubt the complaint originates in the action of the show, in walking, on an enlargement in the nature of a bunion. Erysipelas has supervened upon the injury; and the object is to avoid a gathering... I am on my back, and chafing (* erysipelas, an infection due to the Streptococcus bacillus, could be fatal then if it spread to the blood stream).'

Dolby's reports were favourable. In September the agent decided that an American trip would be feasible and lucrative. The profit could exceed £15000. Dolby was also to consult with James Fields (Dickens's publisher in Boston) as to whether there would be any resentment if Ellen came. The telegram came and was a resounding "No!" to her travelling with him. Yet, even at this late stage Dickens was hopeful. A coded message from Ellen in Florence gave the final answer. She would not be coming.

There was a farewell dinner crammed with celebrities, the Grenadier Guards' Band played, the applause was enthusiastic, and Dickens left the room with the usual tears trickling down his cheek. Kate wrote to wish him well and he replied in a gracious manner. 'I am glad to receive your letter, and to accept and reciprocate your good wishes.' On the 9th of November 1867 Charles Dickens sailed once more for Boston.

Chapter 26

Dickens arrived in Boston on 19th November. 'Even in England,' boasted one of the New York papers, 'Dickens is less known than here; and of the millions here who treasure every word he has written, there are tens of thousands who would make a large sacrifice to see and hear the man who has made happy so many hours.'

Boston had grown, but the old hand of friendship was still there. Previous disputes had been forgotten and, unlike the first visit with Kate, every attention was given to comfort and etiquette - they made a determined effort not to intrude in his privacy. Many of his former friends had died, but the younger authors and artists were equally thrilled to see him. Dickens was also delighted to meet his old friend who had been his secretary on the first trip. One of Dickens's first tasks was to arrange and pay for *The Old Curiosity Shop* to be printed in Braille for the blind of Boston. Mary Boyle, amazingly, managed to keep up the supply of flowers for his button-hole. Such was the enthusiasm that Dickens felt confident of success as the first day approached. He was gambling with his health but felt fine after the three week period of rest.

The opening Reading was in Boston on the 2nd of December; tickets had been rapidly sold out. An immense train of people waited in the freezing street for twelve hours. Dickens had worried that some of the previous animosity and misgivings might remain but the greeting as he entered the room was extraordinarily warm.

Several more Boston lectures followed. 'The young undergraduates of Cambridge (Massachusetts) have made a representation to Longfellow that they are 500 strong and cannot get one ticket. I don't know what is to be done, but I suppose I must read there somehow,' he wrote to Georgina.

So he moved on to New York. At the New York barriers,' he wrote to his daughters, 'where the tickets were on sale…speculators went up and down offering twenty dollars for anybody's place. The money was in no case selected.'

Dickens–mania was at its height. People queued overnight in freezing temperatures. One witness described the scene to a newspaper: 'The pay-place was to open at nine on a Wednesday morning. At midnight on Tuesday a long line of speculators were assembled in queues. At eight there were at least 5000 and at nine each line was more than three quarters of a mile in length'.

Dickens noted that, 'Members of families relieved each other in the queues; waiters flew across the streets and squares from the neighbouring restaurant, to serve parties who were taking their breakfast in the open December air; while excited men offered five and ten dollars for the mere permission to exchange placcs with other persons standing nearer the head of the line!'

'Amazing success, 'he wrote home, 'a fine audience far better than Boston.'

On the 15th a cheerful Dickens sent £3000 to England for banking.

'We go to Boston next Saturday for two more readings and come back here (* New York) on Christmas Day for four more. I am not yet bound to go elsewhere, except three times (for two nights) to Philadelphia. I have had an action brought against me by a man who considered himself injured (and really may have been) in the matter of the tickets. The action was handsomely withdrawn next day, and the plaintiff paid his own costs.'

(*Considering that Christmas had been such a focal point in his year, it typifies the emptiness of home life that Dickens would arrange to be away from his family during the festive season. No doubt he remembered with nostalgia the games, the carols, the punch, the parties, the plays and the merriment; the walks with Forster on Christmas Eve along Aldgate to Bow to see the market stalls - all full of everything that was festive -, and, especially their time together on Christmas Day, when they strolled amongst the poorer people of Somers or Kentish Town – a ritual that extended into many years).

Dickens in 1867: the most famous celebrity face in the World. (Photographs did not catch his humour or laughter. The long exposure time – which could be minutes – made the stern Victorian expression, the only one that could be kept up.)

He wrote to Ellen six times in December and in a letter to Wills said that 'my spirits flutter woefully towards a certain place at which you dined one day not long before I left…I would give £3000 down (and think it cheap) if you could forward me, for four and twenty hours only, instead of the letter.'

Dolby noted a marked depression developing at this stage of the tour. He also noted what Dickens described his reserve of strength as the Reading approached. 'The frequent experience of this return of force when it is wanted saves me a vast amount of anxiety, but I am not at times without the nervous dread that I may some day sink altogether.'

While staying at the Westminster Hotel in Irving Place, New York, he wrote to Georgina, 'Last night I was getting into bed just at 12 o'clock when Dolby came to my door to inform me that the house was on fire. I got Scott (*his dresser) up directly; told him first to pack the books and the clothes for the Readings; dressed, and pocketed my jewels and papers; while the manager stuffed himself out with money. Meanwhile the police and firemen were in the house tracing the mischief to its source in a certain fire-grate. By this time the hose was laid all through from a great tank on the roof, and everybody turned out to help. It was the oddest sight, people had put the strangest things on! After chopping and cutting with axes through the stairs, and much handling about of water, the fire was confined to a dining room in which it had originated; and then everybody talked to everybody else, the ladies being quite loquacious and cheerful. I may remark that the second landlord (from both, but especially the first, I have had untiring attention) no sooner saw me on this agitating occasion, than, with his property blazing, he insisted on taking me down into a room full of hot smoke, to drink brandy and water with him! And so we got to bed again about 2.'

As he surveyed New York, he found it had changed greatly only recognising the Broadway area. Then a ferocious blizzard struck the city, more severe than usually experienced. The railways were closed for days, with snow piled up in enormous walls and sleighs dashed and jingled to and fro.

'I turned out in a rather gorgeous sleigh yesterday with any quantity of buffalo robes.'

Once the transport system got running again, they were off on the tour.

'The railways are truly alarming. Much worse (because more worn I suppose) than when I was here before. We were beaten about yesterday...two rivers have to be crossed, and each time the whole train is banged aboard a big steamer. The steamer rises and falls with the river, which the railroads don't do; and the train is either banged up hill or banged down hill. In coming off the steamer at one of these crossings yesterday, we were banged up such a height that the rope broke, and one carriage rushed back with a run down hill into the boat again. I whisked out in a moment, and two or three others after me; but nobody else seemed to care about it.

The treatment of the luggage is perfectly outrageous. Nearly every case I have is already broken.'

However, the hospitality in Boston touched him when he arrived back – his room being given a homely look for Christmas with flowers garnished by holly, rich in red berries; and, at great effort and expense, the management had purchased mistletoe from a Cunard vessel. It adorned his table as he came down for breakfast.

'In such affectionate touches as this, these New England people are especially amiable.

'Our hotel in New York was on fire again the other night. But fires in this country are quite a matter of course. There was a large one in Boston at four this morning; and I don't think a single night has passed…that I have not heard the Fire bells dolefully clanging all over both cities.'

He read at Boston on the 23rd and 24th of December, and travelled to New York on Christmas Day. He wasn't feeling well and probably low in spirit. He had a heavy cold. The train journey was dreary and, as usual, nerve-wracking for Dickens.

The low action of the heart, or whatever it is, has inconvenienced me greatly this week. On Monday night, after the reading, I was laid upon the bed, in a very faint and shady state; and on Tuesday I did not get up till the afternoon.

When he arrived in New York on the evening of Christmas Day he found a letter from his daughters. 'I wanted it much, for I had a frightful cold (English colds are nothing to those of this country) and was very miserable. It is a bad country to be unwell in. You are one of, say, a hundred people in a heated car (*train) with a great stove in it, all the little windows being closed; and the bumping and banging about are indescribable, the atmosphere detestable, the ordinary motion all but intolerable. I managed to read last night, but it was as much as I could do. Today I am so very unwell that I have sent for a doctor.' He was advised that he might have to stop reading for a while, but decided to carry on.

A week later he wrote to Georgina. 'My cold sticks to me, and I can scarcely exaggerate what I undergo from sleeplessness. I rarely take any breakfast but an egg and a cup of tea – not even toast or bread and butter. My small dinner at 3, and a little quail or some such light thing when I come home at night, is my daily fare; and at the hall I have established the custom of taking an egg beaten up in sherry before going in, and another between the parts, which I think pulls me up. It is snowing hard now, and I begin to move tomorrow.'

The party left for Philadelphia on January 12th 1868.

Dickens had so enjoyed his time in New York.

'I have now read in New York City to 40,000 people, and I am quite as well known in the street there as I am in London. People will turn back, turn again and face me, and have a look at me, or will say to one another "Look here! Dickens coming!" But no one ever stops me or addresses me. Sitting reading in the carriage outside the New York Post Office while one of the staff was stamping the letters inside, I became conscious that a few people who had been looking at the turn-out had discovered me within. On my peeping out good-humouredly, one of them stepped up to the door, took off his hat, and said in a frank way: "Mr Dickens, I should very much like to have the honour of shaking hands with you" – and that done, presented two others. Nothing could be more quiet or less intrusive. In the railway cars, if I see anybody who clearly wants to speak to me, I usually anticipate the wish by speaking myself.'

A further £10,000 was sent to Coutts's bank from Philadelphia. On they went to Baltimore and Washington, but Dickens eschewed travelling all the way to Chicago.

"Good heavens, sir," the great Philadelphia authority said to me this morning, "if you don't read in Chicago the people will go into fits!" "Well," I answered, I would rather they went into fits than I did." But he didn't seem to see it at all.'

The Chicago press had a field day saying that the people were being slighted and only because Dickens did not want to meet his brother's family who lived there. (Augustus had died in1866 and Dickens was, as usual, supporting them.) He did not reply.

There was an amusing episode on one train journey which appealed to Dickens. Dolby reported that 'there was also a small girl who suddenly sat next to him on a train. "God bless my soul," he said, "where did you come from?" She told him how much she liked his books. "Of course," she added, "I do skip some of the very dull parts once in a while; not the short dull parts, but the long ones." Then he took out a notebook and pencil in order to question her about what he called his "long thick books."

He also heard in Washington the story of Abraham Lincoln's dream and premonition before the assassination. He listened transfixed and was to repeat the tale many times afterwards. He loved such strange and almost spiritual coincidences.

On his birthday, his room was filled with flowers. In addition, Dickens had an invitation from the President, Andrew Johnson. Dickens, who initially thought that 'each of us looked at the other very hard,' liked him saying that 'he is a man with a remarkable face, indicating courage, watchfulness, and certainly a strength of purpose. I would have picked him out anywhere as a character of mark.'

As usual Dickens sense of the ridiculous came forth in a letter to Mamie from Washington.

'In the *Carol* a most ridiculous incident occurred. All of a sudden, I saw a dog leap out from among the seats in the centre aisle, and look very intently at me. The general attention being fixed on me, I don't think anybody saw this dog; but I felt so sure of his turning up again and barking, that I kept my eye wandering about in search of him. He was a very comic dog, and it was well for me that I was reading a comic part of the book. But when he bounced out into the centre aisle again, in an entirely new place, and (still looking intently at me) tried the effect of a bark upon my proceedings, I was seized with such a paroxysm of laughter that it communicated itself to the audience, and we roared at one another, loud and long.

Next night I thought I heard (in *Copperfield*) a suddenly-suppressed bark...one of our people instantly caught him up in both hands...and threw him into the entry where the check-takers received him like a game at ball. Last night he came again *with another dog*; but our people were so sharply on the look-out for him that he didn't get in. He evidently promised to pass the other dog, free.'

So the Cities continued throughout February and into March, with the weather at times varying between severe to atrocious...Baltimore, Newhaven, Providence, with stops at Syracuse, Buffalo and then onwards to Niagara Falls - a stop which greatly excited him. However, throughout the preceding days, Dickens was worried that the impeachment of

President Johnson would damage the tour, but it had no effect.

And Dickens's spirit was unflagging.

'It is necessary to the daily recovery of my voice that I should dine at 3 when not travelling; I begin to prepare at 6; and I get back to my hotel pretty well knocked-up, at half-past ten. Add to all this, perpetual railway travelling in one of the severest winters ever known.

Last Sunday evening I left the Falls of Niagara…as there was great thaw, and the melted snow was swelling all the rivers, the whole country for three hundred miles was flooded. On the Tuesday afternoon the train gave in, as under circumstances utterly hopeless, and stopped at a place called Utica; the greater part of which was under water, while the high and dry part could produce nothing particular to eat. Here, some of the wretched passengers passed the night in the train, while others stormed the hotel. I was fortunate enough to get a bedroom, and garnished it with an enormous jug of ginger punch; over which I and the manager played a double-dummy rubber. At six in the morning we were knocked up: "to come aboard and try it." At half-past six we were knocked up again with the tidings "that it was of no use coming aboard or trying it". At eight all the bells in the town were set agoing, to summon us to "come aboard" instantly. As we started, through the water, at four or five miles an hour; seeing nothing but drowned farms, barns adrift like Noah's arks, deserted villages, broken bridges, and all manner of ruin. I was to read at Albany that night, and all the tickets were sold. A very active superintendent of works assured me that if I could be "got along" he was the man to get me along…he then turned on a hundred men in seven-league boots, who went ahead of the train, each armed with a long pole and pushing the blocks of ice away. Following this cavalcade, we got to land at last, and arrived in time for me to read *Carol* and *Trial* triumphantly.'

Springfield, Portland, New Bedford, and other places in Massachusetts, followed. In Boston the sleeplessness and fatigue were becoming unbearable, and he was pleased he did not have to continue into May – 'I think I might have broken down. It is well that I cut off the Far West and Canada when I did.'

Once again he caught a severe cold. 'I have coughed from two or three in the morning until five or six, and have been absolutely sleepless. I have had no appetite besides, and no taste. Last night I took some laudanum, and it is the only thing that has done me any good...I am nearly used up.' Dolby was 'as tender as a woman' and Doctor Barker supervised each day's diet and medication. His diet was, at seven in the morning, in bed, a tumbler of cream with two tablespoons of rum; at twelve, a sherry cobbler and biscuit; at three a pint of champagne. Just before eight, an egg beaten up with a glass of sherry; between the parts beef tea, and at quarter past ten soup and a drink.

On the 3rd of April he recorded in Massachusetts, 'Catarrh worse than ever! And we don't know (at four o'clock) whether I can read tonight.'

On the 7th Longfellow and Fields urged him to cancel that night's reading, but biscuits, sherry and a pint of champagne revived his spirits.

However he was able to write to Mamie from Boston on the 9th of April, the day before his farewell night, 'I not only read last Friday when I was doubtful of being able to do so, but read as I never did before, and astonished the audience quite as much as myself.'

He returned to New York with a severe attack of gout. There was a farewell dinner on the 18th of April. A newspaper reported, 'At about five o'clock on Saturday the hosts began to assemble, but at 5.30, news was received that the expected guest had succumbed to a painful affection of the foot. In a short time, however, another bulletin announced Mr Dickens's intention to attend the dinner at all hazards. At a little after six, having been assisted up the stairs, he was joined by Mr Greeley, and the hosts forming into two lines silently permitted the distinguished gentleman to pass through. Mr Dickens limped perceptibly; his right foot was swathed, and he leaned heavily on the arm of Mr Greeley. He evidently suffered great pain.'

He spoke eloquently and sincerely about the great changes he had seen, the great improvements he had witnessed and promised that in future *American Notes* and *Chuzzlewit* would not be issued without an accompanying mention of the changes he had referred to that night.

He left before the proceedings ended. The following evening he told his last American audience that 'he hoped often to recall them, equally by his winter fire and in the green summer weather, and never as a mere public audience but as a host of friends.'

The applause was tumultuous and overwhelming and continued for many minutes; America had taken Dickens to its heart, as he had for them. He had given seventy-six readings against all the odds. Crowds lined the quayside to see him off, waving and throwing garlands of flowers.

Once more triumphant, he reached home in the first week of May 1868.

Chapter 27

Dickens arrived home in high spirits.

'My doctor was quite broken down in spirits on seeing me for the first time,' he joked, '*Good God*! *Seven years younger*!'

He had dined in Liverpool with Dolby before setting off for London the following day. He first of all visited the Ternans at Peckham; Ellen and her mother having returned from Italy. He stayed a week, visiting London, to catch up with the dramatic version of *No Thoroughfare* at the Adelphi, which was a critical and financial success with over one hundred and fifty performances. He consulted his friend, the actor Fechter about its chances of success in Paris. Fechter was optimistic and borrowed two thousand pounds off Dickens, on the strength of it.

On the 9th of May he went to Gad's Hill. Georgina and Mamie had warned him, while at Peckham, of the welcome awaiting him. His route home was lined with bunting and cheering crowds. He was back in his own familiar surroundings, walking his dogs in a countryside he loved and writing, 'I feel the peace of the countryside beyond all expression.'

And he had new animal friends.

Dickens had always been ambiguous towards cats; his love of birds led him to be so, but this was a change in circumstances that delighted him.

Willamina arrived, having been given to Georgina, as a pretty white kitten. She became devoted to Dickens. When she had kittens in his study, he let them frolic there and when fully grown found them a home, that is, apart from a deaf kitten which he kept. It was called 'the Master's Cat.' Always alarmed that it should loose his master, this kitten would follow inches behind him, like a dog, and spend the day watching him at work.

Willamina: Dickens's cat – late in his life
he became a cat-lover.

But the cats did not usurp his love of dogs (generally large and, by their nature, obviously devoted).

Mrs Bouncer was a white Pomeranian belonging to Mamie, but Dickens spoiled her too, Georgina recalled how 'he was very kind and sweet to her.' (* while touring America Dickens said he dreamed of Bouncer every night). A great favourite was Linda, a St Bernard, who was the most effusive when he returned, 'greatly excited, weeping profusely, and throwing herself on her back that she might caress my foot with her great forepaws.' Mamie recorded 'that she was soft-eyed, gentle and good tempered (*she was kept to keep the vagrants out, who roamed the Dover Road past their house)

Sir Edwin Landseer's only drawing for Dickens, the ferocious dog guarding Dickens's case bears no resemblance to any pet he ever owned.

He went to Paris in May 1868 for the opening of *No Thoroughfare* but was so apprehensive that he sat in a nearby cafe, and caught the early Boulogne train to be home at Gad's Hill the next day. The play, not seen by Dickens, was a huge success.

He was working hard on the magazine, Mondays to Thursdays in London, more so since Wills, the magazines business manager, had fallen from a horse while hunting, and suffered a head injury which kept him out of the office for several months. Dickens also received news that Charles Collins was seriously ill with a stomach cancer (*he lived until 1873). Dickens had resented Collins from the moment he married Katey, often (as Georgina related) ruminating on his daughter's 'dreary unfortunate fate'. Collins was feeble with vomiting and could not leave his room at Gad's Hill. Dickens, for once, showed little compassion and brother Wilkie (Collins) was annoyed. A rift developed between the erstwhile friends and never recovered.

The Ternans were on the move, ending up in Vauxhall Bridge Road after a spell at Worthing. Dickens kept on the Peckham house for a while, and although Ellen accompanied him on his next tour, he no longer lived near (or even with) Ellen.

One of the few surviving photographs
of Ellen Ternan

Dickens felt saddened, either by this relationship or just life in general. During this period Edward ('Plorn') decided to go Australia (to join brother, Alfred), encouraged by his father who noted a lack of determination and application. He left in September 1868. It was a parting that deeply upset Dickens. 'These partings are hard, hard things, but they are the lot of us all.'

Henry reported that his father, "openly gave way to his intense grief" when he took leave of Edward on Paddington Station. Kate also wrote to her son 'I miss you most sadly, my own darling Plorn.' Henry was planning to go to Trinity Hall, Cambridge, and when he won a scholarship the following year, his father was elated.

While in America Dickens had toyed with the idea of a farewell tour in Britain.

'I told the Chappells that when I got back to England, I would have a series of farewell readings in town and country; and then read No More. They at once offered... for a series of 75, six thousand pounds.'

Dickens, in his usual expansive manner, decided that he would do one hundred. Forster, who knew him better than anyone, said that it was not for the money, for 'no man could care essentially less for mere money than he did. However, the necessary provision for many sons was a constant anxiety. It was an opportunity offered for making a particular work really complete before he should abandon it for ever.'

His plan was to make £33,000 in two years from the readings in America and Britain – an amazing sum when one to two hundred pounds a year was an above average working wage (it is worth noting that Nicholas Nickleby had been offered £12 in 1838).

His friends had observed, as the effects of the restful sea voyage had worn off, 'a loss of elasticity of bearing and the wonderful brightness of eye was dimmed at times.'

One day while walking to Forster's house for a meal with Georgina, he suddenly found that he could only read the right half of some letters above a shop doorway. His other foot had become lame, though not as bad as in America.

The Readings were to begin in October 1868 and Dickens began to realise that he would have to conjure up all his reserves of energy to carry him through.

He now made up his mind to raise the stakes.

'I have made a short reading of the murder in *Oliver Twist*, I cannot make up my mind, however, whether to do it or not. I have no doubt that I could perfectly petrify an audience.'

And petrify the audience, he did!

'At Clifton we had a contagion of fainting,'. he told Mamie early in the New Year. 'and yet the place was not hot. I should think we had from a dozen to twenty ladies taken out stiff and rigid, at various times! It became quite ridiculous!

Macready is of the opinion that the Murder is two Macbeths. He declares that he heard every word of the reading, but I doubt it. Alas! He is sadly infirm'

But the exertion was immense. The days after the Readings, he informed Georgina, he had to lie on the sofa all day. And distant journeys, such as Edinburgh, were interspersed with long trips back to London, which also exhausted him.

There were at times glimpses of the old Dickens, Dolby reports him laughing uproariously at parts of *The Old Curiosity Shop* "as if he had never seen it before." Dickens said that it was not his words but the incidents surrounding the writing, he could happily recall (* it was a time, of course, when he lived and entertained with Kate).

On October 24th 1868, the last of his surviving bothers, Frederick, died in Darlington. He succumbed from a lung abscess which burst. He was the younger brother Dickens had taken with him into lodgings; he always felt close to Fred, but was continually worried about his improvidence and irresponsibility.

'He had been tended with the greatest care and affection by some local friends. It was a wasted life, but God forbid that one should be hard upon it, or upon anything in this world that is not deliberate and coldly wrong.'

Georgina in old age, Dickens increasingly corresponded with her. She cared for his family until the end.

Towards the end of 1868 Dolby tried to dissuade him from using the murder scene too often. Dickens, tense and anxious through ill-health, smashed a plate with his knife; then collecting himself, and in remorse embraced Dolby and asked for his pardon.

In the second week in February 1869, while in London, he saw his two doctors. Forster had become close once more and Dickens was relying on his friend's critical observations on each number of the new novel. He wrote to Forster:

'My foot has turned lame again and Sir Henry Thompson will not let me read tonight and will not let me go to Scotland tomorrow. Here is the certificate he drew up for himself and Beard to sign. 'We the undersigned hereby certify that Mr Charles Dickens is suffering from inflammation of the foot (caused by over exertion), and that we have forbidden his appearance on the platform this evening, as he must keep to his room for a day or two.'

In Scotland he consulted the distinguished (foot) surgeon, Mr Syme (Thompson's previous superior). The general opinion was gout. But Dickens preferred to believe it was nervousness and fatigue.

While in Ireland for his final appearance, there was another minor train accident which could have been serious both for himself, Mamie and Katey who were travelling with him. A driving wheel exploded and hurled huge pieces of metal, as shrapnel, through the carriages. Fortunately no one was hurt.

Dickens returned to 5 Hyde Park Place, which he enjoyed, telling Dolby that he liked to hear the wagons at dawn bringing the produce from Paddington Station to the markets. The Ternans were near by (at Vauxhall Bridge Road) and Ellen attended some of the London Readings. The murder scene from Oliver Twist was read up to four times a week at great cost to his health - but Dickens seemed driven to do it, despite the sheer exhaustion afterwards.

His friend Emerson Tennent (to whom he had inscribed his last book) died and at the funeral Forster noted that he was dazed and worn (although, in fairness, Dickens had travelled overnight).

At Chester he was ill with 'giddiness, with a tendency to go backwards and to turn round…with an odd feeling of insecurity about his left leg…and a strangeness of his left hand and arm.' He later said that 'when he was ill in his reading only Nelly observed that he staggered and his eye failed, only she dared tell him.'

He also wrote to Forster, 'Don't say anything in the Gad's direction about my being a little out of sorts. I have broached the matter of course; but very lightly; indeed, there no reason for broaching it otherwise.'

However, a few days later he wrote to Georgina on the 21st of April from Blackpool, 'I have come to this sea beach hotel for a days rest. I am much better than I was on Sunday; but shall want carefully looking to, to get through the readings. My weakness and deadness are all on the left side; and if I don't look at anything I try to touch with my left hand, I don't know where it is. I am in (secret) consultation with Frank Beard who says that I have given him indisputable evidence of overwork which he could wish to treat immediately; and so I have telegraphed for him. I have had a delicious walk by the sea today, and I sleep soundly, and have picked up amazingly in appetite. My foot is greatly better too.'

Dickens rounds off in a cheerful tone

MR. CHARLES DICKENS'S
𝔉𝔞𝔯𝔢𝔴𝔢𝔩𝔩 ℜ𝔢𝔞𝔡𝔦𝔫𝔤𝔰.

Mr. CHARLES DICKENS has resumed his Series of Farewell
Readings at

ST. JAMES'S HALL, PICCADILLY.

The Readings will take place as follows:

TUESDAY EVENING, FEBRUARY 8, The Story of Little Dombey
(last time) and Mr. Bob Sawyer's Party (from Pickwick).

TUESDAY EVENING, FEBRUARY 15, Boots at the Holly Tree Inn;
Sikes and Nancy (from Oliver Twist); and Mrs. Gamp
(last time).

TUESDAY EVENING, FEBRUARY 22, Nicholas Nickleby (at Mr.
Squeers's School, last time); and Mr. Chops, the Dwarf
(last time).

TUESDAY EVENING, MARCH 1, David Copperfield (last time), and
The Trial from Pickwick.

TUESDAY EVENING, MARCH 8, Boots at the Holly Tree Inn
(last time); Sikes and Nancy (from Oliver Twist, last
time); and Mr. Bob Sawyer's Party (from Pickwick, last
time).

TUESDAY EVENING, MARCH 15, FINAL FAREWELL READING,
The Christmas Carol (last time), and The Trial from
Pickwick (last time).

To commence each Evening at Eight o'Clock.

No Readings will take place out of London.

PRICES OF ADMISSION:

SOFA STALLS, 7s; STALLS, 5s.; BALCONY, 3s.;
Admission – ONE SHILLING.

Tickets may be obtained at CHAPPELL & Co.'s, 50, New Bond Street.

The farewell readings were to tax Dickens's health, especially
the 'Sikes and Nancy' scene from *Oliver Twist*.

But things did not suddenly improve, despite his guarded optimism.

At Preston April 22 1869, Dr Beard told Dolby that 'if you insist on Dickens taking the platform tonight I will not guarantee but that he goes through life dragging a foot after him.' The reading was cancelled. The Doctor brought Dickens straight to London for a consultation with Sir Thomas Watson, who advised that, since he was seriously unwell, no readings could be undertaken for several months and that there should be no more rail journeys. He was advised to return to London.

He continued editing the magazine *All The Year Round*; and, in 1869, Chapman and Hall offered him £7500 for a new novel. Dickens decided on the theme of death and murder - and the pain of being in love.

In the early summer of 1869, James Fields (*his American publisher) and his wife came over from America. To give authenticity to the book, Dickens and Fields wandered around the darker side of London where poverty and misery produced vice almost as a necessity to survival. They visited an opium den in New Court, off Bluegate, the den which opens the mystery in *Edwin Drood*. Fields noted, "a haggard old woman blowing at a kind of pipe made of an old penny ink-bottle." Everywhere was sadness, and in a lock-up Dickens found a four year old girl, abandoned or lost, wearing her mother's huge bonnet which had the appearance of 'a sort of straw coal-scuttle' Little had changed for the better, he felt, since his childhood days.

Dickens's new book was to be in twelve parts instead of the usual twenty. He wanted a story concerning the murder of a young man by his uncle, and how the truth of this family slaying would not be revealed until the murderer himself reflected upon the stages of his fatal career in a condemned cell. The plot, with the background of an opium den, bears witness to Wilkie Collins's influence, a resemblance being to *The Moonstone*. Charles Collins was to provide the illustrations, Dickens, in his kindness despite his antipathy, thought that the work might give his son-in-law income as well as take the man's mind off his illness.

In early August he was considering the outline of the novel and began working, in earnest, in September 1869. Dolby wrote that the novel was giving more trouble and anxiety than usual; while Dickens said that he missed writing to a deadline as in former days. But readers of the truncated book will note that there is a felicity in the writing, whatever the background situation was at the time.

The Mystery of Edwin Drood, with its symbolism of Rochester, was unfinished as of 8th June 1870, although several attempts have been made to conclude the mystery. It remains as a fragment to his genius, only half the work having been written. Dickens felt that it might be his last book and the writing is unlike anything he had attempted before, with a fresher style than usual – highlighted by the vividly poetical scenic descriptions that convey the beauty and serenity of Rochester.

He had in the past only written when not acting, but for once he abandoned this rule. Christmas saw him with some of his family, although not well and not joining in the usual games. Henry, however, was amazed, during a memory game, that his father came out with the words, "Warren's Blacking, 30 Strand"; an amused expression on his face intriguing his puzzled son.

Boxing Day had its organised sports with Dickens as a spectator, although he did say that he hoped that he would do it again next Christmas. New Year's Eve was spent at Forster's home.

He saw a production of *No Thoroughfare* (the play written in collaboration with Collins) and went to Paris for the French Production.

Another twelve readings were arranged for London. He continued to rent a house at 5 Hyde Park Place. Sir Thomas Watson had agreed in 1869 that with a long lay-off Dickens could begin again, on condition the railway travel would not tire him. Thus the final twelve readings were delayed until early 1870. They were to begin on January 11th, 1870 at one of his favourite venues, St James's Hall, London, and to end on March 15th.

Forster and Carlyle met him on the 22nd of January and Dickens's arm was in a sling and it remained very swollen on his 58th birthday. Carlyle reported 'Dickens very cheery…he has got, I doubt, some permanent nervous damage from that conquest of the £20,000 in Yankeeland, and is himself rather anxious, now and then, about a foot that goes occasionally wrong (part powerless, I think) and now latterly some fingers of a hand do.'

Dickens still felt weak on his left side and it became commonplace for a doctor and Charley to be present at the Readings. The doctor gave strict instructions for Charley to rush forward if he saw his father falter and bring him off stage, 'or by heaven he'll die before them all.' His pulse raced after each reading, and the doctors were most alarmed when he did the murder scene. Even the prolonged resting on the sofa after the performance was finished, aided with sips of brandy, was barely able to keep him going.

So the readings went on and on, from town to town throughout February, and March. Illness was swift on his heels. The problems were only marginally improved and at the end of March while walking along Oxford Street, the left half of his vision went as he tried to read the signs.

On the 3rd of March he went to Ellen's birthday party at a Restaurant in Regent Street. On the 9th Queen Victoria gave him an audience and presented him, very shyly, with a book she had written. Etiquette kept him standing for ninety minutes while she reclined against a sofa. He told Georgina that 'she was strangely shy and like a girl in manner.' It had been said that the Queen offered him a baronetcy, but there is no record of such an offer; so Dickens joined the ranks of Shakespeare, Cook, Darwin and others luminaries who did not make muster in this respect.

He was still visiting the theatre and at a memorable visit to a circus, on observing an elephant balance on its head, asked out loud, to the amusement of those around, "why they've never taught the rhinoceros to do anything." However, he was increasingly fed up with London and the social round and decided there would be no more engagements for the rest of the year. Friends noted him 'grey-haired and careworn'.

Dickens, despite the opinion of two experts, was adamant that he did not have gout and pointed out to Dr Beard that his 'heart had been fluttered' and it had come on after Staplehurst, and since been aggravated by the constant jarring of rail travel. He wondered if the giddiness he was experiencing was the result of the medicine. Beard was firm in his opinion, 'The medicines cannot possibly have caused them.'

His hand became very swollen and the sling was applied once more. But that did not stop him giving a dinner for all who had worked with him on the tour.

With the last reading in St James's Hall on the 15th of March, over two thousand people gave him a prolonged, standing ovation. Dickens entered, immaculate in evening dress as usual, and stood on the platform, Dolby said, 'evidently much agitated.' It was also remarked that he had never read so well as on that final night. Then Dickens, with tears rolling down his cheeks, told of the fifteen years of the Readings and concluding simply said, "I now vanish for ever more, with heartfelt, grateful, respectful, affectionate farewell.' The audience was stunned for a moment. Then there was 'storm of cheering' as he left the room, which would not stop until he returned to the platform. After the final bow, his kissed his hands to the audience, many applauding wildly with tears in their eyes, and the Readings were finished.

He decided to destroy his reading desk, then changed his mind, Katey begging for it to be given to her. He gave his 'reading books' to Forster.

On the 30th April 1870 he returned thanks for 'Literature' when he addressed the Royal Academy, and he paid a fulsome tribute to Maclise, the dearest of friends, who had died three days before. Although he had drifted away from the Dickens's fold during the last few years, Dickens said that he could not get over his friend's death. The address was described as 'vivacious and brilliant'; some of the old sparkle had returned, albeit temporarily.

One bright note was the gift of a silver table ornament from an admiring business man, who said he had been inspired by Dickens's philosophy on life. On the centre piece were designs of the cheerful seasons - spring, summer and autumn - and although Dickens said that it was one of the most pleasant and gratifying gifts he had ever received, he wrote to Forster , 'I never look at it, that I don't think most of the Winter.'

He had made plans to finish the conservatory, a long held wish, and told a young lady author about Gad's Hill, 'I love the dear old place; and I hope – when I come to die - it may be there.'

The sales of Edwin Drood exceeded all initial expectations, and Dickens was delighted that his change of style had been accepted by his public. He was now inspired and eager to get on, by returning to the quiet of Gad's Hill. He gave up the magazine *All The Year Round* and took a sad farewell of George Dolby, whom he had trusted and admired as a tireless manager.

He was absent for three days in early May, visiting a "sick friend" almost certainly Ellen. He dined with an American minister, met and talked to Disraeli and breakfasted with Gladstone. He had supported Gladstone's liberal stance in the previous November's election but did not really trust any politician saying to Bulwer-Lytton that 'our system fails.' Dickens was very suspicious of Disraeli and had at times, an active dislike of the man.

On the 17th of May he was to attend the Queen's Ball with his daughter. But she went alone.

'I am sorry to report, that, in the old preposterous endeavour to dine at preposterous hours and preposterous places, I have been pulled up by a sharp attack in my foot. And serve me right. I hope to get the better of it soon, but I fear I must not think of dining with you Friday,' he wrote to Forster. 'I have cancelled everything in the dining way this week, and that is a very small precaution after the horrible pain I have had and the remedies I have taken.'

Dickens had been asked to dine with the Prince of Wales and the King of the Belgians, and go to several other meetings and events. In the end, he decided to only meet the Royal guests; although he was so lame he had to be helped into the dining room. However, he seemed in high spirits, being (as one person said) 'bubbling over with fun and conversation', and another reported 'Dickens was in high spirits, brim full of the *joie de vivre*...he was at times still so young and almost boyish in his gaiety.'

Dickens learned of Mark Lemmon's death on the last day he met Forster. They dined together on Sunday the 22nd of May and talked of their friends who had acted in Ben Jonson's play, those many happy years earlier. Dickens commented that, "we are almost alone. And none beyond his sixtieth year, and very few even fifty." 'It's no good talking of it,' said Forster. "We shall not think of it the less," he replied.

His interest in the theatre was undiminished. Throughout May plans had been made for an amateur production at Hyde Park Place. Dickens was everywhere, managing the 'whole thing' as one actor remarked. On June 1st he wrote a few lines to finish the play which was to be performed the following day. He attended the performance, but seemed preoccupied, and was said to have a 'dazed expression'.

Georgina and Mamie noted that Dickens seemed very weary on his return to Gad's Hill. He strolled through the garden, spent some time gazing at the flowers, and contemplated the newly finished conservatory.

The early June days were ones of contentment with Georgina busying herself around the house and

Mamie singing in the evening. But it was sitting and talking with Katey which Dickens adored. One night she said that she wanted to go onto the stage but he hesitated and did not give a firm opinion. In turn he spoke about his hopes for *Edwin Drood* and the success so far, with fifty thousand copies of each issue sold. He confided, "if, please God, I live to finish. I say 'if', because you know, my dear child, I have not been strong lately." He worried about 'not being a better father - a better man', but Katey reassured him and that pleased him. They talked until three in the morning as the light, warm night gave way to dawn's brightness.

On Monday June 6th Katey was to visit London. Seeing her father busy at his writings she left a note. Just as she was to set off in the carriage, she had an uneasy feeling. With a change of heart, and 'an uncontrollable desire to see him once again', Katey rushed back to the chalet; for the first time ever disturbing his writing. But Dickens seemed relieved to see her and held her close for several minutes. "He pushed his chair back from the writing table, opened his arms, and took me into them,' she recalled.

He took his dogs out the same day, and walked with his letters to Rochester. He bought a paper, and surveyed some of the buildings he wanted to use in the novel.

Mamie went to visit Katey on the Tuesday 7th and Dickens, because of fatigue, drove to Cobham Wood, with Georgina. However, he completed a walk round the park and then strolled home.

The men had finished the conservatory and, in the afternoon, he spent time decorating it with Chinese lanterns which had arrived from London. All evening he sat with Georgina, delighted by their brightness and colour.

He reminisced and said he had finally abandoned any idea of living in London and selling Gad's Hill. He wanted people to think of him there; and to be buried in the little graveyard belonging to the Rochester Cathedral, at the foot of the Castle Wall.

The morning of Wednesday, the 8th June 1870, saw Dickens in his chalet working on *Edwin Drood*, surrounded by birdsong, the colours and scents of the garden in full bloom, and the waving leaves near the open windows. He had come a long way in life since those happy childhood days not so far away, in Chatham. He had worked and striven every inch of the way.

Dickens came in for dinner on the 8th of June 1870.

After lunch, against his usual custom, he returned to his desk. As he wrote the final paragraphs, his imagination saw the sun - brilliant as it rose over the old city of Rochester, the ivy gleaming and the rich trees waving in the balmy air, its antiquities and its ruins; its Cathedral and its Castle.

He worked into the late afternoon for once giving up his customary walk. However, before dinner (ordered punctuality, as usual for 6pm) he wrote some letters, one of them to his friend Charles Kent, arranging a meeting the following day.

When Dickens came in for dinner on the 8th of June, Georgina was alarmed. She noticed a change in his colour, and he seemed tired and silent.

"For an hour," he told her, "I have been very ill."

He talked, but his words and thoughts were rambling and disjointed – the sale of a neighbour's house, concern about Macready, wondering if Macready's son was looking after him at Cheltenham. Suddenly he announced that he wanted to go to London.

With this remark he stood up and almost fell. Georgina rushed forward to catch him. She tried to support him to the sofa but he sank heavily onto his left side, "On the ground," were the last words he spoke, it was only ten minutes into the meal.

One servant rode into Rochester to summon the local doctor, Dr Steele. He found Dickens lying on the floor deeply unconscious. The servants brought a couch into the room and he was gently carried there and covered with blankets.

Telegrams brought the two girls rushing home as well as Frank Beard. He verified the diagnosis.

Katey recalls, 'A sudden gloom had fallen upon the place, and everything was changed; only the still, warm weather continued the same, and the sweet scent of the flowers he had so much admired floated in through the open doors of the new conservatory,'

Georgina, Mamie, Katey and Frank Beard sat with Dickens throughout the night but he showed no signs of regaining consciousness. Then Charley arrived and, after a brief consultation with Drs Beard and Steele, was advised to send for a specialist from London. Eventually Dr Reynolds came and gave a gloomy prognosis. Georgina then sent for Ellen Ternan and Mary Boyle. They hurried to the house that afternoon.

The diagnosis was not in doubt; the doctors agreeing that he had suffered a catastrophic stroke. Dickens lay unconscious, slowly breathing, hour after hour. Finally, with faint sigh and a tear slowly trickling down his cheek, he died. It was just after 6 pm on the 9th of June. He was 58.

****

He had wished for a quiet burial at Rochester, or in the little churchyards of Cobham or Shorne. But this was not to be; for the national papers, including the *Times*, demanded otherwise - and the family relented.

His body was taken by a special train to Charing Cross Station in London. After a short service at Westminster Abbey, he was buried in poets' corner. Kate did not attend the service.

Over many years, thousands visited his grave, which was perpetually covered with flowers. The public had loved and admired Dickens for many reasons, perhaps above all, the ability to make them smile at life.

It remains forever, his greatest gift.

The Final Chapter

Charles Huffham Dickens (1812-1870)
'I emphatically direct (said his Will) that I be buried in an inexpensive, unostentatious, and strictly private manner.' He was buried, against his wishes, in Westminster Abbey. *The Times* took the lead, 'Statesmen, men of science, philanthropists, the acknowledged benefactors of their race, might pass away, and yet not leave the void which will be caused by the death of Dickens.' Flowers and letters of sympathy and admiration were sent by the crowds of well-wishers from every walk of life. The Queen telegraphed from Balmoral. Every country in Europe was saddened (Italy went into mourning – 'Nostro Carlo Dickens e morto' the papers declared giving over their front pages to the headline.) In America, Australia and India the response was the same, especially in the United States, which now looked upon Dickens as their own. Directed that his name be inscribed in plain English letters on his tomb without the addition of "Mr" and "Esquire". 'I conjure my friends on no account to make me the subject of any monument, memorial or testimonial whatever." (*when asked in America if they could put up a monument, he had said, "No, knock one down!")

****

The following close circle of family and friends outlived Dickens:

Catherine Dickens (dearest Kate) (1815-1879)

Wife and mother of ten children, married April 1836 and separated in 1858. She travelled on her husband's wild tours including the first in the United States; entertained lavishly with her husband and put up with a constant stream of visitors. After separation, lived with eldest son, Charley, and remained close to Katey; totally estranged from her sister Georgina until just before her own death from cancer. She continued to receive an annual £600s but nothing extra was bequeathed in his Will. Directed Katey to give her personal letters to British Museum, 'so the world may know he loved me once.' She remained attached and loyal to her husband's memory.

****

Charles Culliford Boz (1837-1896).

Eldest son and first child, worked in Baring's bank then went to China to buy tea and set up as a merchant on return. Father strongly disapproved of his marriage to Bessie Evans, daughter of publisher, with whom Dickens had quarrelled. Became bankrupt with Evans when the paper-mill business failed. Given a job on *All the year Round* by Dickens who believed 'he was wanting in a sense of perseverance.' Helped father with final public Readings; bought Gad's Hill but was forced to give it up due to ill health. Died, like his father, from a stroke.

Mary (Mamie) (1838-1896).

Eldest daughter and second born. Named in memory of mother's sister, Mary, who had died suddenly. Lived with Dickens until his death, taking second place in the domestic affairs to Georgina, with whom she continued to live. Edited her father's letters with her aunt. Her gentle nature made her popular; although she did not see her mother for a long while, perhaps under the influence of her father and Georgina.

Kate Macready (Katey) (1839-1929)

Second daughter, nicknamed 'Lucifer Box' because of her fiery temper. Talented in art, she attended Bedford College. Dickens saw a lot of himself in Katey and loved her dearly. She married Charles Allston Collins as a way to independence, which greatly upset her father. When Collins died married a second time to another artist Carlo Perugini. Always spoke her mind and was sometimes lukewarm to Georgina. Lived to ninety.

Francis Jeffrey (Frank) (1844-1886).

Third son who joined Bengal Mounted Police. Came back to England on leave in 1871 and ran up debts, drifted for a while then joined the Northwest Mounted Police. He resigned his commission in 1886 and died not long afterwards.

Alfred D'Orsay Tennyson (1845-1912)

Fourth son. Initially Dickens wanted him to have an army career; sailed to Australia aged twenty leaving a mass of unpaid bills which his father settled. Married to Jessie Devlin in Melbourne (The Belle of Melbourne) who was tragically killed in a carriage accident. He became wealthy and later toured England and America lecturing on his father. Died suddenly in New York from a heart attack.

Sydney Smith Haldimand (1847-1872)

Fifth son, always a favourite with his father, he joined the navy. His chosen career prospered at first but then he began to show all the excesses and the extravagances of his grandfather. As the mountain of debts grew, he appealed for money. Dickens was furious and asked him to keep away from Gad's Hill; sadly he died at sea on the way home, having been granted sick-leave. His lifestyle caused great suffering for Dickens.

Henry Fielding (Harry) (Sir) (1849-1933),

Sixth son and a success. Edited a small fun newspaper with Edward called *The Gad's Hill Gazette*; which amused his father. Athletic at tennis and cricket, robust and clever; he entered Cambridge and won two scholarships and an essay prize, which delighted Dickens. Brilliant career at the Bar and with his fluent French (partly educated in Boulogne) he married Therese Louise Roche. Read his father's works for charity and kept in touch with Georgina, visiting frequently with his wife and two sons. Knighted

Edward Bulwer Lytton ('Plorn')(1852-1902),

Tenth and final child. Sensitive, he did not get on well at school and was given private tuition. He went to Australia to join his brother Alfred but continually wasted money.

(Two of the children died before Dickens: *Dora Annie* (1850-1851) sickly at birth, she died from convulsions. *Walter Landor* (1841-1863), the second son - died in India (believed to be from an aortic aneurysm), had been in the 42nd Highlanders - and also in debt.)

****

Georgina Hogarth (Aunt Georgy) (1827-1917).

The youngest of the three elder Hogarth sisters. When they were first married she frequently visited Charles and Kate; helped from an early age by playing with, and looking after, their children. Took such an active part in the children's care while their parents toured America in 1842 that she was invited to stay - which she did, permanently. She was much blamed for the rift between Kate and Charles, in time taking over the day to day affairs of the house, to the comparative detriment of Kate, while impressing Dickens. His Will directed his children to always remember how much they owed to Aunty Georgy. She was appointed as executor and executrix, along with John Forster, for the Will. Did not speak to her sister until just before Kate's death in 1879 (a lapse of 21 years). Spent the rest of her life editing Dickens's letters for publication and perpetuating his memory.

****

John Forster (1812-1876).
Did not live long after his best friend died; depressed, he mourned away his remaining years. Everything a friend could be – from a poor family (like Dickens) in Newcastle upon Tyne, academically brilliant (like Dickens), became a barrister at Inner Temple and thus was always on hand for legal advice. Embarked on a literary career and loved the theatre and acting (like Dickens), becoming drama critic for *The Examiner.* Unknown to Dickens he was suggested (jokingly) as Pickwick by the publishers Chapman and Hall; had his birthday on Charles and Kate's wedding anniversary; and was born in 1812 (three facts that intrigued Dickens, who believed in fates and coincidences). For almost two decades they had a joint celebration in April, usually only the three

of them. Called for long rides and exhausting walks by Dickens at all hours and did not seem to mind, including the whole-hearted drinking and eating at wayside inns afterwards. Proof-read and gave such invaluable advice on characterisation and plot, that often Dickens could not wait for his friend's opinion. They spent the Festive Season together for many years, when Forster's humour and vociferous personality (and conjuring expertise) matched Dickens's. Married in his forties. For a time their friendship wavered, due to Dickens being under the strong influence of Collins. They were close again during Dickens's final years. Wrote an idealised, rather than truthful, account of the author's life, *The Life of Charles Dickens* (dedicated to his god-daughters Mamie and Katey). It is essential and fascinating reading. His admiration and love of Dickens's friendship and family shine like a beacon in the book.

****

William Harrison Ainsworth (1805-1882) Trained at law but became a publisher and writer; edited *Bentley's Miscellany* after Dickens. The first writer of note to encourage the young Dickens, as a fellow-author, by inviting him to his regular afternoon parties where he met celebrities in art and literature. Good humoured and constantly on-the-go, like Dickens, they often rode out together, usually Forster came along as well.

Letitia Austin (1816 -1893) younger sister of Dickens, after her husband's death (Henry, an architect who helped Dickens's house purchases d.1861), Dickens got her a pension. In later life, Georgina also helped her.

Maria Beadnell (1810-1886): first love who reappeared when the novelist was world famous; married Henry Winter, whose business failed; she asked Dickens for money. He refused and with great irony, replied that her father 'might be induced to do what – I may say to you, Maria – is no great stretch of sentiment to call his duty.'

Henry Burnett (1811-1893) Singer, music-teacher and brother-in-law, married Dickens's elder sister Fanny. Deeply religious dissenter; studied music and entered the Royal Academy of Music in 1832 where he met Fanny (who was excelling there), whom he married in 1837. (Fanny, Dickens's elder sister, whom he loved and admired, died from consumption (tuberculosis) in 1848.)

Thomas Beard (1807-1891). Dickens's only life-long friend; they were shorthand writers in the House of Commons and travelled the country together as reporters. Shy and retiring, perhaps in awe of the great fame, he kept a low profile in contemporary accounts. But Dickens admired him enough to make him his best-man and God-father to his first-born, Charley. To Dickens he was always affectionately known as 'Tom'.

Dr Francis Carr Beard (1814-1893): Thomas's younger brother, became F.R.C.S. and was his medical adviser during the last ten years, was with Dickens at the end.

Richard Bentley (1794-1871) outlived Dickens; started *Bentley's Miscellany* with Dickens as editor in

1837. Fell out over contracts but remained friends, although Dickens was always, to some degree, wary.

Mary Boyle (1810-90). Socialite and related to minor aristocracy, she was a talented actress who often played opposite Dickens. Was a close friend for twenty years; supplied the floral button-hole for his Readings, even in North America; at Gad's Hill when he died. She was always dearest 'Meery'.

Hablot Knight Browne (Phiz) (1815-1882) illustrated Dickens's books for twenty-three years, ten novels in total. Last novel was *A Tale of Two Cities*. There was a cooling of relationships.

Angela Georgina Burdett-Coutts (1814-1906) inherited a great fortune from her banker-grandfather Coutts, daughter of Francis Burdett, Baronet. Devoted her life to philanthropic causes - such as the education of the poor, the reclamation of prostitutes and the prevention of cruelty to children and also to animals. Dickens admired her and her driving ambition to help others, acting for many years as both an adviser and also unofficial almoner and secretary; equally, she admired him. It has been said that there was a cooling relationship after the split with Kate.

Thomas Carlyle (1795-1881) essayist and historian, famous for his book on the French revolution. A close friend, with his wife Jane (d.1866), Dickens enjoyed their company and said that Carlyle's writings had been an inspiration. But he, in turn, often spoke slightingly about fiction writers, including Dickens.

Edward Chapman (1804 -1880) the more literary partner of Chapman and Hall, Dickens's first publisher; the driving force in the publication and support of Dickens. The author broke with the firm after *The Chimes.* Later rejoined.

Wilkie Collins (1824-1889) called to the bar but became an author, contributing to Household Words from 1855. Wrote skilfully, both plays (*The Frozen Deep etc*) and novels (*The Woman in White, The Moonstone* and *Armadale etc.*) Collaborated with Dickens on *The Lazy Tour of Two Idle Apprentices* and *No Thoroughfare.* Curious, almost licentious life style; opium addiction (probably due to the pain caused by his severe gout) marred his later life.

George Cruikshank (1792-1878) first worked with Dickens on *Sketches by* Boz and then *Oliver Twist* in which his drawing of Fagin in the condemned cell was widely admired. Later in life, he claimed to have inspired *Pickwick* and to be the originator of *Oliver Twist.* Dickens flatly repudiated this claim (and rightly). At times a heavy drinker, he could be aggressive. In later years their friendship cooled.

George Dolby. Dickens manager from 1866 to 1870; an amiable, caring, competent man who succeeded in negotiating favourable deals, despite a speech impediment. He sustained Dickens on the British Tour of 1866-1867; the arduous American tour of 1867-1868, and the final British Tour of 1868-1870. He was a welcome visitor to Gad's Hill. Wrote one of the two best biographies of Dickens.

Charles Fechter (1822-1879). Swiss actor-manager, noted for many performances including *No Thoroughfare*. Gave Dickens his Swiss chalet.

James Fields (d 1880) American publisher, persuaded Dickens to undertake reading tours of United States. With wife *Annie* became close friends. He confided in Annie about several matters, including the friendship with Ellen. She became very friendly with Georgina.

Henry William Kolle (1808-1891) Married Anne Beadnell, and was go-between for Dickens with Maria. Was a manufacturer of stoves and ranges. Dickens attended the wedding despite feeling in despair over Maria.

Edwin Henry Landseer (Sir) (1802-1873) A favourite painter of Victoria; best known for his animal portraits. Designed the lions in Trafalgar Square, London.

Edward George Earle Lytton Bulwer-Lytton (Baron)(1803-1873) Novelist, poet, playwright, writer, political reformer. With Dickens founded the Guild of Literature, to help impoverished writers. He encouraged Dickens's amateur productions at his home, Knebworth, and in London. One of Dickens's closest friends, whom he admired for his personality and talents.

William Charles Macready (1793-1873) Distinguished Shakespearean actor and close friend; when in declining health, Dickens was his most frequent visitor and 'conjured back the smile.'

Amongst Dickens's final words was an inquiry about Macready's welfare.

Frederick Ouvry (1814-1881). Solicitor and friend who acted for Dickens on several occasions including the separation from Kate.

Alfred Tennyson (*Baron*) (1809-1892). Writer of epic lyrical poems including *Idylls of the King* and *In Memoriam*, who greatly admired Dickens's skill. His favourite poet.

Ellen Lawless Ternan (1839-1914)
The biggest secret and mystery in Dickens's life. Twenty seven years younger than Dickens, he was forty five, she eighteen, when they met in 1857 and he was very soon infatuated; at the time she was acting in Talfourd's play *Atlanta*. Dickens engaged her (plus her mother and sister) for the play *The Frozen Deep*, although her sister (more talented) caught his attention at first. His infatuation with Ellen led to the break-up of his marriage in 1858. An undistinguished actress, her relationship was ambiguous (a shadowy figure and not referred to by his friends, especially Dolby and Forster – who totally leapt over the relationship in their biographies). The furtive and unsatisfactory relationship, plus her ambivalent feelings towards him, probably caused much sadness to Dickens late in his life. Her personality and attitude certainly created much more welcoming and acceptable heroines in his last books (Bella Wilfer being one; and Estella who taunted Pip (Dickens) another). She accompanied Dickens on certain tours and on holidays, although her formidable and pushy mother was always close at hand, armed with her Victorian morals. Ellen seemed to be able to speak

her mind, especially about his illness and his overwork, when other friends were cowed by the distinguished author. Almost certainly stayed with Dickens, who liked to rent a London home, often close-by. They may have lived together at Slough and possibly at Peckham – if only for brief periods. She may have had the approbation of some of his friends who thought that a woman cohabiting with a married man was tantamount to prostitution. However, became accepted by Georgina and Mamie, but Katey was a friend only to please her father. Sent for when Dickens had collapsed; she remained on speaking terms with Georgina and the family after his death. She was only left £1000 in his Will, which suggests a cooling friendship. Married a clergyman who became a headmaster in Margate. She remained faithful to Dickens, never speaking about their relationship and probably destroying his letters – for none were found. Said she 'loathed the very thought of intimacy' with Dickens, but she was marrying a man of the Church, after all, and had to maintain her innocence. Died from breast cancer.

Edmund Yates (1831-1894). Novelist and founder of the journal *The World*, also wrote for the *Daily News* and *All The Year Round.* Toured America after Dickens's death lecturing on their friendship. Georgina disapproved, no doubt fearing some undesirable facts might come out. She thought Yates 'a harum-scarum creature'. Caused a rift between Thackeray and Dickens.

The last official picture, at the beginning of '*The Mystery of Edwin Drood*': signed 1870. It is fitting that it should end this book.